THE FINANCE OF CANAL BUILDING IN EIGHTEENTH-CENTURY ENGLAND

BY

J. R. WARD

Lecturer in Economic History
at the University of Edinburgh

OXFORD UNIVERSITY PRESS
1974

Oxford University Press, Ely House, London W.1

GLASGOW NEW YORK TORONTO MELBOURNE WELLINGTON
CAPE TOWN IBADAN NAIROBI DAR ES SALAAM LUSAKA ADDIS ABABA
DELHI BOMBAY CALCUTTA MADRAS KARACHI LAHORE DACCA
KUALA LUMPUR SINGAPORE HONG KONG TOKYO

ISBN 0 19 821853 2
© OXFORD UNIVERSITY PRESS

PRINTED IN GREAT BRITAIN
BY WILLIAM CLOWES & SONS LIMITED
LONDON, COLCHESTER AND BECCLES

TO MY PARENTS

ACKNOWLEDGEMENTS

I am grateful to the Archivist of the British Transport Historical Records for permission to consult and cite documents in his custody.

I am also grateful to Dr. R. M. Hartwell, who supervised the preparation of the thesis upon which this book is based, and to Professors P. Mathias and J. R. Harris, who examined the thesis, for their comments and advice.

CONTENTS

ABBREVIATIONS — viii

INTRODUCTION — ix

I. The Finance of River Improvement — 1

II. The Finance of Canal Building — 18

III. The Geographical Location of Investors — 79

IV. The Organization of Canal Finance — 97

V. The Motives of Investors — 126

VI. Landowners and Canals — 143

VII. Canal Finance and English Economic Development — 161

APPENDICES

I. Dividend Payments by Canal Companies — 175

II. Investment in Inland Navigation — 179

III. Subscription to Inland Navigation in Six Towns, 1785–1795 — 180

IV. Changes in the Character of Proprietaries through the Transfer of Shares — 183

V. Bank Finance of Inland Navigation — 186

VI. Sources for the Indices of Traffic Growth — 191

BIBLIOGRAPHY — 195

INDEX — 215

ABBREVIATIONS

A.O.	Archives Office.
B.T.H.R.	British Transport Historical Records, London collection.
B.T.H.R. (York)	British Transport Historical Records, York collection.
Cal. S.P. Dom.	*Calendar of State Papers, Domestic.*
Econ. Hist. Rev.	*Economic History Review.*
H.C.J.	*House of Commons Journals.*
P.R.O.	Public Record Office. (B. Court of Bankruptcy: CUST. Customs Ledgers.)
R.O.	Record Office.

Some navigation company minute books are foliated, others are not. For the sake of uniformity all citations from them have been made by date.

Unless otherwise stated, the location of all navigation company records cited is the London collection of the British Transport Historical Records.

Unless otherwise stated, the place of publication of all printed works cited is London.

INTRODUCTION

THE extension of inland navigation through the building of canals was a powerful force for material progress in eighteenth-century England. Especial interest attaches to the fact that these canals, which elsewhere were usually public works, were here almost wholly the achievement of private men. What were the economic dispositions of a society that could generate and sustain such enterprise? It is the purpose of the following study to answer this question by establishing who financed the canal construction, how they did so, and why.

The modern history of canals in England begins with the Duke of Bridgewater's Worsley–Manchester Navigation in 1759. During the 1760s and early 1770s many other canals were begun in imitation of this. In the later 1770s the economic dislocation associated with the American War of Independence prevented further projects and stopped work on many of those which had already been undertaken. Progress was resumed in the more favourable circumstances of the later 1780s. Its culmination was the 'canal mania' of 1792–3, a brief period of enthusiastic promotion terminated by the commercial crisis consequent upon the outbreak of hostilities with revolutionary France. The projects conceived and planned in the years of peace were largely executed in the following decade of war, although the completion of many extended until 1815, 1820, or even later. Few new lines were promoted after 1793 and England's canal system had been essentially mapped out, though not built, by this date. For the sake of brevity, in the following pages canals undertaken before the American War of Independence will be referred to as of the 'first generation' and those undertaken between the 1780s and 1815 as of the 'second generation'.

This book is devoted exclusively to the study of canal finance; for other, more general aspects of the history of inland navigation the reader is referred to other, more general works.[1] Chapter I surveys the financial history of the

[1] Particularly those of Mr. C. Hadfield, which are listed in the Bibliography.

seventeenth- and early eighteenth-century river navigations and is intended to serve as prologue to an examination of the canals which followed them. Chapter II, which is necessarily tedious, narrates the financial histories of fifty canals and river navigations of the later eighteenth century. Chapters III, IV, V, and VI, are more analytic in form, they investigate, from various points of view, the character and motives of investors, and the financial management of their enterprises. Chapter VII offers certain conclusions drawn from the assembled material and attempts briefly to relate them to the general economic history of the period.

The inquiry is based upon the manuscript records of navigation companies preserved among the British Transport Historical Records, supplemented by material drawn from local and national archives. Attention is concentrated upon the canals of the West Riding of Yorkshire, Lancashire, and the Midlands. It was these areas which served as the cradle of modern industry; there most of England's canals were built as an articulate network to serve its needs. Little is said about the navigations of eastern and southern England or about those few undertakings promoted after 1815. But within these limits of time, space, and subject matter, I have sought to make this study comprehensive.

THE FINANCE OF RIVER IMPROVEMENT

In the history of English river improvement five phases of development may be discerned: first, the isolated undertakings of the early Stuart and Commonwealth periods; second, the schemes of the years immediately following the Restoration; third, those of the later 1690s and early 1700s; fourth, the improvements undertaken between the Treaty of Utrecht and the late 1720s; fifth and finally, those begun in the 1750s and later decades contemporaneously with the canals which are the main subject of this work. After the Restoration it became customary for parliamentary sanction to be obtained for river improvement, and the statistics of legislation from this date are therefore a useful guide to its chronology. The following table indicates the number of rivers which in successive periods were subjected for the first time to Acts for their improvement:[1]

1660–1670 : 12
1671–1696 : 1
1697–1705 : 10
1706–1713 : 1
1714–1727 : 12
1728–1750 : 4
1750–1815 : 22

No attempt is made here to describe the financial history of all navigations. For each phase a number which appear especially characteristic and well documented have been considered, particular attention being paid to the identity and social character of their undertakers and financiers, a task which unfortunately makes for rather awkward reading.

[1] Details from J. Priestley, *Historical Account of the Navigable Rivers, Canals and Railways throughout Great Britain* (1831). See also T. S. Willan, *River Navigation in England 1600–1750* (Oxford, 1936), to which this chapter is heavily indebted.

The Bedfordshire Ouse was undertaken in 1618 by Arnold Spencer[1] who collaborated successively with Thomas Girton of Westminster, vintner, John Jackson of St. Neots, dyer, and Stephen Luxford, a mayor of Bedford. It is not clear how much he spent or how his expenditure was financed but by the 1640s he owed £1,000 to Nathanial Stirrop of London, Esquire, and Francis Read of Willington, Bedfordshire, gentleman, and also £650 to Christopher Rose of Cambridge, Esquire. In 1652 the navigation was assigned to his creditors and in 1674, having fallen into considerable decay, it was sold to Samuel Jemmatt, a former mayor of Reading, who leased it to Henry Ashley, a self-styled tanner and later, gentleman, of Eynesbury, Huntingdonshire. Between that year and 1689 Ashley and his son, an Esquire, Justice of the Peace, landowner, and barrister, restored the navigation to Great Barford and continued it up to Bedford.[2]

The Warwickshire Avon between Tewkesbury and Stratford was undertaken in 1636 by William Sandys, a local landowner. According to a contemporary topographer he spent over £20,000 in three years on the works. By 1641 Sandys had sold lands and was indebted to various persons, including the King to whom '£500 per annum' was due. This obligation may have been connected with the royal grant of a percentage of the duty on sea coals which was to cost him his seat in the House of Commons.[3] In consequence of Sandys's financial difficulties the navigation was taken over by William Say of the Middle Temple, Esquire, one of his sureties, who during the years of the Commonwealth undertook further improvements.[4] At the Restoration Say was attainted as a regicide and the navigation passed through the hands of the trustees of the Duke of York to Thomas, Lord Windsor.

[1] Described in T. S. Willan (ed.), *The Navigation of the Great Ouse between St. Ives and Bedford in the Seventeenth Century* (Bedfordshire Historical Record Society, xxiv, 1946), p. 3, as a landowner of Cople, Bedfordshire, but in a royal grant of letters patent dated 11 Dec. 1638 as of London, gentleman: P.R.O., Chancery Proceedings, C.7/599/3, membrane 3.

[2] Willan, *Great Ouse*, pp. 3–16.

[3] C. Hadfield and J. Norris, *Waterways to Stratford* (Dawlish, 1962), pp. 15–19; M. F. Keeler, *The Long Parliament, 1640–1* (Philadelphia, 1954), pp. 333–4; *Cal. S.P. Dom., 1638–9*, p. 507; ibid., *1641–3*, p. 174.

[4] Also, William Adams of the Middle Temple, Esquire, had an equitable interest in the concern.

Windsor in turn granted two-thirds of the Upper Navigation—
it ran from Evesham Bridge to Stratford—to a syndicate
which included the landowner and projector Andrew
Yarranton, Richard Hunt of Stratford, mercer, Richard
Turton of London, gentleman, Richard Bartlett of Old
Stratford, dyer, and Nicholas Baker of Worcester, mercer.
They were later joined by John Woodin of Stratford. The
group had successfully completed the navigation by the
1670s.[1]

The Restoration was followed by frequent, though largely
ineffectual, legislation for river navigation. Some appointed
undertakers did little or nothing[2] while others expended
much time and money, but without success. The only
permanent extensions of inland navigation effected between
the 1660s and 1690s were those of the Ouse and Avon, as
already described, and of the Welland to Stamford, the last
being the work of the Stamford wine-merchant Daniel
Wigmore.[3] In the following pages two unsuccessful enterprises of the period are described.

The Worcestershire Stour from the Severn to Stourbridge
and the Salwarpe to Droitwich were undertaken in 1662 by
the Earl of Bristol, Thomas, Lord Windsor, and Thomas
Smyth of the Middle Temple, Esquire. In the years which
followed, shares in the concern were subdivided and transferred. New adventurers upon whom they devolved by purchase, and by successive agreements for the completion of

[1] Hadfield and Norris, op. cit., pp. 19–22; P.R.O., Chancery Proceedings,
C.5/198/15, C.5/614/62.

[2] For example, William, Lord Windsor, and Henry Sandys, in the case of Wye
and Lugg; Sir Humphrey Bennett, and others, in the case of the Itchen (Willan,
River Navigation, p. 53); and see C. W. Chalklin, 'Navigation Schemes on the
Upper Medway 1600–1655', *Journal of Transport History*, v (1961), 105–15.

[3] Willan, *River Navigation*, p. 66. Wigmore in his will, proved in 1687, was
styled as of Stamford, Esquire: *Index to Wills Proved in the Prerogative Court of
Canterbury, 1686–93* (Index Library, lxxvii, 1955–6), p. 301. For references to
his wine imports via Boston, Spalding, and the Welland, see P.R.O., Port Books,
e.g. E.190/397/8, 29 Jan. 1675/6, 18 May 1676, E.190/398/6, 29 Feb. 1683/4.
Some Acts of this period related to rivers which appear to have been navigable
already, although they may have required improvement in consequence of fen
drainage: for example, the Little Ouse (T. Badeslade, *The History of the ancient
and present state of the navigation of the port of King's Lynn* (1725), p. 54), the
Waveney (Priestley, *Navigable Rivers*, p. 120), and the Fosdyke (J. W. F. Hill,
Tudor and Stuart Lincoln (Cambridge, 1956), 206–10).

the works, included Samuel Baldwyn of the Inner Temple, Esquire, Timothy Baldwyn, Doctor of Laws, Benjamin Baldwyn of Stoke Castle, Shropshire, gentleman, Sir Clement Clerke of Rudge, Shropshire, John Forth, an ironmonger and alderman of London, George Skipp of Ledbury, Herefordshire, Esquire, and Sir John Poyntz of Iron Acton, Gloucestershire, knight.[1]

Such changes among the proprietors do not appear to have been conducive to the success of the concern. During the 1660s and 1670s at least six separate contracts were made for the completion of the works, and it was later claimed that in all about £8,000 had been laid out on the Stour and £2,000 on the Salwarpe in bringing them to perfection.[2] The first, at least, was navigable for a number of years[3] but successive managers and contractors were handicapped by financial difficulties. Andrew Yarranton, one of this numerous band, recorded his experiences for posterity:[4]

... [following the authorizing Act of 1662] some progress was made with the work, but within a short while after the Act passed it was let fall again. But it being a brat of my own, I was not willing it should be abortive. I made offers to perfect it leaving a third part to me and my heirs forever, and we came to an agreement upon which I fell on it and made it completely navigable from Sturbridge to Kidderminster; and carried down many hundred Tuns of Coales, and laid out near one thousand pounds, and there it was obstructed for want of money which by contract was to be paid.

'I have been at Stourbridge', he had written to one of the undertakers in 1667, 'and I find the want of monies is the thinge that spoyles all.'[5] In May of the same year Lord

---

[1] This paragraph is based upon the collection of partnership agreements and contracts relating to the navigation in Staffordshire R.O., D 1788 (Baldwyn MSS.), pa(rcel). 43, b(undle). 10, pa. 43, b. 3, pa. 59, b. 3, pa. 61, b. 5.

[2] Staffordshire R.O., D 1788, pa. 59, b. 3: *The Earl of Plimouth's Case* (printed broadsheet, n.p., n.d., but *c.* 1700). The Droitwich salt proprietors encouraged the work of the undertakers on the Salwarpe by a grant of salt-water, worth £2,000, Willan, *River Navigation*, p. 66. Their work on the Stour was connected with plans to develop the local coal and iron industries.

[3] According to the parish register of Kidderminster, coal was first brought down from Stourbridge by water in March 1665, *Victoria Country History: Worcestershire* (1906), ii. 252.

[4] Andrew Yarranton, *England's Improvement by Land and Sea* (1677), pp. 65–6.

[5] Staffordshire R.O., D 1788, pa. 59, b. 3, Yarranton to Samuel Baldwyn, 1667.

Windsor complained to Samuel Baldwyn: 'all the Clamours of the whole Country comes to me saying I wrong them and owe them great sums of money'.[1] The wrath of the owners of land taken or damaged without adequate compensation led to obstructive behaviour on their part, which added to the troubles of the undertakers.[2] An undated letter from William Leregoe, one of their agents (and creditors)[3] made

sade account of the navigation of Stowore for want of payment of rentes and damages the Cuntry have discharged the menne for going with the Barges some threatening to cutte the lines others to cutte theyre Legges standing in theyre way with wepones makeinge them to foregoe the way; money oweing in towne and cuntry soe that when the notes come down they are all taken up for debtes . . .

The works were destroyed by floods and attempts at improvement in the 1680s came to nothing.[4] In the winter of 1702-3 a bill was promoted in parliament for the revival of the undertaking by the Earl of Plymouth, Lord Windsor's son, but local owners of land, mills, coal, and salt, petitioned against it and it was lost.[5] The purpose which the navigation had been intended to serve, the development of the coal resources and iron industry of the Stour Valley, was not answered until the completion of the Staffordshire and Worcestershire Canal in the 1770s.

The attempts made to improve the Hampshire Avon from Salisbury to the sea at Christchurch were similarly ill-fated.[6] An Act of 1664/5 had authorized the Lord Chancellor to appoint undertakers, but for ten years nothing was done, it being reported in 1675 that the inhabitants of Salisbury had

---

[1] Ibid., Windsor to Baldwyn, 4 May 1667.

[2] See e.g. ibid., Yarranton to Baldwyn, 5 Dec. 1667. The payment of compensation and purchase money often became a sore point in the early history of river navigation. When a new Act was sought in the early 1700s to revive the Stour the owners of adjacent land objected. The rejoinder of the undertakers was that they should be restrained from making cuts until the land required had been paid for (The Earl of Plimouth's Case).

[3] Staffordshire R.O., D 1788, pa. 59, b. 3, Leregoe to Baldwyn.

[4] Staffordshire R.O., D 1788, pa. 59, b. 3, Articles of Agreement for completing the works, 18 June 1684.

[5] H.C.J. xiv. 7 Off.

[6] This account is based upon T. S. Willan, 'Salisbury and the Navigation of the Avon', Wilts. Arch. and Nat. Hist. Mag. xlvii (1935-7), 592-4; D. A. E. Cross, 'The Salisbury Avon Navigation', Industrial Archaeology, vii (1970), 121-30; P.R.O., Chancery Proceedings, C.5/70/8, C.5/71/15, C.5/78/62.

spent 'all their first vigour in discourse. . . . They talk of nothing but of procuring subscriptions for raising money; and of agreeing with some able persons to undertake the work'.[1] In that year, however, the city's corporation decided to act and declared that it 'shall be concerned £2,000 in the Worke'. It wrote to the Bishops of Salisbury and Chichester, the Earls of Shaftesbury and Clarendon, Sir John Nicholas, Sir Eliab Harvey, and William Chiffinch, telling them 'of the great worke of the navigation undertaken by this Corporation, and of the vast charge they are like to be at about it, in hopes they will be pleased to lend their assistance to so good and publiq a worke'. But the financial burden was assumed by three lesser men: Henry Hedges, surgeon, Thomas Bennet, and Thomas Dennet, gentlemen, all of Salisbury.

They spent about £3,500, partly out of their own resources (no evidence has been noticed of assistance from the corporation of Salisbury) and partly by borrowing on the security of the works or of personal bonds. Sums raised in this way included £350 from Thomas Pitt of the Inner Temple, Esquire, £200 from Woolstone Abbot of Salisbury, gentleman, £100 from James Green of the Close, Salisbury, £100 from John Cooke of Fisherton Anger (a suburb of the city), silkweaver, £58 from John Clements of Symons Inn, London, gentleman, £46 from Barnaby Wilcocks, unstyled, and an unspecified sum from Mary Starr of Salisbury, widow. By the 1680s the river was in use by barges, but its proprietors became entangled in debts and law suits. In 1690 came the report that 'by reason of storms and flood and the present neglect thereof they (the works) dayly run more and more to ruine and destruction'; the river could not be expected to yield a profit; 'especially till after this present war', without a considerable further expenditure. By 1693 all the original undertakers were either dead or brought 'through misfortune low in the world' and the works were in the hands of their creditors: Thomas Pitt of the Inner Temple, Robert Woodward, Doctor of Laws, and Wingfield Brockwell, who has not been identified. These new owners appear to have

---

[1] Cf. Staffordshire R.O., D 1788, pa. 59, b. 3, Yarranton to Baldwyn, 16 Feb. 1676: 'Mr Leregoe is come home. They cannot agree at Salisbury, because soe many men, so many minds.' Yarranton had surveyed the river for the corporation (Willan, 'Salisbury', p. 592).

accomplished little. A bill was introduced in the parliament of 1699–1700 for the revival of the scheme but hostile petitions were preferred by local landowners aggrieved at the damage done to their lands, and it was thrown out.[1] Some work was done which allowed navigation to be resumed after 1700 but about the year 1730 it was abandoned for good.

A common feature of many projects of the 1690s and early 1700s was the initiative of undertakers acting in rather larger bodies than had hitherto been customary. Typically these were the leading inhabitants of the town or towns which stood at the head of the navigation, sometimes acting in their corporate capacity. The Colne was undertaken in 1698 by the corporation of Colchester which raised money on the mortgage of its estates, including £1,200 from the executors of William Hewer of Clapham, Surrey, the former clerk of Samuel Pepys.[2] The undertakers of the river Tone named in the Act of 1699 included seven gentlemen, seven clothiers, five merchants, two grocers, two fullers, two vintners, an ironmonger, a maltster, a dyer, a mercer, and a doctor of physic, all of the parishes of Taunton and Wilton.[3] Under the Act of 1705 the Essex Stour was undertaken by the mayor, aldermen, and ten gentlemen, of the town of Sudbury.[4]

The most important enterprise of this generation and type was unquestionably the Aire and Calder; it is also one of the few for which a reasonably exact measure of the financial contributions of the different occupational groups may be obtained. According to the proud boast of Ralph Thoresby, the historian of Leeds, the improvement was executed 'at the Expence of several private merchants the Proprietors, without calling in the Assistance of the Nobility and Gentry as had been usual in like cases'. This statement is substantially correct: landowners accounted for about £2,000 or 20% of the original subscription; the remainder of the sum required was provided by merchants and a few lesser tradesmen of Leeds and Wakefield.[5]

[1] H.C.J. xiii. 157, 161.
[2] Willan, *River Navigation,* pp. 73–4.
[3] Ibid., p. 56.
[4] 4/5 Anne *cap.* 2.
[5] R. W. Unwin, 'The Aire and Calder Navigation. Part I: The beginning of the Navigation', *The Bradford Antiquary,* n.s. xlii (1964), 57-60.

A few navigations were still made by undertakers acting individually in the older tradition. Thus the merchant Thomas Patten of Bank Hall, Warrington, improved the Mersey from Runcorn to that town in 1694.[1] The case of the upper Trent was similar. Schemes for its improvement between Wilden Ferry and Burton had been in agitation for many years: in 1665 the grand jury of Staffordshire had reported unfavourably upon the project because of the threat which it posed to vested agrarian and commercial interests;[2] in 1699 it nevertheless received parliamentary sanction in answer to the pleas of the townspeople of Burton whose trade was in decline.[3] The undertaker appointed by the Act of that year was Sir William Paget (later, Lord Paget), the proprietor of the town and of local colliery interests. Paget was to provide £600 towards the cost of the works and a further £600 was to come from the inhabitants of Burton. For more than a decade, however, nothing was accomplished, at least not by Paget himself. In 1711 he came to an agreement with George Hayne of Wirksworth, gentleman, apparently a merchant engaged in the salt trade, which declared that, because their difficulty and expense were greater than had been anticipated, the works had not yet been completed:

... the said Navigation hath not since the passing of the said Act been by any person attempted until the said George Hayne hath endeavoured to Navigate on the said River in Wintertime and hath now proposed to undertake at his own charges to make the said River Trent Navigable so as he may have such benefit and advantage of the said Navigation for his own particular use.

This he did, with the assistance of a donation of £600 over six years from Lord Paget.

It appears that by this time the finance of most navigations was entirely in the hands of local men, but Londoners

[1] T. Heywood (ed.), *The Norris Papers* (Chetham Society, ix, 1846), pp. 37–8.

[2] Staffordshire R.O., Q/SO 7, Order Book of Staffordshire Quarter Sessions 1659/60–1667, ff. 123–5.

[3] Staffordshire R.O., D 1734/2/5 ls, Addresses (*c.* 1692 and 1694) of the inhabitants of Burton on Trent to the landowners of Staffordshire and Derbyshire seeking their consent to make the Trent navigable to Burton and promising compensation for damages done in making the improvements. Further details are taken from C. C. Owen, 'The Early History of the Upper Trent Navigation', *Transport History*, i (1968), 233–59.

occasionally took an interest in the rivers of southern England at least. The Itchen, from Winchester to Southampton, had been the subject of an Act of parliament in 1663, although nothing had been done under it. In 1695 the river was undertaken by William Bayley of St. Leonard's, Shoreditch, London, gentleman. The work proving too much for him,[1] in 1701 it passed to Richard Soame, a London merchant. Soame in his turn suffered from financial embarrassments (a commission of bankruptcy was issued against him in 1704), and in 1711 the river came into the hands of his principal creditor, George Huxley, a London attorney. Huxley, in collaboration with Paul Daranda of London, merchant, continued the work of improvement and attempted the development of a trade in coal and corn with the assistance of the money of relatives by whom he was employed as a financial intermediary.[2]

Among the navigations undertaken during the years from 1714 to 1727 was the Derwent from the Trent to the town of Derby. An Act for its improvement was obtained in 1719 in the face of intense opposition from the owners of estates on the river and from the towns of Nottingham, Bawtry, and Chesterfield (Acts had been sought unsuccessfully in 1664, 1675, 1676, 1695, 1698, and 1702). The undertakers named were all prominent tradesmen of the town of Derby.[3] In 1720 an Act was passed for the navigation of the Weaver which appointed a number of landowners as undertakers. However, in consequence of a dispute over the payment of parliamentary expenses they did nothing; it was eventually completed between 1730 and 1733 by three tradesmen of Manchester, Warrington, and Stockport, the works apparently being financed out of their own capital.[4] The Act of 1721 for the Mersey and Irwell between Manchester and

[1] In 1698 Bayley had also undertaken the improvement of the Exe, but he absconded with the money provided by the Corporation of Exeter for this purpose: T. S. Willan, 'English Coasting Trade and Inland Navigation, 1600–1750' (Oxford University D.Phil. Thesis, 1934), p. 322.

[2] P.R.O., Exchequer K.R., Bills and Answers, E. 112/1041/42.

[3] F. Williamson, 'George Sorocold of Derby', *Journal of the Derbyshire Arch. and Nat. Hist. Soc.* lvii (1936), 48–53; Derby Central Library, Derby Canal Coll. no. 15, Deeds of the Derwent Navigation 1720–1.

[4] *The Navigation of the River Weaver in the Eighteenth Century*, ed. T. S. Willan (Chetham Society, 3rd Ser., iii, 157), pp. 22–5, 28–33.

Warrington named forty undertakers who included two Justices of the Peace, thirty-three residents of Manchester (mostly tradesmen), and three of Liverpool (two merchants and an engineer).[1] The undertakers of the Somerset Avon between Bath and Bristol, improved in the years 1725-28 at a cost of £12,000, included two peers, a bishop, seven country gentlemen, seventeen residents of Bath (three 'Esquires', four 'gentlemen', six tradesmen, three women, and a physician), and three residents of Bristol (a 'gentleman', a lawyer, and the timber-merchant John Hobbs who was the principal promoter of the concern).[2]

The Berkshire Kennet, a navigation of these years, is of some interest for the participation of London capital in a provincial undertaking as an effect, it appears, of the speculative excitement associated with the South Sea Bubble. The first Act for the river's improvement,[3] passed in 1715, named as undertakers Richard Cowslade of East Woodhay, Hampshire, Esquire, the author of a number of charitable foundations in the town of Newbury,[4] Thomas Cowslade, Esquire, an Inner Temple barrister and local landowner,[5] Henry Martin, Esquire, a Middle Temple lawyer with local connections,[6] and John Hore, the engineer of the navigation, one of a family of maltsters and propertied men of Newbury and district.[7] Three other undertakers, Bazile Broadwood, Esquire, Thomas Milsom, gentleman, and Thomas Pocock, gentleman, have not been identified, although the last bore the name of a local landed family.[8] The first efforts at improvement were defeated by floods, and by 1720, when a second Act was obtained to extend the time allowed for the

[1] A. P. Wadsworth and J. de L. Mann, *The Cotton Trade and Industrial Lancashire 1600-1780* (Manchester, 1931), pp. 219-20.

[2] AN 1/5, Minutes of the Commissioners 1725-1822, copy of the Deed of Assignment from the Corporation of Bath to the Undertakers, 10 Mar. 1725.

[3] 1 George I Private Act.

[4] *Report of the Commissioners for Inquiring Concerning Charities, Parl. Papers 1837-8*, xxv, 349.

[5] He was described in his epitaph as 'one of the company of Kennet River improvers': Elias Ashmole, *The Antiquities of Berkshire* (1719), ii. 282.

[6] H. A. C. Sturgess (ed.), *Register of Admissions to the Honourable Society of the Middle Temple, 1501-1944* (1949), i. 214, 288.

[7] F. S. Thacker, *Kennet Country* (1932), p. 317.

[8] *Victoria County History: Berkshire*, iv (1924), 58.

completion of the works, control of the concern had passed from the original undertakers to a group of London financiers, apparently through the intermediation of Henry Martin.[1]

The first recorded meeting of the London proprietors was held in June of the same year, when the Bubble was reaching its most extravagant proportions. They appear to have reacted unfavourably to the business methods of their predecessors:[2]

The managing of the Accounts being considered it appears that their having been kept by many hands and withall not well methodized for the purpose has put things into some confusion that we can't satisfie ourselves in such particulars relating to the accounts as is necessary which being matter of consequence is very perplexing to us.

In the aftermath of the South Sea Bubble they found themselves in financial difficulties. By July 1721 William Dale of Covent Garden, one of their number, was £2,000 in arrears in the payment of calls on his share,[3] while a fortnight before, the engineer John Hore had reported from the country of[4]

his Proceedings with the workmen & of the scarcity of both Workmen and Mony that the last he used was borrowed & prest to have some more before Saturday for if should be in want of cash for ye Men fear'd should have more overlookers than labourers.

The undertakers in their turn complained of the 'great scarcity of money' and declared their inability to raise any more at present.[5] A plan had been mooted, presumably when the speculative fever of 1720 was at its height, to put half the navigation in trust as security for 2,000 shares of £30, but this had come to nothing.[6] Nevertheless, by the autumn of

[1] T. S. Willan, 'The Navigation of the Thames and Kennet, 1600–1750', *Berkshire Arch. Journal*, xl (1936), 152–3.

[2] KN 1/1, Minutes of the Undertakers 1720–7, 7 June, 14 June 1720.

[3] Ibid., 11 July 1721.

[4] Ibid., 27 July 1721. For similar complaints of scarcity of money in the country see ibid., 31 Oct., 6 Nov. 1723, 23 Apr. 1724.

[5] Ibid., 4 July 1721.

[6] Willan, 'Thames and Kennet', pp. 152–3. For a similar attempt at this time to 'make a Bubble' of the Douglas Navigation, see Wadsworth and Mann, *Cotton Trade*, pp. 214–17; P.R.O., Exchequer K. R. Bills and Answers, E.112/990/908: Landor Jones of Lincoln's Inn, employed in 1720 by a Middlesex widow to lay

1723 the river was reported as having been made navigable, though the following January 'the Occasions for Money being yet unprovided for' the undertakers welcomed the report from a Mr. Burman which gave them 'expectations of being served by a Friend an attorney employed by a Gentleman in ye country to put out £1,000 or £1,500'. A mortgage of a share in the navigation securing £1,500 at 5% interest was subsequently executed to Dr. George Cheyne of Bath, Doctor of Physic.[1]

By January 1727 the share capital of the concern totalled £36,881[2] and the proprietors included James Ferne of Old Jewry, St. Olave, surgeon[3] (£11,644 invested), William, Lord Forbes, a Scottish peer who in September 1720 had married the daughter[4] of William Dale, a then shareholder (£7,006), James Brain[5] (£3,163), Humphrey Hill[6] (£3,040), and John Midford[7] (£1,578), all merchants of London, Bendal Martin, Esquire, the son of Henry Martin, an undertaker of 1715[8] (£1,376), and William Martyn, apparently Henry's brother, of Plow Court, Lombard Street, attorney[9] (£119). Four of the proprietors, James Milner, Esquire[10] (£2,200), Captain Francis Willis (£2,970), Thomas Evans (£2,609) and Jacob Wyan (£1,175) have not been satisfactorily identified.

Finally, a few later river navigations may be mentioned. The Don Navigation, on which work began in the late 1720s, was financed almost wholly by the merchants, manu-

---

out her money, deals in, among other things, Douglas Navigation shares; P.R.O., PROB 3/20/115: Inventory of Nathaniel Denew, City of Canterbury, Esquire, 1721, listing subscriptions to many of the bubble companies of 1720, including three subscriptions to shares in the Douglas.

[1] KN 1/1, 15 Oct. 1723, 21 Jan., 4 Apr. 1724.

[2] Ibid., 10 Jan. 1727.   [3] *Middle Temple Register*, i, 295.

[4] 'Her fortune of £20 000 was all lost in the South Sea Scheme and other crazy speculations of 1720', G.E.C., *The Complete Peerage* (1926), v. 548.

[5] For his dealings in tobacco in the 1690s, see P.R.O., E. 112/986/708, 710.

[6] Kent's *London Directory* (1736).

[7] For his dealings in tobacco in 1725, see P.R.O., Court of Bankruptcy Order Book, B.1/18, f.160. In 1743 his shares in the river were seized by the Crown to be sold by the Commissioners of the Customs (Thacker, *Kennet Country*, p. 320).

[8] *Middle Temple Register*, i. 288.

[9] Ibid., i. 226; KN 1/1, 2 Mar. 1725.

[10] In 1725 two of the undertakers had been ordered to wait on 'Mr Millner at Tatnum' (? Tottenham) to treat for a 1/16th share in the river, KN 1/1, 16 Nov. 1725.

facturers, and tradesmen, of the towns of Sheffield and Doncaster. Local landowners had offered prolonged opposition to the scheme.[1] Of the £15,075 subscribed under an Act of 1756 for improving the Nene from Northampton to Peterborough, £8,200 (54%) was provided by local landowners and country clergymen, and £6,275 (42%) by residents of the town of Northampton.[2] The Witham Navigation, undertaken between 1762 and 1766 to improve the communication of the port of Boston with the sea, was financed by the corporation and merchants of that town who have been identified as contributing £5,000 of the £6,800 subscribed.[3]

Making the Calder and Hebble between Wakefield and Halifax navigable has first been proposed in 1740 but at that time the opposition of land- and mill-owners was too powerful.[4] The project was revived in 1756 and an authorizing Act followed two years later.[5] Unfortunately, after £56,900, raised on mortgage, had been spent under it, the uncompleted works were severely damaged by floods. In 1769 it was therefore necessary to obtain a further Act incorporating the creditors as proprietors so that additional capital might be raised.[6] The navigation was completed during the 1770s at a total cost of about £70,000. No proper account of the shareholdings has been found but from the record of interest payments to proprietors in 1775 the principal sources of capital may be estimated.[7] The most important were merchants and manufacturers in the clothing trade who contri-

[1] DUN 2/1, Share Ledger 1730–41. T. S. Willan, *The Early History of the Don Navigation* (Manchester, 1965), pp. 1–30.

[2] Calculated from Welland and Nene River Authority, Oundle, Nene Navigation MSS., Book of Assignments 1762.

[3] WTN 1/1, Minutes of the Proprietors 1762–1817.

[4] B.T.H.R. (York), CHN 1/1, Committee Minutes 1756–8 22 July, 24 Aug. 1757.

[5] Wadsworth and Mann, *Cotton Trade,* p. 221; 31 George II *cap.* 72. This Act was referred to in the *Annual Register* for 1760 under 'Projects' p. 144, as evidence that parliament would sanction navigations of whose utility it was convinced, in spite of the opposition which they might arouse, if safeguards were provided for mill-owners and others whose interests were threatened. 'On the other hand', it was conceded, 'there are instances when great opposition in parliament hath frustrated beneficial proposals; but that was many years ago, and at a time when public improvements were not so much encouraged as at present.'

[6] *H.C.J.* xxxii. 102–3; 9 George III *cap.* 71.

[7] B.T.H.R. (York), CHN 4/12, Cash Book 1775–80, ff. 3–5.

buted £30,000–£40,000; landowners[1] accounted for about
£7,000; other proprietors including six clergymen, ten
women, and some physicians and attorneys. Most investors
lived in and about Halifax; a dozen came from Ripponden,
Rochdale, or Manchester, and were no doubt interested in
the improvement of communications to Hull through which
many of Lancashire's consignments to London were made.[2]

Some general conclusions may now be drawn. River
improvement was usually forwarded by mercantile interests;
landowners took little part and indeed were often actively
obstructive. Certainly there were good reasons for this:
navigation might prejudice mills, cause flooding through the
raising of the water-level, or through embankments prevent
flooding when required for the floating of water-meadows,[3]
while artificial cuts separated fields from their farms. To add
insult to injury, many hardpressed improvers could not
afford to pay promptly for the damage which they caused,[4]
and when acting by right of royal patent under the early
Stuarts were associated with the arbitrary policy of the
Crown. Thus Arnold Spencer, undertaker of the Ouse,
'beareing himselfe upon the Authority of this pattent [of
1638] did at first affright ye Country people with it
threatening to bring them before King and Councell if they
opposed him . . .'[5] He entered

other mens' grounds without their consent scoured the ffords between
Eaton and Barford (being common highwayes) and so for 3 or 4 yeares
made the river passable (yet only in times of high water) to Barford
Bridge. But the Country (in a little time) haveing a better understanding
of ye matter the owners of the grounds pulled up his works damed up
ye Cutts Indicted Spencer for scouring the ffords (which were highwayes) and thus began and thus ended . . . all Spencer's right and works
betweene St. Neots and Barford . . .

[1] I have considered as such Sir George Savile, Thomas Thornhill, Esquire, of
Fixby, Samuel Burroughs, Esquire, of Crownest, Lady Salisbury, Francis
Thornhaugh, and F. F. Foljambe.

[2] L. Moffit, *England on the Eve of the Industrial Revolution* (2nd edn., 1963),
p. 150.

[3] The landowners of Wiltshire feared this: see J(ames H(ely), *A Modest
Representation of the Benefits and Advantages of Making the River Avon
Navigable* (1672).

[4] See, for example, above, p. 5).

[5] Bury St. Edmunds and West Suffolk R.O., Cullum MSS., E2/17/1. Spencer
had begun his enterprise in 1618 under an earlier patent. The patent of 1638 was
apparently intended to reinforce it.

The breakdown of royal authority in the early 1640s brought similar attacks on William Sandys and his improvements of the Warwickshire Avon.[1]

It is however perhaps surprising that the hostility or indifference of proprietors was so infrequently relieved by warmer feelings. Might they not have had an interest in the improvement of communications for the contribution it could make to the prosperity of their estates? It seems that only rarely did they find any such interest sufficient compensation for the loss of amenity entailed. Indeed commonly they favoured high transport costs as a defence for the local monopolies of agricultural producers. Whether their unfavourable judgements always followed an entirely rational calculation of economic benefit is to be doubted. One senses at times an atavistic fear of the enterprise of alien commercial forces and of the extension of the market economy. Thus in 1665 the gentlemen of Staffordshire recommended against making the Trent navigable:[2]

As for the pretended new advantage, the profit thereof for goods exported hence will wholly fall to some tradesmen of the Citty of London, who have caused the Country chapmen who of late have sent goods down that river to abate soe much as they save out of the land carriage and for goods imported the advantages will fall to a few tradesmen among ourselves.

The early extension of river navigation proceeded slowly. During the seventeenth century only seven rivers were successfully improved and for some of these the work was drawn out over many decades,[3] while several other projects

1 In November 1641 it was reported that 'the profits upon his river business are likely to be worth nothing, for the owners of land where the river passeth will not suffer any to pass, but shut down the hatches and threaten to arrest any that come upon their ground' (*Cal. S.P. Dom. 1641-3*, p. 174).

2 Staffordshire R.O., Q/SO 7, Order Book of Staffordshire Quarter Sessions 1659/60–1667, f. 125: recommendation of the Grand Jury. In general on the opposition of landowners see Willan, *River Navigation*, pp. 45-6, 138.

3 The Bedfordshire Ouse, Little Ouse, Waveney, Welland, Wey, Upper Thames, and Warwickshire Avon. Also, the Fosdyke Navigation was apparently restored: see above, p. 3, n. 3. It is sometimes alleged that the Somerset Tone was made navigable by John Malet before the Civil War, but the fact that in 1698 his heirs disposed of their interest in the river for £330 does not suggest that any improvements which he may have effected were permanent: Somerset R.O., Tone Commissioners MSS., DD/TC, Box 24, copy of the assignment of interest in the Tone 1698.

failed completely. Their difficulties, as perceived by the undertakers themselves, appear most frequently to have been those of finance: in the words of Andrew Yarranton, 'the want of monies is the thinge that spoyles all'.[1] Of course such assertions prove little. They cannot be considered sufficient evidence that it was a general scarcity of capital in the economy which inhibited river improvement. The true source of the undertakers' troubles might rather have been other circumstances, perhaps a low level of commercial activity which did not offer the prospect of a level of traffic and revenue sufficient to reassure those from whom they sought credit. This raises wider questions about the role of capital accumulation in England's economic development which are best reserved for the concluding chapter. However it must be noted here that at least some of the successfully completed navigations were profitable to their owners. In the 1650s the Wey, on which £15,000 had been spent, yielded £2,000 per annum.[2] Daniel Wigmore devoted £5,000 in the 1670s to the improvement of the Welland which was said in 1695 to have been worth £400–£500 yearly before the outbreak of war with France in 1689.[3] Over the first twenty years after its completion, between 1717 and 1736, the Tone Navigation paid an average annual dividend of 4·8% on its capital of £5,697.[4] On the other hand, the profits on two fifteenth shares in the Warwickshire Avon totalled: 1679–82, £1. 15s. 10d. (very low, because of the 'deadness of trade'); 1683, £14. 11s. 0d.; 1684, £11. 12s. 0d.[5] The figures, although the cost of this navigation is not known, suggest a low rate of return.[6]

Most improvers invested personally sums wholly out of proportion to any direct benefits which they could have

[1] Quoted above, p. 4.

[2] P.R.O., E. 136/10, Exchequer K.R. Decree Book, 20–3 Charles II, f. 101. But this navigation later ran into difficulties.

[3] H.C.J. xi. 388.

[4] Calculated from Somerset R.O., Tone Commissioners MSS., DD/TC no. 1, Treasurer's Memorandum Book.

[5] P.R.O., Chancery Proceedings, C.5/198/15.

[6] It is difficult to reconcile with these figures the claim made by the Countess of Plymouth in 1696 that her rights in the Avon, derived from the Earl of Plymouth, were worth £400 per annum: H.C.J. xi. 376. In 1684 Plymouth's share in the river amounted to nearly one half: P.R.O., C.5/198/15.

expected to derive through the reduction of shipment costs on their own goods; their undertakings must therefore have usually been made for the sake of the income likely to accrue from serving the trade of others. However some, for example the undertakers of the Worcestershire Stour who had local interests in coal and iron, may have regarded their river work as ancillary to other business activities.[1] The fact that so many improvers were ruined suggests that the profits hoped for were high. Thus, again in the case of the Stour, a return of £3,375 per annum was anticipated on an outlay which was probably not expected to exceed £5,000.[2]

Most improvers of provincial rivers were local men but an important minority came from London, whether as financiers of undertakings or as undertakers themselves,[3] and among these Londoners lawyers are conspicuous. They may have been drawn in through their usual business as financial intermediaries, or through work as parliamentary agents. This last point is one upon which further research would be desirable.

---

[1] C. Hadfield, *The Canals of the West Midlands* (Newton Abbot, 1966), p. 58.

[2] Staffordshire R.O., D 1788, Baldwyn MSS. pa. 59, b. 3. The issues raised by these problems of motive are discussed at greater length, with reference to canals, in Chapter V.

[3] In addition to the examples already cited in this chapter see P.R.O., Wey Navigation Claims, E.171/1, nos. 8, 9, 53, 54, 65: shares in the Wey Navigation sold or mortgaged in the 1650s to Londoners by the local undertakers, and loans to the undertakers by Londoners; R. Craig, 'Some Aspects of the Trade and Shipping of the River Dee in the Eighteenth Century', *Trans. Hist. Soc. Lancs. and Cheshire*, cxiv (1962), 100: abortive undertaking of the Dee in the 1690s by Francis Gell of London, merchant; *H.C.J.* xxv. 292–3: unsuccessful petition of 17 Feb. 1747 by Simon Wood, citizen and haberdasher of London, for the right to undertake the Salwarpe.

II

THE FINANCE OF CANAL BUILDING

IN this chapter summary accounts are given of the financial histories of all the principal canal companies, and of a large proportion of the lesser ones.[1] Wherever possible these accounts are preceded by an analysis of the sources of capital upon which they drew, based on the occupations of their proprietors and, in cases where they borrowed substantially, of their creditors. The classification chosen for this purpose is as follows:

I	Peers
II	Landed gentlemen
III	Yeomen, graziers, tenant farmers
IV	Capitalists
V	Manufacturers
VI	Tradesmen
VII	Professional men
VIII	Clergymen
IX	Women

This exercise raises certain problems of method, the first being that of the quality of the sources upon which it is based.

Canals, with only one important exception (the Duke of Bridgewater's navigations), were built by joint-stock companies. Their capital was raised, in the first instance, by making calls on shares which had usually been wholly or largely subscribed for at the time they received parliamentary sanction. This sanction, necessary under the terms of the 'Bubble Act' of 1720, was granted by Acts which served both to incorporate the intending proprietors and to grant (and regulate) the powers which they required to make compulsory purchases of land, levy tolls, etc.[2] The analyses which

---

[1] For some indication of its scope compare it with the complete list of undertakings given by Priestley, *Navigable Rivers, Canals and Railways*.

[2] For details see C. Hadfield, *British Canals* (2nd edn., 1959), pp. 35–8; O. C. Williams, *The Historical Development of Private Bill Procedure and Standing*

follow are in each case based upon the earliest available list of shareholdings, which usually dates from the time at which the Act of incorporation was obtained (often this is the only surviving list). Calls on these shares were made as construction proceeded, the period over which the capital originally authorized was exhausted in this way averaging about five years. During this time shares could and did change hands, the only restriction being that transfers were not permitted in the case of securities on which an unpaid call remained outstanding. Some companies imposed additional controls: that of the Ashby-de-la-Zouch Canal insisted, in order to discourage speculative subscriptions, that no alienation of any share might be made until £15 had been paid on it.[1] However, regulations of this kind are not common. It was thus possible, in principle, for the character of a company as originally constituted to change substantially while its capital was actually being raised (once incorporation had been obtained new proprietors were admissable without any further formality). To what extent did this occur, and how reliable are the original lists of subscribers or newly incorporated proprietors? The secondary market in canal stock is discussed elsewhere;[2] here it is merely necessary to say that, on the evidence of the surviving transfer records, the rate at which shares changed hands was low. Furthermore, new admissions to a company by purchase were usually, taken collectively, of a similar social and occupational character to the original proprietary. The early lists of shareholders may thus be used with some confidence as reliable guides to investments actually made. The problems of 'stagging', of the insertion of fictitious names, and of the very high rates of turnover in scrip which introduce doubts concerning the value of, for example, the nineteenth-century railway subscription contracts[3] do not arise in the case of canal companies.

Orders in the House of Commons, i (1948), 27–37, 43–6; A. B. Dubois, *The English Business Company after the Bubble Act 1720–1800* (New York, 1938), pp. 3ff.

[1] ASCH 1/1, Minutes of the Subscribers 1792–4, 8 Nov. 1972.

[2] Below, pp. 100–8, 183–5.

[3] Cf. S. A. Broadbridge, 'The Early Capital Market: The Lancashire and Yorkshire Railway', *Econ. Hist. Rev.*, 2nd Ser., viii (1955), 201 and references.

The names of subscribers and shareholders are usually given in company records with the addition of their addresses and/or styles, indicating their occupation or social status. Deficiencies in these respects, have, so far as it is possible, been remedied by the use of directories,[1] poll books, local histories, and other miscellaneous sources of information. Additionally, in the case of a number of companies, use has been made of the subscription contracts (lists of persons who had bound themselves to take shares in the undertaking) which, under the terms of the standing orders of both houses of parliament adopted in 1794, were required from that date to be deposited by the promoters of every new scheme.[2] These documents give only the names of the intending proprietors with the amounts subscribed. The task of identifying persons named in company records and subscription contracts has been facilitated by the narrowly circumscribed geographical distribution of the typical proprietary: most investors lived in close proximity to the canals which they financed. It has been further assisted by the organization of many of the lists. In some cases—for example, that of the Staffordshire and Worcestershire canal—the proprietors are listed in their Act of incorporation by rank, the peers coming first, followed by the 'gentry', and finally the tradesmen. In others, for example the subscription contracts of the Rochdale and the Peak Forest Canals, subscribers from particular localities are grouped together. Finally, it is the good fortune of the researcher that the early 1790s, during which the greater part of the canal companies were promoted and incorporated, saw the publication of the *Universal British Directory*, a compilation which, though by no means complete in its coverage, was infinitely superior to anything of its kind which had appeared before, or was to appear for many years afterwards. However, in spite of these auspicious circumstances, by no means all investors can be satisfactorily identified. An obvious problem is that of the more common names (John Smith, etc.) for which more than one identification is possible, if they are not fully described in the company records. Fortunately this does not occur very often,

---

[1] The directories used are listed in the bibliography below, p. 205.
[2] *H.C.J.* xlix. 473–5, 561–2. They are now in the custody of the House of Lords Record Office.

for the range of investors upon which the canal companies drew was limited. When such cases have been met with, the proprietor in question has been classified as 'unknown'. In the 1760s and 1770s satisfactory provincial directories were few and thus the investigation of the early companies has been impeded. With some the lacunae are so great that no analysis has been attempted; with others the proportion of shareholders who remain unknown is disturbingly high. Nevertheless, I believe that the quantity and quality of the available sources are sufficient to validate the exercise. Even the best documented proprietaries usually include a few unidentified investors. Where their contribution is less than five per cent of the company's total capital it has been assimilated into that of their colleagues; where it is more it is presented separately and the per cent figures given are percentages of known investors only.

Identification is the first problem of method, classification is the second. The following remarks may serve to elaborate upon the scheme presented at the beginning of this chapter. Classes I, II, and III, represent the 'landed interest'. Holders of both effective and courtesy titles have been admitted to Class I as peers. Class II comprehends Baronets, Esquires, and 'gentlemen', resident at rural addresses, who have been considered 'landed gentlemen', unless some good reason for not doing so is known. This class is, of course, well served by works of topography and family history.[1] Investors have been usually placed in Class III only if they are styled as yeomen, graziers, or farmers, in company records. As lesser landowners and tenant farmers were beneath the notice of topographers and do not appear in trade directories, they are of all classes the most difficult to identify. Fortunately, however, there is little doubt that the part they played in the finance of canals was slight; in the records of those companies in which the addresses and descriptive additions of proprietors are given in full the suffixes 'yeoman', 'farmer', or their equivalents, are very rare. But occasionally,[2] to identify such investors, use has been made of the Books of

---

[1] Persons resident in the West End of London or in other towns have been admitted to this class if they may be identified from such sources as substantial landowners.

[2] The Grantham and Peak Forest companies, below, pp. 41, 58.

Reference of owners and occupiers of land to be taken by the canal works which promoters were required to deposit, from 1792, with the Clerks of the Peace of the counties affected and, from 1794, with parliament as well.[1]

Classes IV, V, VI, and VII, together may be taken to represent the urban middle classes. Class IV, 'capitalists',[2] includes merchants, bankers, and substantial rentiers. Men sometimes styled themselves 'merchant' without warrant and the authenticity of such pretensions has been checked, where possible, in the trade directories. In inland towns only general merchants have been recognized as 'capitalists', and timber-merchants, wine-merchants, etc., are classified, rather arbitrarily, as 'tradesmen'. In port towns, however, where such specialist merchants are likely to have been engaged in overseas trade and to have been richer than their provincial counterparts, they are considered 'capitalists'. Class V, 'manufacturers', comprehends persons engaged in the rapidly changing and growing industries which produced for mass markets, in particular the woollen, cotton, iron, pottery, and metal-ware manufactures. Brewers, tanners, tailors, wheel-wrights, and others participating in industries which were widely dispersed and served limited markets, have been categorized, along with grocers, mercers, ironmongers, etc., as 'tradesmen'.[3] Class VII, the professions (attorneys, surgeons, apothecaries, etc.), is clear enough. Classes VIII and IX, clergymen and women, are not functional classifications in the sense of those preceding. Clergymen, in so far as their income was derived from glebe, tithes, and personal estates in land (no attempt has been made to distinguish dissenting clergymen, but few have been noticed), might be classified with the 'landed interest'. On the other hand, in some cases their style of life and habits of expenditure may have approximated more closely to those of the urban middle classes with whom, on the evidence of their names, many appear to have had family connections, while the investments

[1] Williams, *Private Bill Procedure*, i. 43–6.

[2] This term was invented in the later eighteenth century, its first known use being by Bentham in 1786: I. R. Christie (ed.), *The Correspondence of Jeremy Bentham*, iii (1781–8) (1971) 454.

[3] No investment has been noticed by a London porter-brewer, so the problem of classification which he would present does not arise.

THE FINANCE OF CANAL BUILDING

of women, invariably, of course, widows and spinsters, were with very few exceptions (an occasional milliner appears) made with wealth derived from the activities of others. It may be noticed that although, to avoid an undue proliferation of categories, these groups have not been subdivided in the analyses offered here, roughly one half of the clergymen and three quarters of the women who appear as proprietors of canals were resident in towns. Thus it seems likely that a considerable proportion of the wealth of the first, and the greater part of that of the second, were derived originally from 'trade'. But considered together these two groups, which accounted between them for only about twelve per cent of the invested capital for which adequate data are available,[1] need not be regarded as presenting any very serious difficulties in the analysis which is attempted here.

All these classifications may be criticized, in detail. The close intermingling of landed and commercial wealth in eighteenth-century England is a commonplace: the fortune of a 'landowner' might have originated in the East or West Indies or in some trade nearer home; a considerable proportion of his income might be derived from coal royalties or the lease of industrial premises. Tradesmen or merchants, especially the most eminent ones, might have substantial interests in real property.[2] I have not attempted the intensive local research which the resolution of the practical ambiguities introduced by these facts would require. Nevertheless, contemporaries admitted the distinction between 'land' and 'trade' and there is no reason why we should not do the same, while remembering that in practice it was blurred at the edges and that it will never be possible to establish the exact provenance of every sovereign which the canal company treasurers received.

The subdivision of the urban middle classes raises questions of its own. In the eighteenth-century economy the functions of commerce, manufacture, and finance were con-

[1] Below, p. 74.

[2] Cf R. Grassby, 'English Merchant Capitalism in the Late Seventeenth Century', *Past and Present*, no. 46 (Feb. 1970), p. 93, n. 17: 'It is extremely rare to find merchants resident in England worth more than £500 without some freehold land . . .'

fusingly interwound. A 'linendraper' at, say, Barnsley might be engaged in putting out to the domestic industry, being thus a 'manufacturer'; at, say, Banbury he would almost certainly be a retailer, and thus a 'tradesman'; but in London he might be engaged in overseas trade and the finance of country manufacturers and shopkeepers, being thus a very substantial 'capitalist'. Or an individual, for example a Manchester merchant-manufacturer in the cotton trade, might combine two functions. Instances of this kind could be multiplied. The problems which they pose can only be met pragmatically; a personal judgement of the circumstances, which space does not permit me to set out *in extenso*, has often supplemented the bald suffixes employed in directories and shareholders' lists. The distinction attempted in the following analyses between Classes IV, V, and VI, must therefore be regarded with particular scepticism.

A further difficulty is presented by the 'urban gentry': persons styled 'Esquire' or 'gentleman' living in towns. These tendentious additions, when employed in shareholders' lists, have wherever possible been checked against the evidence of the directories. Although they were not, on the whole, used lightly they had by the later eighteenth century long since lost their original connotations. For example, as is well known, attorneys at this time almost invariably styled themselves 'gentleman'. A tendency has also been noticed for shopkeepers and others of quite menial standing to assume the mantle of gentility, especially when subscribing to schemes outside their own neighbourhood. Doubts must therefore be entertained as to the value of any analysis in which such pretensions are not scrutinized critically.[1]

However, even when imposters have been eradicated there often remains a residuum of investors who are not recorded in directories as active trades- or professional men and are sometimes included explicitly among the 'gentry' of the town in which they lived. What was their economic status? According to an historian of King's Lynn:

[1] Such as, for example, that of J. R. Killick and W. A. Thomas, 'The Provincial Stock Exchanges, 1830–1870', *Econ. Hist. Rev.*, 2nd Ser., xxiii (1970), 99–100, where 'the intangible mass of gentlemen' and Esquires is found to be the most important single source of subscriptions for three Yorkshire railways and account for half the subscriptions in the 1845 Contracts.

except those of the learned professions, and *very few* besides all the principal families of this town are in fact *tradesmen*, yet even these are here very capriciously and superciliously distinguished into *gentlemen* and *tradesmen*; though the former retale their goods, or sell their commodities in small quantities, as well as the latter . . .

The distinction was founded on nothing more substantial than 'pride, arrogance, ignorance, impertinence, and vulgar servility'.[1] Dr. Newton, considering this problem for a rather later period, though in a town of the 'traditional' kind, concluded that 'the great majority of those described as gentleman [in directories] were professional men or "higher tradesmen", active or retired', though in a few cases the use of the term 'Esquire' instead might distinguish the member of a county family from such persons.[2] It therefore seems reasonable to classify urban 'Esquires', not otherwise identifiable, as 'capitalists', on the assumption that they were substantial rentiers, rather than as landowners, although this procedure might be somewhat unrealistic in, for example, the towns of the Welsh Marches or such centres of English county society as York and Lincoln. Fortunately, perhaps, the size of this problematical class of investors is small. Urban 'gentlemen', not otherwise identifiable, have been distributed proportionately among the tradesmen, professional men, and manufacturers.

From what has been said it will appear that the analyses attempted here entail some difficulties, but it is hoped that their results, although they can only be regarded as approximate, will suffice as a basis for cautious discussion.

In the following pages the canals of the 'first generation' are considered in chronological sequence. The survey of the canals of the 'second generation' is arranged by regions: the East Midlands (including part of Yorkshire), the West Midlands, Lancashire and the adjacent parts of the West Riding,

[1] William Richards, *The History of Lynn* (King's Lynn, 1812), ii. 1168. Italics as in the original.
[2] R. Newton, 'Society and Politics in Exeter 1837–1914', in H. J. Dyos (ed.), *The Study of Urban History* (1968), p. 305. Also, Professor Everitt has written of the emergence in the English provinces by the later seventeenth century of the 'pseudo-gentry': '. . . that class of leisured and commonly urban families who, by their manner of life, were commonly regarded as gentry, though they were not supported by a landed estate'. A. Everitt, 'Social Mobility in Early Modern England', *Past and Present*, no. 33 (Apr. 1966), pp. 70–1.

the South, and South Wales. A few river improvements, for example the Loughborough and the Melton Navigations, which were important and integral parts of the developing canal system, have been considered. The figure which precedes the account of each undertaking indicates roughly how much money was raised by it; the dates indicate the period over which this was done. In addition to receipts from the public in payment for shares and bonds, any outlay from current income on the completion of its works is included in this figure and it is therefore not necessarily the equivalent of the company's formal capitalization. Furthermore, as sums received by each company from proprietors and creditors might be devoted to transfer payments or expenditure on current account, the figure is not necessarily the equivalent of the capital cost of its line.[1] The exact estimation of either of these totals would require, where it is possible, further research which I have not attempted. Nevertheless, the figures given will probably serve in most cases to suggest the order of magnitudes involved. Their source is either my own calculations from company records or, these failing, Mr Hadfield's estimates of the cost of individual lines, printed in the appendices of his regional canal histories. The figures given in my analyses of share capitals refer to the number of shares, whose denominations are given in brackets. On the other hand, analyses of loan capitals, and aggregations of loan and share capitals, are made in units of £100.

I. *The Sankey Navigation* 1755–1761: £18,600

The undertakers named in the Act of authorization[2] were Charles Gore, James Crosbie, John Ashton, John Blackburne, and Richard Trafford, all prominent Liverpool merchants with interests in the coal and salt trades whose development the navigation was intended to serve.[3] The capital of the concern comprised 120 shares on each of which £155 was

---

[1] For an account of these and other problems of estimation, see J. E. Ginarlis, 'Capital Formation in Road and Canal Transport', in J. P. P. Higgins and S. Pollard (eds.), *Aspects of Capital Investment in Great Britain 1750–1850* (1971), pp. 121–30.

[2] 28 George II *cap*. 8.

[3] T. C. Barker, 'The Sankey Navigation', *Trans. Hist. Soc. of Lancashire and Cheshire*, c (1948), 121–55; idem, 'Lancashire Coal, Cheshire Salt and the Rise of Liverpool', ibid. ciii (1951), 83–101.

paid. In 1754 subscriptions for the navigation had been sought at the Exchange in Liverpool,[1] presumably by the undertakers who wished to obtain wider financial support by the disposition of shares. It is not clear to what extent they were successful. By 1766 three shares had been purchased by a Liverpool ironmonger[2] and in 1767 the Liverpool merchant William Trafford owned five (they were valued together at £1,500 and yielded an annual income of £73);[3] but in 1759 John Ashton, one of the original undertakers, had owned 51 of the 120 shares, which he bequeathed to his children.[4] It seems reasonable to suppose, however, that whatever may have been the exact disposition of the shares, the navigation was financed by the trading community of Liverpool.

II. *The Bridgewater Navigations* 1759–1780: £300,000

Capital outlay on the navigations has been regarded as continuing to the accounting year ending 10 January 1780, after which expenditure on this account is described as 'repairing' instead of 'improving'.[5] The total obtained by adding up the figures for the Bridgewater estate's expenditure during these years on the 'navigation and sough account' given in its *General Account* is £255,200; the equivalent figure from the *General State* is £301,300, which includes interest payments, the expenditure of £7,000 on boats, the cost of the Acts of authorization, the value of the Duke's own land, and the salary of his agent John Gilbert. The second figure has been preferred as being more comprehensive. The total 'charge' on the Lancashire estate reached a maximum of £364,805 in January 1786,[6] but this total includes an interest charge of five per cent added annually to its deficit balance. Mr. Hadfield and Mr. Biddle have pointed out that the construction of thirty-three miles of canal, the length of the Bridgewater navigations, between the 1750s and

[1] Wadsworth and Mann, *Cotton Trade*, p. 221.

[2] Barker, 'Sankey Navigation', p. 142, n. 2.

[3] P.R.O., Exchequer K. R., Bills and Answers, E. 112/1530/215.

[4] Barker, 'Sankey Navigation', p. 135.

[5] Details taken from Northamptonshire R.O., E(llesmere). B(rackley). MSS. 1460, 'General Account 1759–1790'; 1461, 'General State of his Grace the Duke of Bridgewater's Navigation, Colliery, Lime and Farm Concerns in Lancashire and Cheshire from Midsummer 1759'.

[6] E.B. MSS., 1461, f. 52.

the 1770s would have required at the level of costs then current much less than the £220,000 often quoted, let alone the sum given here. Such figures must include much expenditure incurred by the Duke through his mining activities and purchases of agricultural land, and they suggest a total outlay on the canals themselves of about £77,500.[1] Although their argument is reasonable I have preferred, in the absence of sources with which Bridgewater's expenditure might be disaggregated, to retain the figure for which there is documentary authority.

To establish exactly what proportion of this expenditure was originally underwritten by the Duke himself would require a more thorough examination of his general finances that has been attempted here. Smiles, in his celebrated and highly coloured account of the enterprise, mentions the £25,000 borrowed from the London bankers Childs and Co. between 1765 and 1769, and numerous smaller sums from his tenants, and from tradespeople in Manchester and Liverpool.[2] In 1769 the debt to Childs was repaid and £35,000 was raised on mortgage from the Sun Fire Insurance Company.[3] However, the largest annual interest charge recorded 'on navigation account' is that of £276 in 1774.[4] In default of a proper investigation of the problem, it may be guessed that 80-90% of the expenditure should be attributed to the Duke himself.

III. *The Trent and Mersey Canal* 1766–1777: £300,000

	I	II	III	IV	V	VI	VII	VIII	IX
Shares: 650 (£200)	44 (7%)	252 (39%)	–	101 (16%)	61 (9%)	58 (9%)	47 (7%)	26 (4%)	61 (9%)
Loan Capital: £166,600	48 (3%)	771 (46%)	–	215 (13%)	37 (2%)	150 (9%)	55 (4%)	207 (12%)	183 (11%)
Total: £296,600	136 (4%)	1275 (42%)	–	417 (14%)	159 (5%)	266 (12%)	149 (5%)	259 (8%)	305 (10%)

[1] C. Hadfield and G. Biddle, *The Canals of North West England* (Newton Abbot 1970), i. 33; ii. 464.

[2] Samuel Smiles, *Lives of the Engineers* (1874 edn.), i. 217–22; Wadsworth and Mann, *Cotton Trade*, p. 222.

[3] A. H. John, 'Insurance Investment and the London Money Market in the Eighteenth Century' *Economica*, xx (1953), 157.

[4] E.B. MSS., 1460, f. 60.

At the time of the incorporation of the company in 1766 only £86,900 of the authorized share capital of £130,000 had been subscribed. This sum was made up by a further subscription among the proprietors at the general assembly of 25 September 1769.[1] Under Acts of 1770, 1775, and 1776, £166,600 was borrowed on mortgage of the tolls, for the purpose of completing the line and constructing the branch to Caldon. The earliest complete list of shareholders and mortgagees which survives is that of 1782,[2] and it is the source for the analysis offered here. An earlier list of the subscribers to the first £86,900 raised[3] suggests that the 1782 list provides an adequate guide to the original composition of the company. There were 240 holders of shares and mortgages (many holding both), the average investment being about £1,200. Most of the large share of landed gentlemen in the loan capital is accounted for by the £42,750 invested by Samuel Egerton of Tatton Park, Cheshire. About £140,000 of the share and loan capital was held in Staffordshire (only £19,300 in the Potteries, but £46,500 at Lichfield), £56,000 in London, and most of the rest in Cheshire.

IV. *The Staffordshire and Worcestershire Canal* 1766–1772: £100,000

Documentation of the share capital of this canal does not survive, but of the 97 subscribers named in the Act of incorporation[4] it has been possible to identify 2 peers, 18 landed gentlemen, 5 clergymen, 5 women, and 32 tradesmen (21 of Wolverhampton, 7 of Kidderminster, 1 of Stourbridge, 1 of Bewdley, and 2 of Birmingham). Of the 35 who have not been identified, it seems likely that many were tradespeople from the towns of the Stour valley below Wolverhampton through which the canal ran, for which adequate comtemporary directories are not available. Wolverhampton provided at least 6 of the early committee members, against only 2 by landowners, and 3 by other towns, and the headquarters of

---

[1] Preamble to 10 George III *cap.* 102.

[2] TMC 2/2C.

[3] In the Archives of Josiah Wedgwood and Sons Ltd., Barlaston, Staffs., a copy of which was kindly communicated to me by Mr. Charles Hadfield.

[4] 6 George III *cap.* 97.

the company were located there, so its financial contribution was probably substantial.[1] Apparently £140 was called on each of the 700 shares.

V. *The Birmingham Canal Navigations* 1768-1798: £250,000

Shares:[2]	I	II	III	IV	V	VI	VII	VIII	IX
500 (£140)	20	98	2	81	117	57	74	3	48
	(4%)	(20%)		(18%)	(23%)	(11%)	(15%)		(10%)
Loans 1784-1798:[3]									
£121,400	—	15	18	317	189	138	117	88	332
		(1%)	(1%)	(26%)	(16%)	(11%)	(10%)	(7%)	(27%)

About 300 shares were subscribed in Birmingham, 100 in the adjacent parts of Staffordshire through which the canal ran, and only 66 outside the counties of Warwickshire and Staffordshire. The average subscription was five shares. The line from Birmingham to the Staffordshire and Worcestershire Canal at Aldersley was completed in 1772 at a total cost of £112,000,[4] the balance over the share capital of £70,000 apparently being raised out of revenue and by borrowing. From the incomplete evidence which is available, it appears that in general the character of the lenders was similar to that of the shareholders (which many of them were).[5]

For the purpose of making the line from Birmingham to Fazeley, and improving the original line, £121,400 was borrowed between 1784 and 1798 on mortgage of the tolls under Acts of 1784 and 1794. This sum was repaid out of revenue between 1800 and 1819; £84,500 (70%) of this loan capital was raised in Birmingham, and only £12,000 (10%) outside Warwickshire and Staffordshire.

[1] From STW 1/1, Committee minutes 1766-85.
[2] BNC, 2/26, Transfer Ledger, 1768-1835; BCN 2/36, Register of Transfers, 1768-73; BCN 4/170, Ledger, 1767-70.
[3] BCN 4/17, Loan Ledger, 1784-1819.
[4] C. Hadfield, *Canals of the West Midlands* (Newton Abbot, 1966), p. 68.
[5] BCN 4/170, ff. 174-9.

VI. *The Coventry Canal* 1768–1790: £90,000

	I	II	III	IV	V	VI	VII	VIII	IX	Unknown
Shares[1]										
500 (£100)	20	54	2	39	71	53	61	58	51	91
	(5%)	(13%)		(10%)	(18%)	(13%)	(15%)	(14%)	(13%)	
Loans 1786–1790[2]										
£37,500	—	27	—	100	77	52	43	47	29	
		(7%)		(27%)	(21%)	(14%)	(11%)	(13%)	(8%)	
Total										
£87,500	20	81	2	139	148	105	104	105	80	91
	(3%)	(10%)		(18%)	(19%)	(13%)	(13%)	(13%)	(10%)	

Of the original subscriptions to shares which have been identified, 218 (50%) came from Coventry, and most of the remainder from the adjacent countryside and the lesser towns along the line of the canal, such as Atherstone and Tamworth. Twenty-two (5%) came from outside Warwickshire. Financially this company was one of the weakest of the early promotions. On the exhaustion of its authorized share capital in 1771, work stopped with the line completed only as far as Atherstone. Part was eventually built by the Birmingham, and the Trent and Mersey Canal companies, and the remainder was completed by the Coventry between 1786 and 1790,[3] work on its section being financed by a loan of £37,500 raised under the Act of 1785. Of this sum £20,200 (54%) was raised at Coventry, and £6,600 (18%) outside the county of Warwickshire (mostly in Staffordshire). The delay in the completion of the line, it was alleged, was due to the disproportionate influence exercised in the company's affairs by proprietors with interests in the collieries of the Atherstone area, who wished to preserve their monopoly of the local market from the competition of Staffordshire coals.[4] However, this course cannot have had the support of the investors of Coventry, who appear to have preponderated, and so some importance should probably be attached to the difficulties of raising additional funds in the circumstances of the late 1770s and early 1780s. The average number of shares subscribed was 4, and holding of loan capital, £600.

[1] CVC 4/23, Treasurer's Accounts 1767–1860, List of those who paid the first call 3 Dec. 1767.

[2] CVC 1/3, Minutes of the Committee and General Assembly 1777–90.

[3] C. Hadfield, *The Canals of the East Midlands* (Newton Abbot, 1966), pp. 17, 23–4.

[4] Hadfield, op. cit., p. 23.

VII. *The Oxford Canal* 1769-1790: £300,000

Shares[1]	I	II	III	IV	V	VI	VII	VIII	IX	Unknown
1,412 (£100)	244	197	–	111	34	275	127	218	107	99
	(19%)	(15%)		(8%)	(3%)	(21%)	(10%)	(16%)	(7%)	
First Loan 1775-1779[2]										
£70,000	117	43	15	40	–	137	54	210	84	
	(17%)	(6%)	(2%)	(6%)		(20%)	(8%)	(30%)	(12%)	
Second Loan 1786-1790[3]										
£60,000	66	12	3	18	–	69	135	201	96	
	(11%)	(2%)		(3%)		(12%)	(23%)	(33%)	(16%)	
Total										
£271,200	427	252	18	169	34	481	316	629	287	99
	(16%)	(10%)		(6%)	(1%)	(18%)	(12%)	(24%)	(11%)	

The Act of incorporation authorized a share capital of £150,000, but only 1,223 shares were originally subscribed. In 1774 the company attempted to issue a further 300 shares,[4] but only 189 were taken. Calls of £100 were made on each share, but the accumulation of arrears of unpaid interest increased the nominal share capital to £178,648 by 1803, the figure given in the *Canal Returns* of 1888.[5] Of the subscriptions of 1769 and 1774 which have been satisfactorily identified, 472 were made in the countryside near the line of the canal, 300 at Oxford, 75 at Banbury, 55 at Woodstock, and 155 at Coventry. During the 1770s many shareholders at Coventry sold out, apparently in consequence of the disputes which took place between the Oxford and Coventry Canal companies.

Of the shares, 115 (8%) were subscribed for outside Oxfordshire and Warwickshire, 70 at London. Local market towns not directly on the line of the canal took little part. For example, only 14 shares were subscribed at Chipping Norton, 5 at Bicester, 4 at Charlbury, and 3 at Witney. The average number of shares individually subscribed for was 7. The loan capital was raised during the periods indicated for the purpose of completing the line, under the authority of Acts of 1775 and 1786. Between 1779 and 1786 work was

[1] Oxfordshire R.O. CH/III/9, Subscription Deed 1768; the lists of proprietors and their holdings in OXC 1/2, Minutes of the Committee and General Assembly 1769-75; Bodleian Library Dep. c. 102, Book of Transfers 1769-93, Dep. a. 16, Accounts 1772-1800, for the second subscription.

[2] OXC 2/2-4, Counterfoils of Mortgage Securities 1775-79.

[3] OXC 2/5-6, Counterfoils of Mortgage Securities 1786-90.

[4] OXC 1/2, 4 July 1774.

[5] *Parl. Papers 1890*, lxiv, 772; Bodleian Library Dep. a. 16.

suspended owing to the financial effects of the American war, with the line between Banbury and Oxford unbuilt. Of the loan, £70,000 (54%) was taken up in the city of Oxford, and £35,000 (27%) elsewhere in the county. The average holding was £800.

The usually large contribution of clergymen to this canal is accounted for by the dons of the Oxford colleges who subscribed for 165 (13%) of the shares, and £35,000 (26%) of the loan capital. With the exception of contributions to the first loan of £2,500 from Pembroke College, £1,000 from University College, and £700 from Brasenose, all these investments were made by individuals. Dons, in particular the Vice-Chancellor Nathan Wetherell, took a leading part in the management of the company in its early years. The substantial investment of the peerage is accounted for by the Duke of Marlborough who subscribed for 50 shares, as did his son (his steward, gardener, and gatekeeper contributed lesser amounts), and also provided £16,900 of the loan capital.

VIII. *The Leeds and Liverpool Canal* 1770–1816: £1,200,000

Shares	I	II	III	IV	V	VI	VII	VIII	IX	Unknown
1,919	10	271	38	582	81	309	209	21	112	286
		(16%)	(2%)	(36%)	(5%)	(19%)	(13%)	(1%)	(7%)	

This analysis is based on a list of subscribers to 1,919 shares in 1769.[1] In consequence of disputes over the course to be taken by the canal some Lancashire subscribers later withdrew leaving subscriptions of £172,400 outstanding.[2] These were subsequently made up to the total of £200,000 required by the Act of incorporation before work could begin.[3] The authorized capital was £260,000, and £60,000 more if necessary. No complete list of shareholders of a sufficiently early date has been found, but it seems likely that the character of the original body of 1769 was not substantially altered by these developments, though—as many of the Lancashire subscribers had been Liverpool merchants— the share of 'capitalists' may have been somewhat reduced.

[1] LLC 1/1, Minutes of the Subscribers 1766–70, ff. 14–30.

[2] LLC 1/2, Minutes of the Committee and General Assembly 1770–82, 20 June 1770.

[3] Ibid., 19 July 1770.

The Yorkshire promoters had opened subscription books at Leeds, Bradford, Keighley, Skipton, Settle, Ottley, Colne, York, Hull, Doncaster, Pontefract, Wakefield, Barnsley, and Sheffield.[1] Most support came from the Aire valley and Colne through which the line was to run: 930 shares were taken there—312 at Skipton, 261 at Bradford, 137 at Colne, 129 at Leeds, and 91 at Keighley—but only 190 elsewhere.[2] The subscriptions from Lancashire (740 shares excluding Colne and district) were largely drawn from Liverpool (650), whose merchants (369) account for the large share of 'capitalists' in this canal. Most of the other subscribers in this class were Quaker merchants and woolstaplers of Bradford, the original promoters of the scheme.[3] Of the subscribers who have not been identified, many were probably yeomen, clothiers, and petty retailers, groups poorly served by contemporary directories, whose contribution may thus be understated. The average number of shares subscribed individually was 3.

During the initial phase of construction between 1770 and 1777, in which $61\frac{1}{2}$ miles of the line were completed, about £300,000 was spent.[4] By 1776 £242,901 had been raised by calls totalling £114 on 2,059 shares. In 1775 and 1776 shares in addition to the original subscription, apparently about 200, had been issued.[5] After this date, lesser sums were borrowed on mortgage of the tolls, some of the committee members giving their personal guarantees as additional security.[6] During the years in which the calls on the original subscriptions were paid the character of the company

[1] LLC 1/1, 9 Jan. 1769.

[2] These figures include subscriptions at these towns made by inhabitants of the neighbouring countryside.

[3] For a general account see H. F. Killick, 'Notes on the Early History of the Leeds and Liverpool Canal,' *Bradford Antiquary*, n.s., Part II (July 1897), 169–238; J. R. Harris, 'Liverpool Canal Controversies 1769–1772,' *Journal of Transport History*, vol. ii, no. 3 (May 1956), pp. 158–74.

[4] Priestley, *Navigable Rivers*, p. 424; £232,016 by 1775 according to LLC 4/6, Statistical History of the Leeds and Liverpool Canal, f. 34. The length of the canal from Leeds to Liverpool as eventually completed was 127 miles; this included 7 miles of the Upper Douglas Navigation and 11 miles of the Lancaster Canal, Priestley, op. cit., p. 421.

[5] Killick, op. cit., p. 232; LLC 1/2, 28 July 1775.

[6] Ibid., 27 Mar. 1778, 25 Sept. 1778, 24 Sept. 1779; LLC 1/3, Minutes of Committee and General Assembly 1782–1790, 21 July 1784: by this time the debts of the company totalled £17,000 to £18,000; The Prior's Kitchen, Durham, Backhouse MSS., 289–90.

changed to some extent. Between 1770 and the end of 1776 358 shares were transferred to investors resident outside Lancashire and Yorkshire: 207 to London and 108 to Norwich. The purchasers were mostly bankers and merchants: Gurneys, Peckovers, and other Quaker connections of the Bradford promoters. The woolstapler John Hustler, the treasurer of the company until his death in 1790,[1] acted as an intermediary in this process, buying up shares locally and disposing of them elsewhere. Between 1770 and 1777 about 200 passed through his hands. Nearly 100 went to the London bankers Smith, Wright, and Grey, or their clerk, who in turn passed most of them on to investors in London and the Home Counties.[2] This process continued. By 1800 less than half of the stock was owned in the counties through which the canal ran, its geographical distribution being as follows: Yorkshire 32%, Lancashire 14%, elsewhere in the North 2%, London and Middlesex 20%, the Midlands and South 17%, Norfolk 14% unclassified 2%.[3]

Work was resumed in 1790 and continued until the completion of the line in 1816. It was financed by the issue of a further 697 shares, with a par value equivalent to those already outstanding, at prices of £180 and £160, to be subscribed for by the existing proprietors;[4] by borrowing on mortgage (the debt reached a maximum of £442,154 in 1822);[5] and by toll income. Proper records relating to the disposition of the loan capital do not survive. Although ownership of the stock was by this time geographically widely dispersed, the impression given by a later notebook recording transfers of mortgage securities is of sources of finance essentially local and middle class.[6] Of 64 mortgagees mentioned only 13 were resident outside Yorkshire and Lancashire: these included four members of families of Coalbrookdale ironmasters, and a Quaker woolstapler of

[1] LLC 1/4, Minutes of the Committee and General Assembly 1790–3, 24 Nov. 1790.

[2] LLC 2/1, Transfer Ledger 1770–1819.

[3] G. H. Evans, *British Corporation Finance 1775–1850* (Baltimore, 1936), p. 162, analysis of a list of holders of Original Shares in 1800.

[4] LLC 1/5, Minutes of Committee and General Assembly 1793–98, 17 Oct. 1794, 15 Sept. 1797.

[5] LLC 4/6 f. 79. It was finally liquidated in 1847.

[6] LLC 2/11, 'Leeds and Liverpool Canal Mortgage Book', 1820–30.

Cirencester. Of local investors, women (23 mentioned), and yeomen, farmers, and graziers (15), appear to have been more than usually prominent.

Mention may also be made here of the Bradford Canal, built under the authority of an Act of 1771[1] at a cost of about £9,000, to link the town of that name with the main line of the Leeds and Liverpool Canal. From the names of those incorporated as proprietors it is clear that it was financed for the most part by merchants and tradesmen of Bradford.

IX. *The Chesterfield Canal* 1771–1777: £150,000

At the time parliamentary sanction was sought only £55,000 had been subscribed towards the estimated cost of £97,000.[2] On the passage of the Act of incorporation, subscription books for the completion of the authorized share capital of £100,000 were opened at Chesterfield, Retford, Worksop, and at Messrs. Lancaster, Bax, and Ellil, lead merchants of London.[3] The Quakers of the London Lead Company, who were leading promoters of the scheme (it was intended to facilitate the shipment of lead),[4] appear to have had some success in disposing of shares among their connections in the metropolis.[5] However, no more than about 10% of the shareholders have been satisfactorily identified as Londoners, though this may in part be accounted for by the fact that contemporary directories do not deal adequately with tradesmen of less than the first rank.[6] The financial weight of the company appears to have rested at Chesterfield, with lesser contributions from its lead-mining hinterland, and from Worksop, Retford, and Gainsborough. The inadequacy of the sources precludes a systematic analysis of the social composition of the com-

---

[1] 11 George III *cap.* 89.

[2] *H.C.J.* xxxiii. 133.

[3] CHC 1/1, Minutes of the Committee and General Assembly 1771–80, 18 Apr. 1771.

[4] G. C. Hopkinson, 'The Development of Inland Navigation in South Yorkshire and North Derbyshire 1697–1850,' *Trans. Hunter Arch. Soc.* vii (1956), 236–40.

[5] See, for example, the 2 shares taken by the Quaker timber-merchant Jacob Hagen, Bodleian Library, MS. Eng. Misc. b. 41, Account Book, f. 27.

[6] The most complete list of shareholders is CHC 1/1, 24 Jan. 1774.

pany, but it appears that, although the canal passed through the 'Dukeries', the contribution of landowners to the share capital was modest, perhaps not amounting to much more than 10% of the total. Investors in this class included the Dukes of Devonshire (35 shares) and Newcastle (30), Lord Scarsdale (5), Sir Cecil Wray, the M.P. for Retford (10), and Godfrey Clarke, the M.P. for Derbyshire (20). £100 was apparently called on each share, and about £50,000 borrowed on mortgage.[1]

X. *The Stourbridge Canal* 1776–1783: £43,000

Shares[2]	I	II	III	IV	V	VI	VII	VIII	IX
300 (£143)	43	31	4	40	101	28	29	3	21
	(14%)	(10%)	(1%)	(13%)	(34%)	(10%)	(10%)	(1%)	(7%)

Subscriptions were drawn almost entirely from Stourbridge, Kingswinford, and Oldswinford (glass-makers of the two latter parishes account for most of the contribution of manufacturers), and the adjacent countryside, with a few (22 shares) from Birmingham. The average individual subscription was 4 shares. When the authorized share capital of £30,000 was spent, £4,500 was borrowed on bond, which was repaid by making further calls on the proprietors under the Act of 1782.[3]

XI. *The Dudley Canal* 1776–1797: £200,000

Shares[4]	I	II	III	IV	V	VI	VII	VIII	IX
2,074 (£100)	138	259	19	380	618	210	223	118	109
	(7%)	(12%)		(19%)	(30%)	(10%)	(11%)	(6%)	(5%)

Between the incorporation of this company in 1776 with an authorized capital of £7000 and 1797 when the last call was made, a total sum in excess of £200,000 was raised by three successive creations of shares for the purpose of financing the modest line as originally conceived, and two substantial extensions. Briefly, under the original Act of 1776 £13,000 was called on 70 shares, under that of 1785

---

[1] CHC 1/1, 30 Nov. 1778.

[2] STN 1/1, Minutes of General Assembly 1776–1826, 1 June 1776, list of subscribers; STN 2/1, Transfer Book 1776–1827.

[3] 22 George III *cap.* 14; STN 1/3, Committee Minutes 1776–83, 1 Jan. 1782 ff.

[4] DDC 1/2, Minutes of the Committee 1776–85 and General Assembly 1776–1846, list of proprietors 1 Oct. 1798.

£38,325 was called on 219, and under those of 1793 and 1797 £155,000 was called on 900.[1] In 1798 the capital was consolidated into 2,074 shares of £100. The distribution of these recorded at the time of the General Assembly of 1 October 1798 is the basis of the analysis offered here. Of the shares, 673 (32%) were held in Birmingham, 616 (30%) in Worcestershire, 312 (15%) in Staffordshire, 222 (11%) in London, and 251 (12%) elsewhere. The average holding was 9 shares.

XII. *The Stroudwater Navigation* 1776–1779: £41,000

Shares[2]	I	II	III	IV	V	VI	VII	VIII	IX
200 (£150)	3	20	3	25	72	45	14	5	13
		(10%)		(13%)	(36%)	(23%)	(7%)	(3%)	(7%)

Of the shares, 35 were held outside Gloucestershire, most of the remainder in the clothing centres of that county (90 at Stroud). The average holding was 2 shares.

XIII. *The Loughborough Navigation* 1776–1779: £9,000

Shares[3]	I	II	III	IV	V	VI	VII	VIII	IX	Unknown
70 (£120)	10	13	–	–	–	39		4	3	1
	(14%)	(20%)				(56%)		(6%)	(4%)	

Of the shares, 37 were subscribed at Loughborough, and all the rest locally, in Leicestershire, Nottinghamshire, and Derbyshire. The average individual subscription was 2 shares. In 1779 £600 was borrowed on mortgage from Edward Dawson, the steward of the Earl of Huntingdon (both were shareholders).[4]

XIV. *The Erewash Canal* 1777–1779: £21,000

Shares[5]	I	II	III	IV	V	VI	VII	VIII	IX	Unknown
154	5	53	–	–	–	63		7	16	10
	(3%)	(37%)				(44%)		(5%)	(11%)	

[1] 16 George III *cap.* 66; 25 George III *cap.* 87; 33 George III *cap.* 66; 37 George III *cap.* 13; DDC 1/2, 6 June 1776, 24 June 1792, 5 Sept. 1796.

[2] Gloucestershire R.O., D 1180 3/1, Register of Shares and Share Transfers, 1774–1809. 28 shares held by persons resident in towns styled Esquire or gentleman, not otherwise identified, have been distributed equally between groups IV, V, VI, and VII.

[3] LBN 1/1, Minutes of the Committee and General Assembly 1776–97, second foliation, ff. 1–2, list of subscribers to 69 shares.

[4] LBN 1/1, 19 Oct. 1779.

[5] EWC 1/1, Minutes of the Committee and General Assembly 1777–98, ff. 1–4, list of subscribers.

With the exception of 3 shares taken by a Birmingham man all the subscriptions were made locally, in Derbyshire, Nottinghamshire, Leicestershire, and Rutland. Some proprietors (23) of the Loughborough Navigation contributed (they were interested in increasing the supply of coal to their line). The average subscription was 2 shares. It is not clear how much was called on each share, but a certain amount was borrowed.[1] The figure for the total cost given here is that of Mr. Hadfield.[2]

XV. *The Cromford Canal* 1789-1795: £82,000

Shares[3]	I	II	III	IV	V	VI	VII	VIII	IX
460 (£145)	10	133	40	47	48	46	42	45	49
	(2%)	(30%)	(9%)	(10%)	(10%)	(10%)	(9%)	(10%)	(10%)

Of the shares, 400 (87%) were subscribed for in the counties of Nottinghamshire and Derbyshire. Most of the investors from further afield clearly had local interests or connections. The average subscription was 6 shares, and £11,120 was borrowed locally for the completion of the line, the lenders resembling the proprietors in occupational character.[4]

XVI. *The Nottingham Canal* 1792-1796: £85,000

Shares[5]	I	II	III	IV	V	VI	VII	VIII	IX
497 (£150)	30	126	–	24	90	148	30	22	27
	(6%)	(25%)		(5%)	(18%)	(30%)	(6%)	(4%)	(5%)

Of the shares, 307 (60%) were subscribed for in the town of Nottingham; most of the remainder were taken by local landowners or their connections for whom 200 shares were reserved;[6] £10,000 was borrowed.[7] Information concerning the lenders is not available. The average subscription was 3 shares.

---

[1] EWC 1/1, 3 Aug 1780 1 May 1781.
[2] *Canals of the East Midlands*, p. 41.
[3] CRC 1/1, Minutes of the Committee and General Assembly 1789-99, ff. 11-14, list of subscribers.
[4] CRC 1/1, ff. 120, 129, 135, 154, 157.
[5] NC 1/2, Minutes of the Committee and General Assembly 1792-97, list of subscribers.
[6] See below, pp. 153-4.
[7] NC 1/2, 13 Dec. 1796.

XVII. *The Leicester Navigation* 1791–1794: £80,000

Shares[1]	I	II	III	IV	V	VI	VII	VIII	IX
507 (£140)	43	116	20	92	39	96	63	11	27
	(9%)	(22%)	(4%)	(18%)	(8%)	(19%)	(12%)	(2%)	(5%)

Of the shares 411 (81%) were subscribed in Leicestershire, of which 211 (42%) in the town of Leicester, where the navigation terminated. By 1798 £7,000 was due on mortgage, £2,000 to the treasurers, the two Leicester banks of Bentley and Co. and Boultbee and Co., £3,500 to the clerk of the company, the attorney Edward Carter, and the remainder apparently to tradesmen of the town of Leicester.[2] The average subscription was 3 shares.

No account of the subscribers to the closely-connected Leicestershire and Northamptonshire Union Canal (1793–1809: £200,000) appears to survive, but it seems likely that the sources of finance on which it drew were similar, though as it was a more speculative concern, the contribution of landowners may have been less, and subscribers from further afield may have secured admission.[3] A list compiled in 1810 of 36 shareholders in arrears in the payment of calls includes 3 resident in London, 3 in Birmingham, the rest being local.[4]

XVIII. *The Melton Navigation* 1791–1797: £40,000

Shares[5]	I	II	III	IV	V	VI	VII	VIII	IX
250 (£120)	26	62	19	10	–	80	25	19	9
	(10%)	(25%)	(8%)	(4%)		(32%)	(10%)	(8%)	(4%)

Of the shares, 180 were subscribed in Leicestershire, 48 in Nottinghamshire and Derbyshire. The cost in excess of the original share capital of £25,000 was apparently met partly by extra calls and partly by income.[6] The average subscription was 3 shares.

[1] LCN 1/1, Minutes of the Committee and General Assembly 1790–1, 21 July 1791, list of subscribers. A few more shares were subscribed. In 1798 the first dividend was paid on 502 shares of £140 and 9 of £110 (LCN 1/3, Committee and General Assembly Minutes 1795–1801, 1 Jan. 1798).

[2] LCN 1/3, 25 Sept., 15 Dec. 1797, 9 Mar. 28 Dec. 1798.

[3] Subscriptions were received at Leicester, Loughborough, Harborough, Northampton, Coventry, and Birmingham (*Leicester Journal*, 12 Oct. 1792). For the varying attitude of landowners, and the varying opportunities of 'outsiders' at this time see below pp. 87–90, 157.

[4] LNC 1/9, General Assembly Minutes 1805–44, 21 May 1810.

[5] Leicestershire R.O., Acc. No. 336/1, Register of Shareholders.

[6] Hadfield, *Canals of the East Midlands*, pp. 93–4.

XIX. *The Oakham Canal* 1793-1803: £70,000

Shares[1]	I	II	III	IV	V	VI	VII	VIII	IX	Unknown
545 (£130)	70	94	10	32	–	66	91	41	–	141
	(17%)	(23%)	(3%)	(8%)		(16%)	(23%)	(10%)		

Only 150 shares were subscribed for away from the immediate vicinity of the canal, of which 75 were at Leicester. Of the 44 owners of land on the line of the canal, 32 subscribed. The average subscription was 4 shares.

XX. *The Horncastle Navigation* 1792-1803: £50,000

Shares[2]	I	II	III	IV	V	VI	VII	VIII	IX
462 (£100)	–	146	23	116	–	89	46	28	14
		(31%)	(5%)	(25%)		(19%)	(10%)	(6%)	(3%)

These figures include the 266 shares subscribed under the original Act of 1792, and the further 196 taken by the old proprietors under that of 1800,[3] to meet an increase in the cost of the line over that which had been anticipated. Of the shares, 162 (28%) were subscribed in the town of Horncastle, 83 at Boston, 16 at London, and the remainder in the neighbouring countryside. The average subscription was 8 shares.

XXI. *The Grantham Canal* 1793-1802: £150,000

Shares[4]	I	II	III	IV	V	VI	VII	VIII	IX	Unknown
750 (£150)	40	177	78	52	–	146	74	72	19	92
	(6%)	(27%)	(12%)	(8%)		(22%)	(11%)	(11%)	(3%)	

Of the shares whose holders have been identified, 130 (17%) were subscribed for at Grantham, 100 (13%) at Nottingham, and almost all the rest in the adjacent countryside (only 21 from outside Nottinghamshire and Lincolnshire). The average subscription was 4 shares. Out of 132 owners of land on the line of the canal, 62 took the opportunity to subscribe.[5] £34,240 was spent on capital account out of toll income,[6] and by 1800 £6,250 was due on mortgage as follows:[7]

[1] This analysis is derived from that of D. H. Tew, *The Oakham Canal*, (Wymondham, 1968), pp. 30-2.

[2] Lincolnshire R.O., T.L.E. I/1/7-8, Share Register, and Dividend Book 1813-61.

[3] 32 George III *cap*. 107; 39, 40 George III *cap*. 109.

[4] GCN 1/1, Minutes of the Committee and General Assembly 1793-1809, 7 Mar. 1793, list of subscribers.

[5] Leicestershire R.O., Q.S. 72/3, Grantham Canal Book of Reference.

[6] GCN 1/3, Minutes of the Committee and General Assembly 1835-54, f. 138.

[7] GCN 1/1, 7 Aug. 1800.

I	II	III	IV	V	VI	VII	VIII	IX
2	9	7	6	–	23	7	3	5½

XXII. *The Derby Canal* 1793–1796: £100,000

Shares[1]	I	II	III	IV	V	VI	VII	VIII	IX
600 (£150)	20	141	79	66	54	126	69	23	22
	(3%)	(24%)	(13%)	(11%)	(9%)	(21%)	(12%)	(4%)	(4%)

Of the shares, 256 (43%) were subscribed for in the town of Derby, and almost all the remainder in the adjacent countryside. Only 78 (13%) were taken up outside the county. The average subscription was 2 shares. Of the owners of land on the line of the canal, 98 were entitled to 152 shares; only 21, entitled to 33 shares, failed to exercise this option.[2] The subscribers included 4 self-styled labourers, and a serving man, who took one share each.

XXIII. *The Ashby-de-la-Zouch Canal* 1794–1804: £170,000

Shares[3]	I	II	III	IV	V	VI	VII	VIII	IX
1,500 (£100)	114	395	106	147	70	307	153	85	123
	(8%)	(26%)	(7%)	(10%)	(5%)	(20%)	(10%)	(6%)	(8%)

Two-thirds of the shares were subscribed for in the parts of Leicestershire and Derbyshire served by the line, and in addition, support was received from Birmingham and Wolverhampton (64 shares), Leicester (60), Derby (49), Coventry (34), and London (117). The average subscription was three shares. This company, like the Derby Canal, was unusually 'democratic' in character. Investors included two serving men, a labourer, a postilion, and the 'Measham Sick Club', each of which took one share.

In 1801–2 a further £21,676 was raised on mortgage of the tolls as follows:[4]

I	II	III	IV	V	VI	VII	VIII	IX
2	42·5	3·8	111	10	18	19	7	3·46
(1%)	(20%)	(2%)	(51%)	(5%)	(9%)	(9%)	(3%)	(2%)

XXIV. *The Barnsley Canal* 1793–1808: £150,000

Shares[5]	I	II	III	IV	V	VI	VII	VIII	IX	Unknown
720 (£160)	24	196	–	145	40	31	83	8	40	153
	(4%)	(34%)		(26%)	(7%)	(5%)	(15%)	(2%)	(7%)	

[1] Derby Central Library, Derby Canal Collection, Transfer Book.

[2] Derby Canal Collection, no 48. For the rights of owners of land to be taken by the canal to subscribe, see below, pp. 153–7.

[3] ASCH 2/1, Share Register.

[4] ASCH 2/2, Register of Mortgages.

[5] BYC 1/3, Minutes of the Committee and General Assembly 1792–1806, ff. 2–3.

This analysis is based on a list made in 1792 of the first 594 shares subscribed. Of the shares, 158 were subscribed at Wakefield, 89 at Barnsley and most of the rest in the neighbouring countryside. The average subscription was 7 shares. The 'undemocratic' character of the company reflects the fact that the canal was promoted by the undertakers of the Aire and Calder Navigation, who were mostly land-owners, rentiers, and merchants, in order to increase the supply of coal, and many took shares. Preference was given to landowners and, as Priestley correctly remarked, almost all in the neighbourhood subscribed.[1] By 1797 the original share capital of £72,000 had been exhausted, and £20,000 was then raised by voluntary calls on some of the proprietors, this sum being later converted into a loan stock. By 1807 a further £4,340 had been borrowed at interest, and £12,000 spent out of toll income. The debts were discharged, and an additional sum raised to complete the line, by making compulsory calls of £60 per share under the authority of an Act of 1808.[2]

XXV. *The Grand Junction Canal* 1793–1815: £1,800,000

No documentation of the share capital of this canal survives. The Act of incorporation,[3] authorizing a capital of £500,000 and £100,000 more if necessary, named 414 proprietors of whom it has been possible to identify 7 as peers, 24 as landed gentlemen, 31 as 'capitalists', 24 as manufacturers, 73 as tradesmen, 60 as professional men, 27 as clergymen, and 4 as women. In addition shares were sub-sequently issued to 148 owners of land on the line of the canal.[4] The total number allocated on this account is not clear. The Act (Clause 33) granted an option of one share to the proprietor of each complete furlong of land taken, up to a maximum of ten, and it appears that this was exercised by about half of those entitled to do so.[5] The length of the

---

[1] Priestley, *Navigable Rivers*, p. 59; BYC 1/3, 29 Oct. 1792.

[2] 48 George III *cap*. 13; W. N. Slatcher, 'The Barnsley Canal: its first twenty years', *Transport History*, i (1968), 48–66.

[3] 33 George III *cap*. 80.

[4] GJC 1/39, Minutes of the General Assembly and General Committee 1793–8, 1 June 1793.

[5] Estimated from the account of owners of land on the line of the canal given in the Book of Reference, Middlesex R.O., Deposited Plans.

canal as originally authorized was 109 miles. At the original subscription meeting in July 1792 £100,000 out of a capital (which was subsequently enlarged) of £350,000 was reserved for the owners of land.[1] It appears, however, that as elsewhere,[2] the depression of share prices after 1793 made many reluctant to participate. In June 1794, 225 shares which might be distributed to landowners were held in trust for the company, and in 1798, 164 remained.[3] It may perhaps be tentatively guessed that collectively they took about 15% of the 4,323[4] shares which had been subscribed by 1795: roughly 300 through their participation in the original subscription, and 400 under Clause 33. As regards the relative importance of the other classes of proprietors, it is probable that the figures offered above provide an adequate guide. The original subscribers were all obliged to take a 'set' of ten shares, though later transfers brought differentiation in the size of holdings which may to some extent have increased the proportionate contribution of 'capitalists'. For example, by the time of the General Assembly of 16 September 1793 the bankers William Praed (of Tyringham and London) and Philip Box (of Buckingham) held respectively 55 and 22 shares, while the Coventry merchant Jeremiah Lowe had 54.[5] The average subscription, including those in right of land taken, was about 8 shares, though this may have been subsequently increased by a slight tendency towards concentration.

This canal was a product of the canal mania in the East Midlands (the original promotion meeting was held at Stony Stratford),[6] and the fact is reflected in the geographical distribution of subscriptions. Landowners along the whole length of the canal took shares, but of the other proprietors named in the Act of incorporation who have been identified,

[1] *Leicester Journal*, 27 July 1792.

[2] See pp. 52, 67, 156–7.

[3] GJC 1/39, 3 June 1794, 5 June 1798.

[4] The figure is that given in Buckinghamshire R.O., D/W 96/12.

[5] For the evolution of holdings see the record of attendances and proxies in the minutes of the General Assemblies GJC 1/39–40. References to sets of subscriptions to 10 shares occur frequently in advertisements in Midland newspapers during the years 1792–3. e.g. *Leicester Journal*, 31 Aug. 1792.

[6] Ibid., 27 July 1792. For the canal mania in the East Midlands, see below, pp. 86–92.

44 were resident in Leicester, 40 in Coventry,[1] 23 in Birmingham, 12 in Market Harborough, 11 in Banbury, 10 in Buckingham, 6 in Aylesbury, and lesser numbers in such towns as Daventry, Rugby, Melton Mowbray, Loughborough, and Derby. Although the line terminated on the Thames at Brentford, the contribution of Londoners was insignificant: only 15 have been identified in the Act.

By 1811 expenditure on the canal works totalled £1,646,000.[2] No figure for the outlay by 1815, in which year two additional branch lines were completed, has been found. That of £1,800,000 given above is a guess based on the amount of work which appears to have been done in the intervening period. This expenditure was financed approximately as follows: £465,700 was raised by calls totalling £100 on each of the original shares; £225,000 by the creation of additional half-shares under the Act of 1796;[3] £165,000, £100,000, and £108,920 by successive issues, under Acts of 1801 and 1803[4] of interest-bearing loan-notes, carrying the option of conversion into single shares with the par value of £100, at prices of respectively £100, £250, and £280;[5] £234,500 by the creation of 2,345 shares of £100 in 1803; £75,512 (an addition of 6·25% to the capital as it was then constituted) by a further issue of loan-notes in 1804–5; and, finally, £160,000 by the issue of 887 shares at the price of £180 each in 1811.[6] This last creation was described as an issue of one share for every 12 already held, suggesting that the nominal share capital, as it finally emerged, was about £1,153,000, though as some shares had been issued at more than par, a rather larger sum had in fact been raised on this account. In 1820, 11,807½ shares were outstanding; in 1888 the ordinary share capital was returned as £1,130,000. The documents required for making complete sense of these various figures do not appear to have survived; in particular,

[1] In 1807 42 proprietors resident at Coventry requested that their dividends be paid through a bank there. GJC 1/42, Minutes of the General Committee 1805–12, 10 July 1807.

[2] Hadfield, *East Midlands*, p. 270.

[3] 36 George III *cap*. 43.

[4] 41 George III *cap*. 71; 43 George III *cap*. 8.

[5] For further details about these issues see below, pp. 123–5.

[6] This included the reissue of 215 shares which had been bought up by the Commissioners for the Sinking Fund.

there are no records of the activities of the Commissioners of the Sinking Fund, who were responsible for the liquidation of the loan-notes.[1] It may be guessed that by 1815, about £1,200,000 had been raised by the issue of shares, a floating capital constituted by the loan-notes of about £200,000 to £300,000 was outstanding, and that the balance of expenditure had been financed out of toll income.[2]

There are no records relating to the disposition of this additional capital.[3] The existing proprietors were granted a right of pre-emption on the successive issues of shares and loan-notes, which they appear in general to have exercised.[4] It thus seems likely that the social character of the company remained much as it had been in 1793. There is however evidence of a tendency for the interest of Londoners to increase. In 1800 a proposition was received from the Stock Exchange for taking £10,000 worth of shares at a premium of 25% (2,500 worth were granted at a premium of 28%).[5] Of the recorded applications made to the General Committee in 1803 by holders of shares or loan stock, or their nominees, for admission as subscribers to the £234,500 share issue of that year, nearly a half (19) were by Londoners, most of the rest coming from the Midlands (20), and, in addition, one each from Yorkshire, Bristol, and Liverpool.[6] At this time the company usually advertised in newspapers in London, Oxford, Coventry, Northampton, Leicester, Derby, Birmingham, and Liverpool.[7]

---

[1] This account has been based on references in the minutes of the General Committee: GJC 1/40 (1798–1802), 15 Apr. 1800 ff., GJC 1/41 (1802–1805), 8 June 1802 2 Nov. 1802, 9 Nov. 1804, 12 Feb. 1805, GJC 1/42 (1805–12), 29 Oct. 1811; GJC 1/43 (1812–28), 9 Nov. 1820; *Parl. Papers 1890*, lxiv, 762, The Sinking Fund was established 21 Jan. 1805 (GJC 1/41).

[2] By 1888, £692,498 had been spent 'from time to time' out of income (*Parl. Papers 1890*, lxiv, 762).

[3] The share register of 1809–37 (GJC 2/2) catalogued among the records of the Grand Junction Canal is in fact that of the Grand Union Canal. See below pp. 83–4.

[4] Authorities as in Note 1 above. For holdings of the half-shares of 1796 see the record of attendances and proxies at General Assemblies in GJC 1/39–40.

[5] GJC 1/40, 15 Apr. 1800.

[6] GJC 1/41, ff. 154, 163, 168, 183, 188.

[7] GJC 1/41, 4 Dec. 1804.

XXVI. *The Worcester and Birmingham Canal* 1791–1815: £610,000

Shares[1]	I	II	III	IV	V	VI	VII	VIII	IX	Forfeit
1,800 (£139)	70	314	6	478	128	308	165	61	263	7
	(4%)	(17%)		(27%)	(7%)	(17%)	(9%)	(3%)	(15%)	

The earliest surviving list of shareholders is one of 1798 which is the source for this analysis. Of the 254 proprietors incorporated by the Act of 1791,[2] 144 held shares at this time, so it seems likely that an adequate guide to the original composition of the company is given. Of the shares, 406 (23%) were held in the city of Worcester and 142 (8%) elsewhere in the county, 285 (16%) at Birmingham, 218 (12%) in Staffordshire, 146 (8%) at Bristol, 270 (15%) at London, and 326 (18%) elsewhere. The average holding was 6 shares.

The authorized capital of the company was £180,000 and £70,000 more if necessary. This additional sum was raised by further calls on the shares. After 1798 work proceeded slowly owing to the difficulty of raising money. The Act of that year[3] authorized the company to raise £149,929. 1s. 1½d. by the subscription among the proprietors of 1,259 half-shares of £69. 8s. 10½d. each, or by mortgage of the tolls or the issue of annuities, while that of 1804[4] sanctioned the additional subscription of £49,680 (27. 10s. 0d. per share). However, the terms of the proposed enlargements of the capital, which amounted to additional subscriptions at par, were evidently, because of the circumstances and prospects of the company, insufficiently attractive to receive support. It was reported by Phillips in November 1802 that 'the Worcester and Birmingham canal shares of £140 had fallen to nothing; a plan for the completion is in agitation; the shares have risen tb £40'.[5]

The resumption of work was eventually financed by the issue of 4,200 shares priced at £40 under the Act of 1808.[6] The only account of the distribution of these shares which

[1] Birmingham Ref. Lib. 72298, *A List of the Proprietors of the Worcester and Birmingham Canal Navigation on the First Day of June, 1798.*

[2] 31 George III *cap.* 59.

[3] 38 George III *cap.* 31.

[4] 44 George III *cap.* 35.

[5] J. Phillips, *A General History of Inland Navigation* (1803 edn.), p. 270.

[6] 48 George III *cap.* 49.

has been found is that of November 1808,[1] at which time only 3,229 had been subscribed (the remainder appear to have been taken up in the following year). It was as follows:

Shares	I	II	III	IV	V	VI	VII	VIII	IX
3,229 (£40)	60	344	39	637	592	848	479	105	125
	(2%)	(11%)	(1%)	(20%)	(18%)	(26%)	(15%)	(3%)	(4%)

Of this issue, 767 (24%) of the shares were held at Birmingham, 622 (19%) at the city of Worcester, 526 (16%) elsewhere in Worcestershire, 309 (9%) in Staffordshire, 111 (4%) at Bristol, 468 (15%) at London, and 426 (13%) elsewhere. Although the proprietors of the original shares were given a right of pre-emption,[2] most failed to exercise it, and at this time held only 1,073 (33%) of the new issue. On a comparison with the distribution of shares in 1798, landowners, women, and the inhabitants of Bristol, appear to have displayed least resilience as investors, while the enthusiasm of manufacturers, tradesmen, and professional men, in particular those of Birmingham and Kidderminster, had increased.

In 1813 the company sought to raise a further £50,000 by the issue of debentures of £40, convertible into shares or mortgages within three years of the completion of the canal. However, difficulties were experienced in filling the subscription for this issue (£38,013 worth of the securities were outstanding in 1818), and the company came to rely increasingly on advances from its treasurers, the Birmingham bankers Messrs. Startin and Smith. By 1815, when the partners declared their determination not to extend the overdraft, £27,096 was due and the company was obliged to obtain a further Act[3] to raise £90,000 for the repayment of this and other debts, and for the completion of the works. As a result, £30,000 was raised by an additional call of 5% on each share, and £36,000 by the sale of annuities at the rate of 10% per annum (later converted into mortgages at 5%).[4]

---

[1] Birmingham Ref. Lib. 366657, *A List of the Proprietors of the Worcester and Birmingham Canal Navigation on the 26th November 1808.*

[2] WOBC 1/1, Minutes of the General Assembly 1791–1834, 17 Nov. 1807.

[3] 55 George III *cap.* 66.

[4] This paragraph is based on WOBC 1/1, 5 Jan. 1813, 6 July 1813, 3 Jan. 1815, 4 July 1815, 2 Jan. 1816, 6 Jan. 1818, 6 Mar. 1818; WOBC 1/6, Minutes of the Committee 1812–16, 24 Nov. 1814, 28 Dec. 1814.

XXVII. *The Wyrley and Essington Canal* 1792-1800: £80,000

Shares[1]	I	II	III	IV	V	VI	VII	VIII	IX
600 (£125)	–	158	–	130	63	56	97	62	34
		(26%		(22%)	(11%)	(9%)	(16%)	(10%)	(6%)

Under the original Act of 1792, 200 shares were created and 600 were added under that of 1794 to finance an extension of the line. Of the latter, 200 were allotted without any payment being demanded to the proprietors of original shares, apparently because of the premium at which these stood.[2] Only the 600 shares on which calls were paid have been considered here. Of these 169 (28%) were subscribed at Wolverhampton and 267 (45%) elsewhere in Staffordshire. The average subscription was 5 shares. In 1803, £8,300 was borrowed on mortgage (in part to meet a deficiency on shares which had not been fully paid up) from 6 tradesmen and 4 women, all apparently of the town of Wolverhampton.[3]

XXVIII. *The Stratford-upon-Avon Canal* 1793-1816: £300,000

Shares[4]	I	II	III	IV	V	VI	VII	VIII	IX
1,200 (£150)	50	326	53	165	27	280	138	108	53
	(4%)	(27%)	(4%)	(14%)	(2%)	(23%)	(11%)	(9%)	(4%)

Of the shares, 302 (25%) were subscribed for at Stratford, 95 (8%) at Birmingham, 470 (39) elsewhere in Warwickshire, and 333 (28%) outside the county. The average subscription was 6 shares. Between 1793 and 1802 £153,771 was raised by calls of £150 on each share, a deficiency of nearly £30,000 occurring through forfeitures and the non-payment of calls. Work was then suspended for some years, the line being finally completed between 1809 and 1816 at a further cost of about £143,000. This work was financed by the issue of 2,606 shares at the price of £30, the sale for a total sum of £45,000 of annuities at rates of up to 10% per annum, and

[1] WEC 1/1, Minutes of the General Assembly 1793–1840, ff. 1, 22–4, lists of proprietors 10 May 1792 and 10 May 1794.

[2] 32 George III *cap.* 81; 34 George III *cap.* 25; WEC 1/1, 10 May 1794.

[3] WEC 1/1, 10 Nov. 1803.

[4] SCN 1/1, Minutes of the General Assembly 1793–1856, ff. 1–7, list of proprietors 1793.

by incurring debts of £20,000.[1] Information about the sources of this capital is not available.

XXIX. *The Warwick and Birmingham Canal* 1793–1800: £160,000

Shares[2]	I	II	III	IV	V	VI	VII	VIII	IX	Unknown
693 (£100)	15	40	5	94	91	160	79	56	20	133
	(3%)	(7%)		(17%)	(16%)	(28%)	(14%)	(10%)	(4%)	

This analysis is based on a list of the subscribers to 693 shares named in the Act of incorporation.[3] Subsequently, 278 more shares were issued, 76 to owners of land on the line of the canal,[4] bringing the total number outstanding to 971. Of the original subscriptions to shares which have been identified, 236 (42%) were made at Birmingham, 110 (20%) at Warwick, and the remainder elsewhere in the county of Warwickshire. The average subscription was 4 shares. In 1797, after £100 had been paid on each of the original shares, 840 additional half-shares of £50 were taken up among the proprietors,[5] and in 1798 £20,000 was raised on loan from the same source.[6] By 1800, £9,350 of this sum had been converted into stock, and more shares had been sold.[7] The capital, as it finally emerged, was composed of 1,000 full shares and 1,000 half-shares.

XXX. *The Warwick and Napton Canal* 1794–1800: £80,000

Shares[8]	I	II	III	IV	V	VI	VII	VIII	IX	Unknown
795 (£100)	3	132	—	87	100	161	57	21	27	207
		(22%)		(15%)	(17%)	(27%)	(10%)	(4%)	(5%)	

This analysis is based on the original subscription of 1794. After the issue of more shares (including 71 to owners of land on the line of the canal which have been included in the figure of 132 given above), and a number of forfeitures, 795

---

[1] C. Hadfield and J. Norris, *Waterways to Stratford* (Dawlish, 1962), pp, 76–7, 83, 90.

[2] WBC 1/1, Minutes of the General Assembly 1793–1812, ff. 1–7, list of proprietors 1793.

[3] 33 George III *cap.* 38.

[4] WBC 1/1, 17 June 1793, 24 Sept. 1793.

[5] Ibid., 27 Jan. 1797.

[6] Ibid., 27 Mar. 1798.

[7] Ibid., 30 Sept. 1800.

[8] House of Lords R.O., Deposited Plans, Warwick and Braunston Canal (later Warwick and Napton) Subscription Contract, 1794 to a total of about 700 shares.

were outstanding in 1801 after the completion of the line.[1] This canal was closely associated with the Warwick and Birmingham company, whose proprietors had preference in subscribing for 3 shares each. Of these 107 did so. The company was therefore dominated financially by investors from Birmingham who took 247 (41%) of the shares whose subscribers have been identified. Most of the remainder were taken in the town of Warwick and elsewhere in the county. The average subscription was 3 shares.

XXXI. *The Shropshire Canal* 1788-1792: £50,000

Shares[2]	I	II	III	IV	V	VI	VII	VIII	IX
500 (£100)	40	45	–	73	230	28	18	10	56
	(8%)	(9%)		(15%)	(46%)	(6%)	(4%)	(2%)	(11%)

This canal was promoted and largely controlled by the ironmasters of Coalbrookdale, and their connections: the Reynolds, Rathbones, and John Wilkinson, who account for the large contribution of 'manufacturers'. Of the shares 391 (78%) were taken up in Shropshire, and 50 (10%) in Staffordshire. The average subscription was 9 shares.

XXXII. *The Shrewsbury Canal* 1793-1797: £65,000

Shares[3]	I	II	III	IV	V	VI	VII	VIII	IX
500 (£125)	20	205	–	129	50	40	13	24	19
	(4%)	(41%)		(26%)	(10%)	(8%)	(3%)	(5%)	(4%)

Of the shares, 459 (92%) were subscribed in Shropshire and Staffordshire. The average subscription was 8 shares.

XXXIII. *The Ellesmere Canal* 1793-1805: £500,000

No list of proprietors of an earlier date than 1822 appears to survive, and no systematic attempt has been made to identify or analyse the 1,240 subscribers to the original share capital of £400,000 named in the Act of incorporation.[4] This undertaking was one of the most remarkable promotions of the canal mania. It had originally been set on foot by a group of local men but drew substantial support from the principal

[1] WNC 1/1, General Assembly Minutes 1794-1810, 27 May 1794, 29 Sept. 1798, 30 Sept. 1801.

[2] SHPC 1/1, Committee and General Assembly minutes 1788-1858, 12 June 1788, list of proprietors.

[3] SHRC 1/1, Committee and General Assembly Minutes 1793-1847, 1 July 1793, list of proprietors.

[4] 33 George III *cap.* 91.

centres of excitement: Birmingham and the towns of the East Midlands.[1] In order to accommodate the enthusiasm manifested at the subscription meeting of 10 September 1792, at which £967,700 was promised, the capital was enlarged from £200,000 to £300,000, and later £400,000, and the proposed line was extended. Surplus subscription deposits were ordered to be returned at Derby, Leicester, Northampton, Stony Stratford, Coventry, Birmingham, and Shrewsbury. At a meeting in December 1792 Leicestershire subscribers to the amount of £60,000 were represented. Of 145 proprietors present in person or represented at the General Assembly of 29 October 1794 about 40 (i.e less than one-third) were local men, 25 were residents of the town of Leicester, 20 of Birmingham, 13 of Derby, with lesser numbers from such towns as Market Harborough, Lichfield, Nottingham, Coventry, and Loughborough.[2]

Of the share capital, £40,000 (10%) was reserved for—and initially accepted by—the owners of land on the line of the canal.[3] However, many later declined to take up their allotments, or to pay the calls, and for this reason, and on account of 'the insolvency of some other of the original Subscribers', by 1802 there was a deficiency of £70,000 in the company's stock.[4] The Act of that year[5] empowered it to meet this by additional calls on the shares which remained outstanding, and £133 was eventually called on 3,330 shares, the balance of expenditure being financed by a loan of £10,000 from the treasurers, by the issue at the price of £70 each of about £20,000 worth of optional notes, and toll and other income to the amount of £48,586.[6] In 1813 the company was amalgamated with the Chester Canal. Although their patience was sorely tried (the first dividend, of £4 per

1 Hadfield, *West Midlands*, pp. 167–9; and see below, pp. 86–92.

2 Hadfield, loc. cit.; ELC 1/4, Minutes of the Promoters 1791–3, 6 Sept., 25 Sept., 28 Dec. 1792; ELC 1/5 Minutes of the General Assembly 1793–1812, 29 Oct. 1794.

3 ELC 1/4, 25 Sept. 1792, 11 Jan. 1793; ELC 1/5, 3 July 1793.

4 *H.C.J.* lvii. 101.

5 42 George III *cap.* 20.

6 Hadfield, op. cit., p. 179; ELC 1/5, 5 Mar. 1806, 24 July 1807; ECC 1/7, Ellesmere (later Ellesmere and Chester) Canal, Minutes of the Subcommittee of Accounts and Finance 1805–46, 5 Feb. 1806.

share, was not declared until 1815),[1] the distant investors appear to have remained loyal. In 1822 the geographical distribution of the 3,500 shares, which by this time had become concentrated in the hands of 714 holders, was as follows: Leicestershire 704 (20%), elsewhere in the Midlands 814 (23%), Shropshire 619 (18%), Cheshire 491 (14%), London 529 (15%), elsewhere 343 (10%).[2]

XXXIV. *The Montgomeryshire Canal* 1794–1797: £71,100

Shares[3]	I	II	III	IV	V	VI	VII	VIII	IX
711 (£100)	70	306	4	95	–	96	65	52	23
	(10%)	(43%)		(13%)		(14%)	(9%)	(7%)	(3%)

Shares were taken in the towns on or near the line of the canal: Montgomery, Newtown, and Welshpool, and in the neighbouring countryside. Only about 80 were subscribed outside the counties of Montgomeryshire and Shropshire. The average subscription was 9 shares. In 1797, after £100 had been called on each share, work was suspended with only two-thirds of the line completed. The remainder was built between 1815 and 1820, at a cost of £53,390, by investors acting as a separate company.[4]

XXXV. *The Herefordshire and Gloucestershire Canal* 1791–1798: £105,000

Shares[5]	I	II	III	IV	V	VI	VII	VIII	IX
750 (£140)	10	244	–	105	–	222	100	56	13
	(1%)	(33%)		(14%)		(30%)	(13%)	(7%)	(2%)

Of the shares, 277 were subscribed in Herefordshire, 209 in Gloucestershire, and 233 (31%) elsewhere (83 at Bristol). The average subscription was 4 shares. In 1798, after the authorized capital had been exhausted, and the line completed only between Gloucester and Ledbury, 16 out of 34 miles of its intended course, work was suspended. The line to Hereford was built between 1839 and 1845 at a further cost

---

[1] ECC 1/7, 13 Nov. 1815.

[2] E. A. Wilson, 'The Proprietors of the Ellesmere and Chester Canal Company in 1822', *Journal of Transport History*, vol. iii, no 1 (May, 1957), pp. 52–4.

[3] House of Lords R.O., Deposited Plans, Montgomeryshire Canal Subscription Contract 1794; MONC 1/1, General Assembly Minutes 1794–1839, 7 July 1794, admission of additional proprietors.

[4] Hadfield, *West Midlands*, pp. 194–5.

[5] HGN 2/5, Calls Book 1791–98.

of £141,500, this sum being raised by the issue of further shares, by loans on mortgage, and out of toll income.[1]

XXXVI. *The Gloucester and Berkeley Canal 1793–1799: £112,000*

Shares [2]	I	II	III	IV	V	VI	VII	VIII	IX
1,179 (£100)	10	216	–	313	177	206	180	60	17
	(1%)	(18%)		(27%)	(15%)	(17%)	(15%)	(5%)	(1%)

Of the shares, 417 (35%) were subscribed in the city of Gloucester, 197 (17%) elsewhere in the county, 250 (21%) in Worcestershire, 135 (11%) in Shropshire, and 91 (8%) at Birmingham. The average subscription was 11 shares. The authorized share capital was £140,000. One-fifth of this was reserved for the owners of land required by the canal. However, in consequence of the depreciation of the company's scrip following the commercial crisis of 1793, many failed to exercise their option, and a deficiency in the subscription resulted.[3] Only 1,179 shares were eventually taken. This stock was further depleted by the failure of some of the proprietors (in every case, apparently, persons engaged in trade) to complete the payment of the calls on them, and by 1799 only £112,000 had been raised by calls of £100 on each share.[4] Out of 18 miles of the intended line, 12 remained unbuilt and work was suspended. The company's scheme to raise additional funds by a lottery was rejected by parliament,[5] and the attempt to obtain £80,000 by the issue of depreciated shares under the Act of 1805 failed, apparently because the stipulated price (£60 per share) was too high.[6] The line was finally completed between 1818 and 1827 at a further cost of about £328,000, financed by advances totalling £160,000 from the Exchequer Bill Loan Commissioners, by loans from other sources, and by the issue of additional shares.[7]

---

[1] C. Hadfield, *The Canals of South Wales and the Border* (Cardiff, 1960) pp. 204–6.

[2] GBC 2/1, Calls Book 1792–1829.

[3] See below, p. 156.

[4] 58 George III (Local and Personal) *cap.* xvii.

[5] C. Hadfield, *The Canals of Southern England* (1955), p. 184; *H.C.J.* lxii. 183.

[6] 45 George III *cap.* 104. In 1798 it has been reported that the shares stood at a discount of 80% (GBC 1/1, Minutes of the General Assembly 1793–1823, 26. Mar. 1798).

[7] Hadfield, op cit., pp. 185–7.

XXXVII. *The Manchester, Bolton and Bury Canal 1791-1810: £160,000*

The 94 proprietors named in the Act of incorporation[1] included 2 peers, 10 landowners, 13 'capitalists', 27 manufacturers (25 of these being engaged in the cotton industry), 10 tradesmen, 10 professional men, 5 clergymen, and 5 women. Of those who have been identified, 27 were resident in Manchester, 25 in Bolton, and 6 in Bury. Between 1791 and 1796 the authorized capital of £67,700 was raised by calls on the 477 shares. Thereafter additional sums were raised without parliamentary sanction by voluntary subscription among the proprietors, including 3 calls of 7·5% made between 1796 and 1798. By 1805 a total debt of £31,345 in excess of the authorized capital had been incurred in this way. The Act of that year[2] sanctioned an enlargement of the stock by £80,000 for the purpose of liquidating this liability and completing the works. The sum was raised by calls on the proprietors between 1805 and 1808, and in 1810 £10,000 was borrowed on mortgage of the tolls.[3]

XXXVIII. *The Lancaster Canal 1792-1820: £800,000*

The Act of incorporation[4] names 112 proprietors of whom it is possible to identify about half as merchants and substantial tradesmen of the town of Lancaster,[5] with roughly half a dozen contributions from both Kendal and Liverpool. It is clear that (for no obvious reason) this list is incomplete. For example, at the first general assembly of the company's proprietors 257 holders of only £275,200 of the authorized share capital of £414,100 were present or represented.[6] The company was notable for the very large investments of individual Lancaster merchants. Many held 50 shares, while a few (for example Abraham Rawlinson and John Dilworth) held 100 or 120. It seems likely that the contribution of 'capitalists' was substantial, though, as no

[1] 31 George III *cap.* 68   [2] 45 George III *cap.* 4.

[3] V. I. Tomlinson, 'The Manchester, Bolton and Bury Canal,' *Transactions Lancs. and Cheshire Antiq. Soc.* lxxv-lxxvi (1965-6), 252-9.

[4] 32 George III *cap.* 107.

[5] Cf. J. F. Curwen, 'The Lancaster Canal,' *Trans. Cumberland and Westmoreland Arch. Soc.,* n.s., xvii (1917), 31, '... the town of Lancaster providing an overwhelming proportion' of the subscriptions.

[6] LC 1/8, Minutes of the General Assembly 1792-1822, 3 July 1792.

complete list of proprietors has been found, it is not possible to give statistical support to this impression.

On each of the 4,141 shares £85 was called. The full £100 could not be raised because £60,000 of the authorized capital was reserved under the terms of the Act for expenditure on the line to Kendal, a work which was postponed in consequence of the financial difficulties experienced by the company. In 1797 a plan was set on foot to raise the additional £15 per share by a voluntary loan from the proprietors on mortgage of the tolls, and by July of that year it was reported that the proprietors of 2,139 shares had subscribed.[1] However, this course was inadequate. In 1800 it was reported that the company had been unable to raise the supplementary capital of £200,000 authorized by the Act of 1792 in the manner prescribed (by mortgage, additional calls, or the admission of new proprietors to shares at par), and the Act of that year permitted it to meet this deficiency by the creation of new shares at the price of £30 each or 'whatever rate or value per share as should from Time to Time be the current or saleable Value of Shares',[2] and 4,141 new shares of £30 were created in the manner thus authorized, 3,607 of which were accepted by proprietors in proportion to their current holdings, all but 107 of the remainder being disposed of among them by auction.[3] In 1804 a further 4,000 shares were created at the price of £12 each, which were apparently distributed in the same way.[4] Also £270,000 was borrowed on mortgage under the Act of 1819[5] for the purpose of completing the line to Kendal.

No documents recording changes in ownership of the share capital have been found. It may have become rather more widely dispersed than it appears to have been in 1792. Of 238 shares which were declared forfeit, or against whose proprietors prosecutions were ordered to be commenced for non-payment of calls in 1796, 140 were held in Lancaster, 22 in Manchester, 20 in Liverpool, 16 in Derby, 14 in London,

[1] LC 1/8, 31 Jan., 4 July 1797.
[2] *H.C.J.* lv. 282, 39, 40 George III *cap.* 57.
[3] LC 1/8, 7 Jan. 1800, 6 Jan. 1801, 2 Aug. 1803.
[4] LC 1/8, 29 Mar. 1804.
[5] 59 George III *cap.* 64.

and 29 elsewhere.[1] In the company's letter books reference is occasionally made to proprietors resident in London and the Home Counties,[2] and in 1797, when accommodation was being urgently sought from local bankers to finance the completion of the works to Preston before the following winter, the clerk exclaimed: 'Surely some means can be pointed out by some of our friends in London how we can obtain this Temporary Aid'.[3] However, although this exceptionally ambitious undertaking may have drawn capital from a distance to a greater degree than most of the Lancashire canals, there is no reason to suppose that such assistance was ever of more than secondary importance.[4]

XXXIX. *The Ashton under Lyne Canal* 1792–1807: £210,000

Of the 121 proprietors named in the Act of incorporation[5] it has been possible to identify 91. These include 2 peers, 1 landowner, 7 'capitalists', 42 manufacturers (33 of these being cotton manufacturers), 22 tradesmen, 6 professional men, 4 clergymen, and 7 women. Of these 63 were resident at Manchester and 18 at Ashton under Lyne.

By 1798 £90,000 had been raised by calling £135. 17s. on each of the 600 shares.[6] Under the Act of that year[7] the capital was enlarged by £30,000, apparently by the issue of interest-bearing promissory notes convertible into shares if not repaid within 5 years. That of 1800[8] allowed £20,000 to be raised on mortgage of the tolls but it was only found possible to borrow £8,677 in this way.[9] The Act of 1805 recited that the share capital raised and the debts due totalled £158,654, and enlarged the authorized total of the former from £170,000 to £210,000.[10] Further calls were evidently

---

[1] LC 1/8, 5 July 1796.

[2] e.g. LC 8/2, Letter Book 1794–7, f. 587 (9 Nov. 1796); LC 8/3, Letter Book 1797–1808, ff. 285, 290, 294 (21 Sept., 23 Sept., 1 Oct. 1800).

[3] LC 8/2, f. 679 (30 Mar. 1797).

[4] For the cases of the Leeds and Liverpool, and the Rochdale Canals, see pp. 35, 63, 123.

[5] 32 George III *cap.* 84.

[6] AC 1/1, Committee Minutes 1798–1815, 28 July 1798.

[7] 38 George III *cap.* 32.

[8] 39, 40 George III *cap.* 24.

[9] AC 1/1, 10 Mar. 1802, 30 Apr., 28 May 1802, 17 Jan. 1803, 2 Mar. 1804.

[10] 45 George III *cap.* 11.

made on the proprietors in the following years.[1] In 1888 the capital of the company was returned as £286,750.[2]

XL. *The Peak Forest Canal* 1794–1805: £250,000

Shares[3]	I	II	III	IV	V	VI	VII	VIII	IX	Unknown
806 (£100)	–	115	37	31	391	49	43	16	21	103
		(16%)	(5%)	(4%)	(56%)	(7%)	(6%)	(3%)		

Of the shares whose subscribers have been identified, 243 (42%) were taken at Manchester, 146 (25%) at Stockport and district, 31 (5%) at Ashton under Lyne, and 166 (28%) by owners of land on the line of the canal, not all of whom were merely 'landowners'. The company was closely connected with that of the Ashton under Lyne Canal, 73 out of 121 (60%) of whose proprietors took shares.[4] The average subscription was 4 shares. Persons engaged in the cotton industry account for all but 38 (10%) of the shares subscribed by 'manufacturers'.

Only £80,600 of the authorized share capital of £90,000 was originally subscribed. By 1800 £80,045 had been raised by calls of £100 on each share (of which 9 had been forfeited for the non-payment of calls). In the circumstances of the time it was found to be impossible to raise the further sum of £60,000 in the manner prescribed by mortgage of the tolls, and so, under the Act of that year,[5] the deficiency of £69,955 in the total authorized capital of £150,000 was made up by the issue of 1,594 additional shares (twice the number then outstanding) at an arbitrarily determined price, 'in order to induce all the proprietors to take up their proportion of the new shares.'[6] This measure was, however,

[1] e.g. AC 1/1, 28 May, 2 Sept. 1805.

[2] *Parl. Papers, 1890*, lxiv 796.

[3] House of Lords R.O., Deposited Plans, Peak Forest Canal Subscription Contract 1794. Landowners have been identified through the Book of Reference (loc. cit.). Proprietors of small amounts of land crossed by the canal have, unless otherwise identifiable, been classed as 'yeomen'.

[4] From a comparison of the names in the latter's Act of incorporation with the former's subscription contract.

[5] 39, 40 George III *cap.* 38.

[6] PFC 1/1, Committee Minutes 1794–1800, 20 June 1800. According to J. Phillips, *A General History of Inland Navigation* (1803 edn.), p. 343, the company's shares stood at a premium of £10. In 1798 £36,540 had been raised among the proprietors by a voluntary loan of £50 per share, PFC 1/1, 2 Mar. 1798 ff.

found to be insufficient. In October 1801 orders were given for the preparation of a bill to be submitted to parliament authorizing the raising of a further £50,000 by the creation of new shares.[1] The application was however postponed because the times were thought unpropitious, in particular because opposition was apprehended from the mill owners,[2] and instead it was agreed by a number of proprietors to advance £10 on their shares as a voluntary loan, the other members of the company allowing the payment of interest on this sum preference over the dividend.[3]

In 1802 negotiations were begun with the cotton manufacturers Samuel Oldknow and Richard Arkwright for the conclusion of an agreement under which they were to finance the construction of the locks at Marple, required to join the upper and lower levels of the canal. It was at first proposed that their advances should be serviced by rebates on the tonnages payable by their goods carried on the company's canal and railways: a rebate of $\frac{1}{4}$ when they should total £4,000, $\frac{1}{2}$ at £8,000, $\frac{3}{4}$ at £12,000, and at £16,000 or, it was later suggested, £20,000, the whole.[4] The advances were to be repaid over a period of 21 months after the completion of the works, the tonnages being restored in the same proportions. While it is clear that the construction of the locks was financed by Arkwright, the committee minutes (the only source available) leave it in some doubt whether it was on precisely these terms. In March 1803 it was proposed that the sum inserted in the contract be £30,000,[5] and in April, that Oldknow and Arkwright be allowed a lease (i.e. a composition) of £1,200 per annum for the tonnages which should be due from them during the following four years. At the

[1] PFC 1/2, Committee Minutes 1800–7, 16 Oct. 1801.
[2] PFC 1/2, 13 Nov. 1801.
[3] PFC 1/2, 25 Nov. 1801.
[4] PFC 1/2, 24 Nov. 1802, 19 Jan. 1803. For Oldknow's connection with the canal company, and with Arkwright on whom by this time his financial dependence was complete, see George Unwin, *Samuel Oldknow and the Arkwrights* (Manchester, 1924), especially pp. 200–2, 224–8. Oldknow is said (ibid., p. 227) to have held 52 shares in Dec. 1794 (he appears for 65 in the subscription contract), and 261 by 1800. Arkwright does not appear in the subscription contract, but by the 1800s was a committee member, and so no doubt a shareholder.
[5] PFC 1/2, 21 Mar. 1803.

same time it was suggested that they give the company
£24,000 with which to undertake the works, repayable with
interest within four years.[1] Terms had apparently been
settled by August when the clerks were finally ordered to get
the agreement executed.[2] In September an order was given
for the canal, its tolls, limeworks, and other ancillary assets,
to be leased to Oldknow and Arkwright for 15 years, on
unspecified terms.[3] In October 1805 it was reported that the
company was prepared to give Arkwright a mortgage for the
money he had advanced 'and that the Committee wish it to
be made up to twenty seven thousand pounds which it is
expected will finish the works respecting the Locks. . . .'[4]

It is not possible from these fragmentary references to
make complete sense of what were clearly long and complicated negotiations. It appears, however, that Arkwright
was granted some kind of concession with regard to the tolls,
in addition to legal interest, in consideration of his advances.
No example of an arrangement of this kind has been noticed in
the history of any other canal. Under the Act of 1805 the
company's capital was enlarged by £60,000, apparently by
making additional calls among the proprietors, in part no
doubt for the purpose of repaying this debt.[5]

XLI. *The Huddersfield Canal* 1794–1811: £400,000

Shares[6]	I	II	III	IV	V	VI	VII	VIII	IX	Unknown
1,819 (£100)	–	72	28	379	476	300	123	10	18	413
		(5%)	(2%)	(27%)	(34%)	(21%)	(9%)	(1%)	(1%)	

Of the shares whose subscribers have been identified, about
250 (18%) were taken at Huddersfield, 500 (37%) elsewhere
in Yorkshire, 160 (12%) in Manchester, 340 (25%) elsewhere
in Lancashire, and 100 (8%) outside these counties, mostly in
the adjacent parts of Cheshire. Most of the Lancashire and
Yorkshire subscribers were resident in manufacturing centres
on the line of the canal, including Oldham, Ashton under

[1] PFC 1/2, 18 Apr. 1803.
[2] PFC 1/2, 26 Aug. 1803.
[3] PFC 1/2, 13 Sept. 1803.
[4] PFC 1/2, 7 Oct. 1805.
[5] 45 George III *cap.* 12; PFC 1/2, 27 Mar. 1805.
[6] House of Lords R.O., Deposited Plans, Huddersfield Canal Subscription
Contract 1794.

Lyne, and the clothing parish of Saddleworth. The average subscription was 5 shares.

The Act of incorporation[1] authorized a capital of £184,000 and £90,000 more if necessary; £100 was called on each share but in 1798 it was reported that 'by the Bankruptcy of several of the Proprietors of Shares in the said Canal, by the Deaths of others of the Proprietors of Shares insolvent and from the Circumstances of several of the Proprietors having left the Kingdom, it is become impossible to procure payment of the whole of the money subscribed for executing the said Canal and its Works'.[2] By 1799 the deficiency on this account exceeded £19,000, and it had been possible to raise only £15,482 on mortgage.[3] The Act of 1800[4] permitted the company to raise the residue of the £274,000 originally authorized by making additional calls on the old shares and creating new ones.

On each of the 1,666 shares which remained outstanding £20 was called and an equivalent number of new shares of £30 were created, the proprietors being granted a right of pre-emption in proportion to their holdings: 1,448 were accepted on this account.[5] In 1804 when, after further forfeitures, 1,612 of both old and new shares remained, the disposition of the latter was as follows:

Shares[6]	I	II	III	IV	V	VI	VII	VIII	IX
1,612 (£30)	—	68	6	844	229	298	115	30	22
		(4%)		(53%)	(14%)	(19%)	(7%)	(2%)	(1%)

Of these 603 (38%) were held in Yorkshire, 423 (26%) in Manchester, 287 (18%) elsewhere in Lancashire, 109 (7%) in London, 109 (7%) in the Midlands, and 81 (5%) elsewhere. The average holding was 6 shares.

From the account of those who accepted new shares in 1801 it is possible to identify the subscribers for 1,202 of the shares in the subscription contract of 1794, which, taking into account the forfeitures that had taken place, suggests

[1] 34 George III *cap.* 53.
[2] HUC 1/1, General Assembly Minutes 1794–1815, 16 Feb. 1798.
[3] Ibid., 16 May 1799.
[4] 39, 40 George III *cap.* 39.
[5] HUC 1/1, 25 June 1801.
[6] HUC 2/1, 'A Book Containing an Account of the New or Additional Shares in the Huddersfield Canal'.

that in the intervening years the composition of the company had not substantially changed. However, some of the proprietors assigned away their right to subscribe to the new issue while others, having subscribed, transferred their shares. A tendency towards the concentration of holdings is thus manifested: in the subscription contract of 1794, 367 persons are named, in 1801, 338 accepted new shares, but by 1804 this issue was in the hands of only 260 holders. Many had been bought up by merchants, particularly those of Manchester, and although some self-styled merchants may also have been manufacturers, thus exaggerating the extent to which the contribution of 'capitalists' had increased at the expense of the latter class in the decade 1794–1804, there can be little doubt that it was the lesser manufacturers, especially the clothiers, who had taken more than 200 shares in the original subscription of 1794, but who held only 75 of the new issue in 1804, who had suffered most from the financial vicissitudes of the period.

In 1804, 3,224 additional shares (one for each share already outstanding) of £8. 13s. were issued.[1] Finally, under the Act of 1806 a further £100,000 was raised by calling £16 on each of the 6,448 shares.[2] The capital structure may be summarized thus:

	Amount Called	Amount Raised
1,612 Original Shares	£120	£193,440
1,612 New Shares (1801)	£30	£48,360
3,224 New Shares (1804)	£8 13s.	£27,887
6,448 Additional Calls	£16	£103,168
Total		£372,855

The indeterminate amount raised on shares which became forfeit, expenditure out of toll income, and an overdraft with the treasurers which totalled £5,608 in 1812,[3] have been taken into consideration to produce a guess of £400,000 as the total cost of this line. Priestley's figure of 'upwards of £300,000'[4] is apparently too low.

[1] HUC 1/1, 28 June 1804.
[2] 46 George III *cap.* 12; HUC 1/3, Committee Minutes 1801–19, 24 Apr. 1806 ff.
[3] HUC 1/3, 26 Mar. 1812.
[4] Priestley, *Historical Account . . .*, p. 372.

XLII. *The Rochdale Canal* 1794–1821: £770,000

Shares[1]	I	II	III	IV	V	VI	VII	VIII	IX	Unknown
2,919 (£100)	10	48	–	274	1117	265	251	61	94	799
		(2%)		(13%)	(53%)	(13%)	(12%)	(3%)	(4%)	

The manufacturers were drawn equally from the cotton and the woollen trades with a few from such ancillary industries as dyeing and printing. Of the shares whose subscribers have been identified, about 1,000 (46%) were taken in Manchester, 700 (32%) in Rochdale, 290 (13%) in Coventry, 100 (5%) in Birmingham and district, and 72 (3%) in Leicester.[2] The average number of shares subscribed was 9.

As the records of the company were not available to this writer,[3] it is not possible to describe its financial history in any degree of detail. Evidently, £100 was called on the original shares, but the company found it impossible to raise the authorized supplementary capital of £100,000 in the manner prescribed (by mortgage or the creation of new shares at par).[4] Authority was therefore obtained[5] in 1800 to raise this sum among the proprietors by the issue of interest-bearing promissory notes of £30 each, convertible into stock if not repaid within 8 years. Members of the company were circularized with an offer in 1804 of these securities.[6] Under the Act of 1804 an attempt was made to raise £70,000 by an issue of shares of £20, which were apparently made available to both the proprietors and the public at large.[7] Neither of these attempted enlargements of the capital appears to have met with much success. The Act of 1806[8] recited that only £328,900 had been spent by that date, £143,050 still being needed for the completion of the works, which the company was thereby authorized to raise, either by additional calls of £25 on each share, or by the issue of what were in effect preference shares of the same

---

[1] House of Lords R.O., Deposited Plans, Rochdale Canal Subscription Contract 1794.

[2] This contribution from the Midlands is discussed below, pp. 89–90.

[3] They are in the hands of the Rochdale Canal Co., 75 Dale St., Manchester.

[4] By the original Act of incorporation, 34 George III *cap.* 78.

[5] By the Act of 40 George III *cap.* 36.

[6] Lancashire R.O., DD Bo/289.

[7] 44 George III *cap.* 9; DD Bo/290.

[8] 46 George III *cap.* 20.

amount.[1] In 1888 the share capital was stated as £481,355 (5,663 shares of £85) and at the same time it was reported, on the authority of the 'old records', that after the canal had been opened throughout its length in 1804 'in consequence of political complications the greatest difficulties were experienced in raising additional fixed capital' for the purpose of perfecting the works and repaying debts. It was therefore necessary to apply the whole of the net revenue for the succeeding 7 years, and the bulk of the net revenue for a further 10, to the task of making necessary improvements. In addition large sums were obtained on open loan and subsequently repaid out of revenue.[2]

XLIII. The Thames and Severn Canal 1783–1793: £230,000

Shares[3]	I	II	III	IV	V	VI	VII	VIII	IX	Unknown
1,300 (£100)	25	135	—	550	16	2	62	25	170	315
	(3%)	(13%)		(56%)	(2%)		(6%)	(3%)	(17%)	

This canal was remarkable, to a degree which attracted contemporary comment, for the extent to which it drew capital from outside the district through which it ran. About 320 (25%) of its shares were subscribed for by proprietors of the Staffordshire and Worcestershire Canal and their connections, who were interested in the completion of a navigation between the valleys of the Severn and Thames which their concern would be well situated to supply with traffic, especially coal. Of the other subscriptions which have been positively identified, 600 (61%) were made at London. Apart from a handful of landowners, the only local subscribers who have been noticed are Thomas Bailiss (1 share) and William Capell (10 shares), both clothiers, and Richard Aldridge, tallow-chandler (2 shares), all of Stroud. Only 5 proprietors of the adjacent Stroudwater Navigation, an essentially local undertaking incorporated by an Act of 1776,[4] appear as subscribers to this canal.

[1] Promissory notes of £25 each, bearing interest at 5%, or rights to the full dividend whenever it should exceed that rate.

[2] Parl. Papers 1890, lxiv, 773. £261,565 had been spent out of revenue by 1888.

[3] Gloucestershire R.O., T.S. 166, Minutes of the General Assembly 1783–1822, lists of proprietors at the time of the first General Assembly, 24 June 1783.

[4] 16 George III cap. 21; Gloucestershire R.O., D 1180 3/1, Stroudwater Navigation Register of Shares and Share Transfers 1774–1809; see above p. 38.

According to Phillips[1] the line had been surveyed in 1782

at the desire of several opulent private persons, chiefly merchants of
London (not the corporation), who had no local interest in either of
the counties of Wilts and Gloucester, through which the canal
passes. . . .

So favourable an idea was entertained by the citizens of London of the
utility of this junction of the Thames with the Severn, that if its
completion had called for a million instead of 130,000£ the fund would
have been presently subscribed. The connections of one mercantile
house alone subscribed 23,000£ and several others 10,000£ each.

This last sentence refers to the investments of the partners of
the firm of Chambers, Rolleston, and Sargent, 38 Mincing
Lane.[2]

It is probable that the figures which have been offered
above significantly understate the metropolitan contribution.
Many of the subscribers who have not been satisfactorily
identified[3] seem far more likely from their names and the
size of their investments to have been London merchants, or
their relations, than provincial tradesmen. They may not have
appeared in contemporary directories because they were
members of partnerships or in retirement. Of the subscriptions which have not been identified, a total of only £900
were made in amounts of less than £1,000. The average
subscription was 20 shares, the highest for any company
investigated in this work. £13,000 of the sum attributed to
women was subscribed by the female connections of London
merchants. It therefore seems reasonable to suppose that
London's share of the total capital approached 70%, and that
most of its contribution was made by 'capitalists'. After
1793, when the canal had been completed, meetings of the

---

[1] *General History of Inland Navigation*, p. 212.

[2] Christopher Chambers took 50 shares, Frances Chambers 50, Sophia
Chambers 30, Robert Rolleston 50, John Sargent 50. As the maximum individual
subscription allowed was 100 shares, Frances and Sophia Chambers may have
been nominees. In 1777 Sargent, Chambers, and others, were partners as African
merchants, P.R.O., Chancery Proceedings, C.12/1741/32. In 1763 Sargent was a
partner with George Aufrere, another subscriber to the Thames and Severn, in
trade with North America, L. B. Namier, *England in the Age of the American
Revolution* (1930), pp. 292–3.

[3] For example, John Lewis Boissier, 1742–1821 (£2,000), Captain of
Dragoons, son of Jean Daniel Boissier, a protestant refugee who was buried at
Putney in 1770 (*The Genealogist*, vi (1882), 173).

proprietors were held in London because it was difficult to get a quorum in the Cotswolds.[1]

On each share £100 was called and a further sum was raised, mostly from the proprietors, on mortgage of the tolls. By 1808 £104,425 was due on this account, in addition to £60,905 arrears of unpaid interest, some of which had been capitalized as half-shares, and other liabilities totalling £28,562. Part of these debts were paid off and the remainder converted under an Act of the following year into 1,150 'Red' or preference shares.[2]

XLIV. *The Andover Canal* 1789–1796: £48,000

No records of this canal survive, but the 62 (out of 73) proprietors named in the Act of incorporation whom it has been possible to identify include 1 peer, 12 landed gentlemen, 5 'capitalists', 4 manufacturers, 26 tradesmen, 9 professional men, 4 clergymen, and 1 woman, 36 of these being residents of the town of Andover. The authorized share capital was £35,000 and in addition £13,000 was raised on mortgage of the tolls.[3]

XLV. *The Kennet and Avon Canal* 1794–1810: £950,000

Shares[4]	I	II	III	IV	V	VI	VII	VIII	IX	Unknown
3,500 (£137)	92	190	–	1255	–	1016	215	68	53	611
	(3%)	(7%)		(43%)		(35%)	(7%)	(2%)	(2%)	

This undertaking had first been promoted locally in the counties of Wiltshire and Berkshire in the late 1780s and early 1790s, abandoned, and then revived at the time of the canal mania in December 1792 by a small group of merchants and other capitalists of the city of Bristol, the so-called White Lion Junto, which apparently attempted to monopolize the shares.[5] This group was obliged by the pressure of public opinion to open the subscription more widely. The distribution of shares eventually agreed upon was 1,167 to the

[1] H. G. W. Household, 'Thames and Severn: Birth and Death of a Canal' (Bristol University M.A. Dissertation 1958), p. 354.

[2] 49 George III *cap.* 112; Household, op cit., pp. 350–68.

[3] 29 George III *cap.* 72; J. E. H. Spaul (ed.), Andover Documents no. I, *The Andover Canal* (Andover Local Archives Committee, 1968); Hadfield, *Southern England*, p. 84.

[4] House of Lords R.O., Deposited Plans, Kennet and Avon Canal Subscription Contract 1794.

[5] Hadfield, *Southern England*, pp. 71–8.

White Lion subscribers, 1,167 to persons later admitted to the scheme (for the most part, it appears, lesser tradesmen of Bristol), and 1,166 for the subscribers to the original promotion of 1790, and owners of land on the line of the canal.[1] In fact the latter group does not appear to have taken up its full entitlement. Of the subscriptions to shares which have been identified, about 80% were made at Bristol. Most of the remainder originated in Wiltshire and Berkshire as the contributions of landowners and the inhabitants of towns along the proposed line: Marlborough, Devizes, Chippenham, etc. The average subscription was about 4 shares.

At the time the Act of incorporation was sought, a number of the shares reserved for landowners had not been taken.[2] In order to complete the subscription these were vested in some of the committee members (mostly Bristol merchants) as trustees for their eventual disposition. However, 'in consequence of the depreciation of the value of shares in the said undertaking' $177\frac{1}{2}$ of these trust shares remained unclaimed and were liquidated in 1797.[3] On this account, and through defalcations and forfeitures on the part of other proprietors (mostly persons engaged in trade), the number of original shares was reduced to 3,000, on each of which £137. 4s. 7d. was called.[4]

Under the Act of 1801, 3,000 new shares were created, which were disposed of among the proprietors in proportion to their holdings of original shares.[5] Under that of 1805 a further £200,000 was raised by the issue of additional shares at £30, and interest-bearing optional notes at £50, which were also reserved in the first instance for the proprietors. Because of the difficulty experienced in completing the

[1] KAC 1/1, Minutes of the Promoters 1788–94, 29 Jan. 1793. The White Lion subscribers numbered 59, the later admissions—who were rationed to one, two, or three shares each—several hundreds. Cf *Felix Farley's Bristol Journal*, 5 Jan., 3 Feb. 1793.

[2] KAC 1/9, Minutes of the Committee of Management 1794–1805, 13 June 1797. 327 shares were unclaimed 17 Feb. 1794 (KAC 1/1).

[3] KAC 1/9, 13 June 1797.

[4] Forfeitures are recorded in KAC 1/9.

[5] 41 George III *cap.* 23. Authority was given for the creation of a further 1,000 shares 'to be disposed of at the Discretion of the General Committee in the most advantageous manner' but these were never issued (KAC 1/9, 16 Dec. 1800, 20 Mar. 1802).

subscription for these issues, their offer prices were twice temporarily reduced to, respectively, £20 and £33. 6s. 8d., and they were made available for a brief period to the general public.[1] A further 4,000 shares of £20 were created under the Act of 1809, to be subscribed freely by all, whether proprietors or not, on the payment of a premium of £4 per share.[2]

Documents recording changes in the ownership of the original shares, and thus the sources of subscriptions to most of the later issues, are lacking. However, there are grounds for supposing that the interest of Londoners in the canal (insignificant in 1794) increased, mainly at the expense of the Bristol proprietors. The Act of 1801 contains the unusually exact stipulation that the new shares were to be disposed of through sale by auction, not less than 20 or more than 50 in a day 'at the Exchange Coffee House, or some other suitable place in Bristol, or at Garraway's Coffee House or some other suitable place in London, to be selected by the Committee of Management' (though in fact it appears that no shares were disposed of in this way). In 1802 a Londoner was elected to the committee of management of the Eastern District.[3] In 1807 an (unsuccessful) attempt was made to dispose by auction of 42 forfeited shares at Garraway's, but apparently nowhere else.[4]

The highly speculative schemes of 1809–11, in which the Kennet and Avon company was closely interested, for the extension of the navigation from Newbury to London, and from Bath to Bristol, had their origins to a considerable extent in the short-lived mania for joint-stock promotions which affected London during those years.[5] Of 1,166 original shares on which the dividend of 1815 was not claimed, 288 were held in Bristol, 327 in Wiltshire, and 343 in London and the Home Counties (the Londoners including a few stockbrokers).[6] It thus seems probable that the completion

[1] 45 George III *cap*. 70; KAC 1/9, 16 August 1805; KAC 1/10, Minutes of the General Committee of Management 1805–18, 29 Oct., 17 Dec., 18 Dec. 1805, 6 Apr. 1806, 18 Aug., 18 Sept. 1807, 27 Jan. 1808.

[2] 49 George III *cap*. 64; KAC 1/10, 3 July, 26 Sept. 1809.

[3] KAC 1/9, 23 Mar. 1802.

[4] KAC 1/10, 3 Mar. 1807.

[5] See below pp. 82–3.

[6] KAC 2/1, Register of Unclaimed Dividends 1814–51.

of the Kennet and Avon Canal, at its inception an exclusively provincial promotion, was materially assisted by capital from the metropolis.

XLVI. *The Wilts and Berks Canal* 1795–1810: £250,000

Shares[1]	I	II	III	IV	V	VI	VII	VIII	IX
782 (£100)	59	257	–	108	–	248	39	59	12
	(8%)	(33%)		(14%)		(32%)	(5%)	(8%)	(2%)

The subscription was for the most part made up in the towns along the line of the canal, such as Abingdon, Wantage, and Chippenham, and in the adjacent countryside. Only 172 (22%) of the shares were taken by investors from outside the counties of Wiltshire and Berkshire. These included a contingent of 8 from the Midlands (Daventry, Rugby, Stony Stratford, Towcester, Birmingham) with 44 shares, and 3 from Bristol with 40, two of whom, however, with 30 shares, forfeited for non-payment of calls. The average subscription was 5 shares.

In its financial history this company was singularly unfortunate. The Act of incorporation,[2] obtained in 1795, long after the enthusiasm of the canal mania had evaporated, authorized a capital of £111,900, with the unusually lavish supplementary provision of a further £150,000 if necessary. The estimate of expense[3] was £111,953, though this included £9,000 for part of the line to be built at the cost of the Kennet and Avon Canal. According to the subscription contract[4] only £74,950 had been promised towards this expense. Subscribers for 228 shares had withdrawn;[5] these included 4 or 5 Bristolians for about 40 shares, but the remainder were apparently local men resembling in social character those who remained loyal. After the contract had been made up, a number of subscriptions were added, bringing the total number of shares taken to the 782 analysed

[1] Subscription Ledger 1793–1803, Swindon Public Library, Wilts and Berks Canal Collection, no. 13. Unless otherwise stated, all documents cited in this section are from this collection.

[2] 35 George III *cap.* 52.

[3] House of Lords R.O., Deposited Plans, Wilts and Berks Canal 1795.

[4] Loc. cit.

[5] See Subscription Ledger, f. 1, 'List of those who paid subscriptions and dropped the undertaking'.

here.[1] However, through defalcations on the part of the proprietors, which in most cases resulted in forfeiture, only 642 of these were fully paid up.[2] Such forfeitures were in most cases made by persons engaged in trade, whose effective contribution is thus slightly exaggerated by the figures given above.

By the end of 1810, the year in which the canal was opened, nearly £250,000 had been spent on the works.[3] The additional funds required had been raised by the issue of shares at successively lower prices: 463 at £60 (which, together with 20 at £65 taken by the Marquis of Lansdowne, raised £29,080), 755 at £40 (£30,200), 1,838 at £25 (£45,950), and, finally, 3,494 at £12. 10s. (£43,455).[4] In 1802-3 £20,120 had also been raised on notes bearing interest at 5% repayable in June 1811 and carrying until March 1807 the option of conversion into one share for each £100 lent. But, as the current price of the company's shares was much lower than this, the option was not exercised and the notes were paid off after 1811, though in 1817 £3,500 still remained due.[5] Of these notes £13,000 (65%) were taken up outside the counties of Wiltshire and Berkshire: £8,100 in London by 15 merchants and tradesmen, and £4,000 in Bristol by one clergyman. As Mr. Hadfield had remarked,[6] the impression is given that 'local financing is only just holding its own against the influence of London'.

Although there is evidence from other sources that London capital was taking a growing part in the canals of southern England during the first decade of the nineteenth century,[7] the apparent extent of its intervention here is surprising and, in the absence of minute books or other documentation, inexplicable. As already indicated, the original body of proprietors was overwhelmingly local in its composition; it included, apart from the Earl of Radnor, who

[1] On the evidence of a comparison of the subscription contract with the Subscription Ledger.

[2] No. 2, Account of Receipts and Disbursements 1795-1805. In 1801 it was alleged that only £61,512 had been raised, and only 741 shares originally subscribed: *H.C.J.* lvi., 40.

[3] No. 32 Ledger 1810-17, f. 3.

[4] Ibid., f. 5.

[5] No. 12, Register of Optional Notes 1802-3

[6] Hadfield, *Southern England*, p. 158.

[7] See pp. 81-5.

had an estate at Highworth, only three persons resident in London, all of whom were evidently family connections of local subscribers. As usual in such cases,[1] the existing proprietors appear to have reserved for themselves—and in general to have exercised—a right of pre-emption on the later issues, and, although the nature of the evidence available makes it impracticable to demonstrate this statistically, it is clear that these issues did not substantially alter the original character of the company.[2] For example, about half of the shares at £25 and £12. 10s., disposed of between 1807 and 1810, were taken up among the long-suffering subscribers of 1795; most of the other recipients may be identified as local men and women, in many cases probably holders by assignment of the original shares. Only 6 of the 15 metropolitan subscribers of 1802–3 participated in these issues. The only explanation which can be suggested for the latter's enthusiasm for the optional notes is that the privileges attached to them made them more widely negotiable than ordinary shares, and, possibly, that they had been popularized among the moneyed men of London by the Grand Junction Canal which was employing them very extensively during this period.[3]

Proprietors of the Wilts and Berks provided £15,000 towards the cost of the North Wilts Canal (1813–1819: £33,000) which connected its line to the Thames by a branch from Swindon. Lesser contributions were received from proprietors of the Thames and Severn Canal (£5,000), and the Bollo Pill Railway (£500), all of these concerns being interested in the development of a through traffic in coal from the Forest of Dean to southern England, and the avoidance of the unsatisfactory navigation of the Thames above Oxford.[4] Under an Act of 1821 the North Wilts and

---

[1] See below, pp. 120–1.

[2] The names of the subscribers to these issues, with the amounts subscribed, but without addresses or styles, are given in No. 2, Account of Receipts and Disbursements.

[3] See pp. 45, 123–5.

[4] House of Lords R.O., Deposited Plans, North Wilts Canal Subscription Contract 1813; Household, 'Thames and Severn' (thesis), p. 395; Hadfield, *Southern England*, pp. 159–60. The Bollo Pill Railway was a Forest of Dean tramway. For the 'Wilts and Berks Interest' and the development of collieries and tramways in the Forest for the purpose of supplying their line with coal, see Hadfield, *South Wales*, p. 212.

the Wilts and Berks were amalgamated, the latter's purchase of the former being financed by the issue of 10,000 additional shares at £5 each, bringing the total number outstanding to 20,000.[1]

XLVII. *The Glamorganshire Canal* 1790-1794: £103,600

Shares[2]	I	II	III	IV	V	VI	VII	VIII	IX
600 (£172)	–	85	4	175	256	29	17	4	30
		(14%)		(29%)	(44%)	(5%)	(3%)		(5%)

Of the shares, 267 (44%) were subscribed locally, 36 (6%) at Brecon, and 297 (50%) in England (196 in London). Most of this large proportion of 'outside' capital was, however, contributed by persons connected with the local iron industry, most notably Richard Crawshay and his family (131 shares). The average subscription was 8 shares.

XLVIII. *The Neath Canal* 1791-1799: £40,000

Shares[3]	I	II	III	IV	V	VI	VII	VIII	IX
248 (£107)	–	55	–	71	28	33	37	17	7
		(22%)		(29%)	(11%)	(13%)	(15%)	(7%)	(3%)

Of the shares, 127 (51%) were subscribed locally, 30 at Brecon, and 91 in England, 71 of these being taken by a group of investors of Birmingham and its neighbourhood, brought in through manufacturing connections. The average subscription was 6 shares. The balance of the expenditure in excess of the sum raised by the calls on the shares was financed through toll income, and payments by Lord Vernon, who was granted in return £600 and a rent charge of £105 p.a.[4]

XLIX. *The Swansea Canal* 1794-1798: £53,000

Shares[5]	I	II	III	IV	V	VI	VII	VIII	IX
530 (£100)[6]	–	148	–	112	66	138	34	23	9
		(28%)		(21%)	(12%)	(26%)	(6%)	(4%)	(2%)

[1] 2 George IV *cap.* 97.

[2] National Library of Wales, Dept. of MSS., Deposit 91B, Glamorganshire Canal Minute Book 1790, ff. 1–3, list of subscribers.

[3] Glamorganshire R.O., D/D NCa 84, Neath Canal Minute Book 1791–1856, f. 1, list of subscribers.

[4] Hadfield, *South Wales*, pp. 64–6.

[5] House of Lords R.O., Deposited Plans, Swansea Canal Subscription Contract 1794; Stock Account in SWC 4/1, Ledger 1794–1813.

[6] A nominal share capital of £53,300 eventually emerged, after some shares had been forfeited for non-payment of calls, and additional ones issued, but it appears that only £60 was paid on each of the original shares. See Hadfield, op. cit., p. 49, and H. Pollins, 'The Swansea Canal,' *Journal of Transport History*, i (1954), 144.

Of the shares 371 (70%) were subscribed at Swansea, Neath, and district, 32 elsewhere in Wales, and 127 in England, mostly at London and Birmingham. The average subscription was 6 shares.

L. *The Brecknock and Abergavenny Canal* 1793-1812: £200,000

Shares[1]	I	II	III	IV	V	VI	VII	VIII	IX
1,000 (£150)	19	414	14	150	26	103	144	106	24
	(2%)	(41%)	(1%)	(15%)	(3%)	(10%)	(14%)	(11%)	(2%)

Finance for this canal was overwhelmingly local, only 88 shares being subscribed for in England. Its most prominent supporters, apart from the local landowners, were the inhabitants of the town of Brecon where 233 shares were subscribed. Contributions were received from 5 out of 6 of the town's physicians, 8 out of 12 of its lawyers, 5 out of 9 of its 'gentry', and 4 out of 11 of its clergymen. The average subscription was 4 shares, on each of which £150 was paid. The sum of £50,000 was borrowed on mortgage for the completion of the line between 1809 and 1812, including £30,000 from the ironmaster Richard Crawshay (the contribution of ironmasters to the original subscription had been negligible), £8,100 from Lady Fern, £2,000 from the Duke of Beaufort, and lesser sums from others.[2] In addition, by October 1814 an overdraft of £11,600 had been run up with the treasurer, the Brecon banker Walter Wilkins.[3]

Between 1755 and 1815 about £17,000,000 were raised by undertakings for the construction of canals and the improvement of rivers. In the preceding pages analyses have been offered indicating the sources of about £5,000,000 of this total. It is probable that in some respects this sample is not entirely representative of the total population of navigation capital from which it is drawn. Firstly, there is the £300,000 attributed to the Duke of Bridgewater and thus to the Class I of peers. In the sample investigated this sum accounts for 60% of the £497,200 known to have been invested by peers. But Bridgewater's enterprise was unique of its kind; it has no equivalent among the navigations not

---

[1] BAC 1/1, Minutes of the General Assembly 1793-1823, list of subscribers 1793.

[2] BAC 1/4, Minutes of the Committee 1802-10, 17 Aug. 1809.

[3] Below, p. 187.

investigated in detail here and the aristocracy's share in the capital of those joint-stock canals for which data are available was uniformly low (4·2%). Its inclusion here must therefore tend to exaggerate the contribution made by peers. Secondly, in the sample, navigations of the 'first generation' and, among the 'second generation', those serving principally agricultural as distinct from commercial interests are disproportionately represented.[1] Thus while analyses have been completed for 55% of the 'first generation' of navigation capitals, the equivalent proportions for 'agricultural' and 'commercial' navigations of the 'second generation' are respectively 43% and 23%. The social composition of investment in the three types of navigation differed significantly and it seems desirable to take account of this fact. Therefore, in arriving at an estimate of the average share of the different classes in navigation investment over the period 1755–1815, the appropriate adjustments have been made to offset these biases. The result yielded is as follows:

Shares of the Classes (*per cent*)									Capital Raised (*£000s*)	Percentage Analysed
I	II	III	IV	V	VI	VII	VIII	IX		
5·4	17·3	1·6	21·4	14·7	17·6	10·0	5·5	6·5	17,201	28·9

It may be disaggregated according to the generation and type of navigation (see Table I).

TABLE I

A. *'First Generation' Navigations: England 1755–1780*

I	II	III	IV	V	VI	VII	VIII	IX	Capital Raised (*£000s*)	Percentage Analysed
20·2	20·8	0·7	13·7	7·6	13·4	8·0	7·8	7·8	2,149	54·8

B. *'Second Generation' Navigations: England and Wales 1780–1815*

1. *Total*

3·5	18·2	2·0	21·5	14·6	18·3	10·3	5·7	6·1	15,052	25·2

2. *Analysis by Type:* (a) *'Agricultural'*

5·8	30·4	3·8	12·8	4·9	19·4	11·1	7·7	4·2	2,003	42·8

(b) *'Commercial'*

2·8	14·7	1·5	24·0	17·4	18·0	10·1	4·8	6·6	13,049	22·7

[1] In Appendix II I list the navigations which I define as 'agricultural' and give the sources for other statements made here.

3. *Analysis by Region:* (a) *East Midlands*

6·2	24·1	5·6	13·3	6·3	18·1	12·2	8·0	6·2	4,945	18·1

(b) *West Midlands*

3·4	19·4	1·0	20·3	13·5	17·4	11·2	5·9	7·9	2,584	57·1

(c) *Lancashire*

0·2	5·4	1·6	18·3	43·9	15·6	10·1	2·0	3·0	2,597	18·2

(d) *Southern England*

3·7	11·4	—	41·5	0·3	28·7	6·9	3·1	4·5	4,176	13·7

(e) *South Wales*

1·3	26·1	0·7	19·1	23·5	10·1	8·5	5·5	5·0	749	49·8

These statistics may be compared with contemporary estimates of the distribution of the national income. The following analysis is based upon Joseph Massie's account for 1759–60:[1]

(figures in £ millions)

I	II	III	IV	V	VI	VII	VIII	Total
8·72		16·95	3·4	4·2	9·9	3·92	0·65	47·74
18·3%		35·5%	7·3%	8·8%	20·7%	8·2%	1·4%	

These figures exclude from consideration all incomes of less than £40 per annum, except those of the 120,000 'freeholders' averaged at £25 per annum. But £100 per annum might be postulated as a more realistic 'threshold' below which individuals would be unable to afford an investment in a canal. A recalculation of Massie's data to exclude lesser incomes yields the following results:

I	II	III	IV	V	VI	VII	VIII	Total
8·72		4·75	3·4	1·0	2·7	1·4	0·2	22·17
39·3%		21·4%	15·3%	4·5%	12·2%	6·3%	0·9%	

A similar analysis may be derived from Colquhoun's account for 1814:[2]

(figures in £ millions)

I	II	III	IV	V	VI	VII	VIII	Total
5·16	39·02	73·85	47·43	35·78	44·63	40·86	5·32	292·05
1·8%	13·4%	25·3%	16·2%	12·3%	15·3%	14·0%	1·8%	

All incomes of less than £100 per annum have been excluded from consideration. The £28 million attributed by Colquhoun to 'Gentlemen and Ladies Living on Incomes' has been divided equally between Classes II (country gentlemen) and IV ('capitalists'). His class of manufacturers includes

[1] Taken from P. Mathias, 'The Social Structure in the Eighteenth Century: A Calculation by Joseph Massie', *Econ. Hist. Rev.*, 2nd Ser., x (1957–8), 42–3. The same occupational classification is used as in the analysis of navigation capital.

[2] P. Colquhoun, *A Treatise on the Wealth, Power and Resources of the British Empire* (1814), pp. 124–5.

tanners, brewers, tallow-chandlers, etc., and therefore is not strictly comparable with mine.

The most obvious conclusion to be drawn from all this is that the investments of the principal occupational classes were roughly proportional to their shares of the nation's larger incomes. As an important exception to this rule the contribution of tenant farmers and small landowners (Class III) was disproportionately small. Presumably their agricultural activities usually employed whatever capital they could accumulate. Also clergymen (Class VIII) were, I do not know why, disproportionately active as investors.

The relative importance of the different classes varied according to time and place in a more or less predictable fashion. Thus the distribution of investment in the 'first generation' of canals approximates to the analysis of incomes derived from Massie's calculations; the distribution of investment in the 'second generation' is closer to that derived from Colquhoun's. The share of the principal landowners (Classes I and II) was greater in the 'first generation' than in the 'second generation'; the shares of most other classes, particularly of manufacturers (Class V), were correspondingly less. Such differences may be attributed to the contemporary progress of industrialization. Similarly, the contribution of landowners was greatest in the more rural areas, such as the East Midlands, or where, as in South Wales, they had important mineral interests; that of manufacturers was greatest in centres of industry, most notably in Lancashire.

The part taken by landowners in the canals of southern England appears rather less considerable than might have been expected. To some extent this may merely reflect biases in the unsatisfactorily small sample of capitals for which analyses have been completed, but it must indicate also the importance of commercial capital from London and Bristol in the history of the canals of this region.[1] The shares estimated for 'capitalists' (Class IV) and tradesmen (Class VI) here exceed those attained elsewhere.

---

[1] Some evidence for this has already been cited: above, pp. 64–6, 68–71. For further evidence see below, pp. 80–5: the Basingstoke Canal, and London's joint-stock boom of 1807–11 which, apart from several ephemeral promotions, yielded the Regent's and the Wey and Arun Canals.

As manufacturers played so important a part in the contemporary transformation of the economy their investment in canals may be particularly discussed. Efficient means of communication were important to the pioneers of the new forms of industry because characteristically they sought economies of scale and so required unimpeded access to wide markets. But manufacturing on a large scale could pose problems of finance as well as problems of transport: for example, some of the more adventurous manufacturers found it difficult to insert the unusual volume of their business into the 'credit circle', the network of mutual accommodation between traders, by which the circulating stocks of the traditional mercantile and handicraft economy had been financed. Possibly, as a result, the demands made by the need for improved communications were burdensome to these men; they might have been glad to stand back and let them be provided by other classes which were financially less constrained.[1]

But it appears that the share of manufacturers in the finance of canals rather exceeded their share of the nation's large incomes; the investments of some of the most ambitious industrialists, of Lancashire's cotton-spinners, for example, were very substantial indeed.[2] Furthermore, there is no evidence that as a class manufacturers found it particularly difficult to produce the sums for which they subscribed. The problems experienced in raising sufficient capital by proprietaries in which they were numerous did not surpass those faced by undertakings of a more 'agricultural' or 'commercial' complexion; the canals of Lancashire and South Wales were completed as quickly as, or rather, no more slowly than their counterparts elsewhere. The only example which has been noticed of a large-scale manufacturer who may have suffered from his canal building is Samuel Oldknow, but the causes of his business failure were as much entrepreneurial

[1] Such suggestions have been made by S. Pollard, 'Fixed Capital in the Industrial Revolution in Britain' *Journal of Economic History*, xxiv (1964), 299–314.
[2] Above, pp. 57–63. Although it could be argued that as so large a proportion of the benefits from canals was likely to accrue to them they might reasonably have contributed even more.

and technological as financial, and the extent of his involvement in the Peak Forest company had been unusual.[1]

However, although it may not have been true in general that manufacturers found it burdensome to finance the creation of infra-structure, it may have been true in particular cases. The Staffordshire pottery industry took only a very modest part in the Trent and Mersey Canal upon which its own fortunes were in large measure based; Josiah Wedgwood, among others, agitated for its promotion and built his factory on its banks but at first took none of its shares.[2] So it can be argued that for individual manufacturers subscription to canals was optional: if they had money to spare from their principal activities, as many evidently did, then they could invest it, but, if not, then they were under no obligation to starve their businesses to secure the provision of necessary means of communication. A broadly-based investing public existed which could carry the burden for them. Perhaps the careers of some eighteenth-century industrialists were facilitated by the freedom of manoeuvre thus granted to them.

---

[1] See above, pp. 59–60, and Unwin, *Samuel Oldknow*.

[2] Above, p. 29, and A. L. Thomas, 'Geographical Aspects of the Development of Transport and Communications affecting the Pottery Industry of North Staffordshire during the Eighteenth Century', *Collections for a History of Staffordshire* (1934), 1–157. Wedgwood was not a proprietor of the Trent and Mersey at the time of its incorporation, although by the early 1780s he had acquired 11 of its shares and £1,000 of its loan: TMC 2/2A, 2B, 2C, Lists of Shareholders and Mortgagees, 1781–4.

III

THE GEOGRAPHICAL LOCATION
OF INVESTORS

Canals were generally financed by persons resident in the localities which they served.[1] Most companies had a residuum of proprietors from further afield who may usually be accounted for as the personal or commercial connections of local men,[2] or as persons with interests in the neighbourhood, such as landed property, who happened to live elsewhere.[3] The important departures from this pattern were of two kinds: those resulting from the concerted intervention of London capital in the provinces, and those resulting from the special circumstances of the canal mania of 1792–3. These will be considered in turn.

London finance played a modest but significant part in four of the 'first generation' of canals: the Duke of Bridgewater's, with the advances to him from Childs and Co. and the Sun Fire Office, the Trent and Mersey, the Leeds and Liverpool, and the Chesterfield. The first case may be attributed to the privileged position in the market for capital enjoyed by the great landowner and the second, perhaps, to the exceptional dexterity and vigour of a publicity campaign in which Josiah Wedgwood was involved,[4] while the third, which engaged in addition investors from Norfolk, and the fourth, reflect the participation of members of the Society of Friends and the possibilities for the long-distance recruitment of capital offered by the exceptional cohesion of the sect.[5]

[1] See Chapter II, which is the source for unsupported statements made in this chapter about particular canals.

[2] For example, London silk-merchants in the Coventry Canal, and London cider-merchants in the Herefordshire and Gloucestershire.

[3] The interest of London- and Birmingham-based manufacturers in some of the canals of South Wales may be regarded as an example of this.

[4] Cf. Meteyard, *Life of Wedgwood*, i. 345 ff., for his work as a publicist for the Trent and Mersey.

[5] For an illustration of the aptitude of its members for joint-stock investment see Bodleian Library, MS. Eng. Misc. b. 41, Account Book 1736–74 of the Quaker Jacob Hagen, a Southwark timber-merchant. He had 2 shares in the Leeds

During the 1780s Londoners took a substantial interest in two canals of the Thames valley: the Thames and Severn, and the Basingstoke. The former has already been considered[1] and requires no further discussion here.

In 1788, when the Kennet and Avon Canal was in agitation, a pamphleteer sought support for what appears to have been commonly, and correctly, regarded as a scheme of doubtful profitability by instancing the Basingstoke Canal: although it had been estimated that its capital cost of £82,000 would be serviced by a revenue of only £7,800, a yield of 7·5% gross of repairs, etc. (this estimate itself proved most over-optimistic):

> yet the whole sum of £82,000 has been already subscribed, not by the neighbouring gentlemen only, but by persons wholly unconnected with that country; merchants and bankers in London, and other great towns; men too well acquainted with the subject, and with the value of money, to engage in a project which has not a reasonable prospect of advantage.[2]

Because of the peculiar history of the undertaking it is impossible to verify this statement properly. The original Act of incorporation of 1778 names only 33 subscribers, most of them identifiable in the usual way as local landowners, clergymen, and tradespeople.[3] However, plans to begin work were postponed in consequence of the American war, and nothing more was done until the months of late 1787 and early 1788 when the authorized capital of £86,000 was subscribed by 150 persons.[4] No complete list of these proprietors appears to have survived, but general assemblies were usually held in London, at the Crown and Anchor Tavern, Strand. Of 53 persons attending such a meeting in

and Liverpool and 2 in the Chesterfield Canal, and shares in the Pennsylvania Land Company, the London Lead Company, the Dovegang Committee (Lead Mining), and three copperas companies, all apparently Quaker-influenced or Quaker-controlled enterprises.

[1] See above, pp. 64–6.

[2] *Observations on a scheme for extending the Navigation of the Rivers of Kennett and Avon . . by a Canal from Newbury to Bath* (Marlborough, 1788), p. 13. In 1789 it was alleged, by a hostile source, that the Basingstoke Canal subscribers were 'daily selling out their shares at a considerable loss': *Hampshire Chronicle*, 18 May 1789, quoted J. E. H. Spaul (ed.), *The Andover Canal*, p. 5.

[3] 18 George III *cap.* 75.

[4] P. A. L. Vine, *London's Lost Route to Basingstoke* (Newton Abbot, 1968), p. 42.

August 1792 it is possible to identify at least half as residents of the metropolis.[1] On the other hand, a General Assembly held in November of the same year at Basingstoke was attended by only 16 proprietors, who found it necessary to make a special request that the payment of interest due to them should be made through a local bank, instead of at London as was usually the case.[2] It was perhaps the Thames and Severn and the Basingstoke Canals which Arthur Young had in mind when he wrote in 1794 of the modern tendency for canal companies to be controlled by 'any company of merchants who live at a distance and subscribe their money'[3] though this was not in fact as common as he seemed to think.

In spite of these early incursions, London, as already indicated, took no real interest in the promotions of the canal mania, even in those of southern England: the initial investments of its inhabitants in the Wilts and Berks, and, so far as it is possible to judge, the Grand Junction and the Kennet and Avon were negligible.[4] They took only 27 of the 400 shares in the ill-fated Salisbury and Southampton Canal subscribed for in October 1794.[5]

There are however signs that in the following years their involvement increased. In November 1796 reference is made to Mr. Christopher Rollestone's Inland Navigation Office at Tokenhouse Yard, London, where canal stock was traded.[6] The evidence for the encroachment of London capital during the early 1800s in the Grand Junction, Kennet and Avon, and Wilts and Berks companies has already been reviewed.[7]

---

[1] Birmingham Ref. Lib. 568603, f. 40. See also f. 43. These are part of the canal papers of the Revd. John Rose Holden of London who had 10 shares in the Basingstoke. During the mania he bought 1 share in the Warwick and Birmingham, and subscribed for 5 (3 as a landowner) in the Grand Junction. See also Nottinghamshire R.O., DDVC 67/12–16, five Basingstoke Canal shares of Peter Vere of Kensington.

[2] Birmingham Ref. Lib. 568603, f. 41.

[3] A Young, *General View of the Agriculture of Sussex* (1794), p. 425.

[4] See above, pp. 45, 67–9, 70–1.

[5] E. Welch, *The Bankrupt Canal*, Southampton, Southampton Corporation Civic Record Office, Southampton Papers, no. 5 (1966), pp. 5–7.

[6] LC 8/2, Lancaster Canal Letter Book 1792–7, ff. 587, 593. In the *Universal British Directory* (1790), Rollestone is styled insurance broker in the same place. For the 'Navigation Offices' of 1792–3, see pp. 106–8.

[7] Above, pp. 46, 68–9, 70–1.

In 1804 notice was given of the sale by auction at Garraway's Coffee House, London, of 13 shares in the Leeds and Liverpool, 5 in the Forth and Clyde, and unspecified numbers in the Grand Junction, Peak Forest, Ashton, Oldham, Shropshire, Wilts and Berks, Oakham, and Surrey Iron Railroad.[1] The 1803 edition of Phillip's *General History of Inland Navigation* includes reports of the prices of shares in companies throughout the country, suggesting the existence of a fairly wide market.

Londoners took most interest in canals, or at least in their shares, during the joint-stock boom of 1807–11 which was in any case an essentially metropolitan phenomenon.[2] Canal shares were first put on the official lists of the Stock Exchange in 1811.[3] In the same year the attorney Henry Fry of Bedford Place included among the causes of his bankruptcy £4,645 'lost on Sundry Shares with the Portsmouth and Gosport Berks Wilts East Kent Stamford Waterworks' (i.e. canals).[4] In proceedings relating to the liquidation of the assets of a Worthing (Sussex) bank which had failed, including 10 shares in the Ellesmere Canal (they had been purchased in 1793 at a premium of 10 guineas each) mention is made of Mr Scott of Bridge Street, London, 'a person much employed in the sale of Canal Property', and also of Mr. Woolfe of Change Alley, 'a broker in such shares'. Mr. Scott arranged for their sale by auction.[5]

The many speculative canal schemes promoted in southern England during these years drew heavily upon the enthusiasm

[1] *Leeds Mercury*, 23 Apr. 1804.

[2] B. C. Hunt, *The Development of the Business Corporation in England 1800–1867* (Cambridge, Mass., 1936), pp. 14 ff.

[3] E. V. Morgan and W. A. Thomas, *The Stock Exchange: its history and function* (1962), p. 100.

[4] P.R.O., Proceedings under Commissions of Brankruptcy, B. 3/1677. Reference is made to the Portsmouth and Arundel, not authorized until 1817 (57 George III *cap.* 63), the Wilts and Berks, a canal of the 1790s which was issuing additional shares at this time (above pp. 70–1), the Weald of Kent (52 George III *cap.* 70), authorized but never built. For the Stamford canal schemes unsuccessfully agitated at this time, see Samuel Edwards, *Extracts from Harrod's History of Stamford relating to the Navigation of the River Welland . . .* (1810), p. 13.

[5] P.R.O., Exchequer K.R., Bills and Answers, E. 112/2015/204. From November 1809 the current prices of shares in canal, dock, and waterwork companies 'at the office of Mr. Scott, no. 28, New Bridge Street' were regularly given in the *Gentleman's Magazine*. See also the price list of shares issued in 1830 by Wolfe, Brothers, Stock and Share Brokers, 23 Change Alley, printed in Hadfield, *British Canals* (1959), p. 178.

of London, even when they were local in origin. One of the best-documented of these is the proposed eastern extension of the Kennet and Avon Canal from Newbury to London. Although it had the approbation of the original Kennet and Avon company, control was evidently in the hands of the Committee of the London District whose first recorded act was to order the closure of the subscription book there,[1]

having observed that the Subscription entered at Messrs. Whitehead and Co. (London bankers) were likely to have increased to an amount beyond any possible demands for the proposed Eastern Extension of the Kennet and Avon Canal and that if the Subscription Book had remained open it might have occasioned much inconvenience and load the Market with an immense amount of Scrip highly injurious to this undertaking and to a large Body of the Subscribers.

The books at other places, however, were to remain open 'to persons not residing within 20 miles of London'. The project was short-lived. Within a year it was reported that 'the peculiar Circumstances of the Times have considerably impeded the Subscriptions authorized to be entered into'[2] and in 1812 it was wound up without an Act having been obtained, as was the contemporaneous English and Bristol Channels Ship Canal promotion which had opened subscription books at London and Chard.[3] The Bath and Bristol Canal and Bristol Waterworks, on whose committee Londoners had 5 out of 15 seats, at least obtained an Act but it was decided in July 1811 'in consequence of the general distress of trade' to postpone putting it into effect, and nothing was ever done.[4] Similarly, most of the £571,800 subscribed for the Bristol and Taunton Canal evidently came from London, many of the residents of Bristol perhaps having learnt a lesson from their experience with the Kennet and Avon, but the line was never built.[5] One of the very few of the canals promoted at this time to be successfully completed was the Grand Union which connected the lines of

[1] KAC 1/7, Minutes of the Committee for the Eastern Extension 1809–16, 19 Dec. 1809.

[2] Ibid., 1 Dec. 1810.

[3] P.R.O., E. 112/1951/1093.

[4] BBC 1/1, Committee Minutes 1811–19, 17 July 1811; 51 George III *cap.* 167.

[5] House of Lords R.O., Deposited Plans, Bristol and Taunton Canal Subscription Contract 1811. 46 of its London subscribers were also subscribers to the Grand Union Canal.

the Grand Junction and the Leicestershire and Northampton-shire Union. The distribution of subscriptions to the 2,250 shares in 1809 was as follows: London and Middlesex 1,662 (74%), the Midlands 426 (16%), elsewhere 162 (7%). The subscribers were overwhelmingly persons engaged in manu-factures, trade, and the professions: they included no owners of land on the line of the canal. The average subscription was 9 shares.[1]

Although there is no doubt as to the degree of London's enthusiasm for canal undertakings during this brief period, its importance in the general history of their finance should not be exaggerated. The most economically advantageous way in which its capital could have been employed would have been to assist the completion of those canals of the 1790s which had run into financial difficulties. Tooke, it is true, mentions a 'Company for purchasing Canal Shares and lending money for completing Canals' among the promotions of 1807, but, as might be expected, this bubble scheme left no recorded mark.[2] It appears that to some extent such assistance was forthcoming from London in more orthodox ways, but probably only to those canals which were near at hand: the Wilts and Berks, Grand Junction, and Kennet and Avon.[3] The completion of the indigent Stratford-on-Avon Canal, on which work had been suspended since 1802, was undertaken after 1809, perhaps partly in consequence of the speculative excitement of the times. The leader of its revival was the versatile William James at whose London land agency office subscriptions for the new issue of £30 shares were receivable; they were also to be taken locally at Birmingham, Daventry, and Stratford.[4] No information has been found as to the disposition of these shares so it is impossible to tell how

---

[1] House of Lords R.O., Deposited Plans, Grand Union Canal Subscription Contract 1810; GJC 2/2, Share Register 1809–37.

[2] Quoted Hunt, *Business Corporation*, p. 14. See *H.C.J.* lix. 111, for the unsuccessful petition of 24 Feb. 1804 for a 'Canal Society Incorporation' to undertake the same task. It was referred to M.P.s for Lancashire constituencies, perhaps an indication of its source.

[3] Above, pp. 46, 68–9, 70–1.

[4] Hadfield and Norris, *Stratford*, pp. 85 ff.; SCN 1/3, Committee Minutes 1798–1829, 13 June 1814. James also became extensively involved in the promotion of railways: E.M.S.P., *The Two James's and the Two Stephensons* (1861; new edn., Dawlish, 1961).

many were taken up in the metropolis. Most of the evidence on this point relating to other canals of the Midlands and North is of a slightly earlier date. It is not encouraging. In 1802 the Ashton under Lyne Canal sought to raise £15,000 on mortgage in London, without success.[1] Where it is possible to analyse exactly the distribution of a new issue of shares the importance of London capital is found to be residual: 7% in the case of the Huddersfield (1804), 15% in that of the Worcester and Birmingham (1808).[2] It would therefore be unreasonable to attach much importance to the fact that in the records of other companies, for example, the Lancaster,[3] and the Peak Forest,[4] mention is made incidentally of proprietors resident there.

Thus the speculation of 1807-11 is to be seen as ephemeral, and not as the manifestation of a long-term tendency for the interest of London investors to increase, or for the capital market on which the canal companies drew to become substantially wider or more elaborately organized. The handful of promotions undertaken successfully in the post-war years were thoroughly 'traditional' in form. All but 13 of the 320 shares of the Pocklington Canal (1815-18: £32,000) were subscribed in the adjacent parts of Yorkshire, the character of the subscribers being as follows:

Shares[5]	I	II	III	IV	V	VI	VII	VIII	IX
320 (£100)	40	114	15	11	–	49	41	18	32
	(13%)	(35%)	(5%)	(4%)		(15%)	(13%)	(6%)	(10%)

Or, to take the case of a long-distance 'commercial' canal, in 1827, 70% of the 4,000 shares in the Birmingham and Liverpool Junction (1826-35: £800,000) were held in its immediate vicinity, the counties of Warwickshire, Staffordshire, Shropshire, and Cheshire, but only 564 (14%) in London.[6] It is true that in 1825 the subscription to the Grand Western Ship Canal was made up in London as well as locally, and, to a lesser extent, at Liverpool and Manchester, and that its scrip was traded on the Stock Exchange, but

---

[1] AC 1/1, Committee Minutes 1798–1815, 10 Mar. 1802, 28 May 1802.
[2] Above, pp. 48, 61.   [3] Above, p. 57.
[4] PFC 1/2, Committee Minutes 1800–7, 19 June 1804.
[5] B.T.H.R. (York), POC 2/1, Shareholders' Register.
[6] P.R.O., Chancery Masters' Exhibits, C. 108/204, Printed List of Shareholders in the Birmingham and Liverpool Junction Canal, 7 July 1827.

parliamentary sanction was refused, apparently because the scheme savoured too much of speculation.[1] The London and Birmingham Canal promotion of 1829–30 was ephemeral and rejected out of hand, it having been found that the main part had been taken by impecunious *habitués* of Exchange Alley: in the caustic words of the parliamentary committee of inquiry, 'needy and indigent persons, of inferior station in life, deeply engaged in bubble companies and gambling transactions . . .'[2]

The effect of the canal mania in widening the horizons of investors will now be considered. Although in the early 1790s, and especially in that *annus mirabilis* 1792, navigation schemes were promoted throughout the country, the 'canal mania', in the sense of an indiscriminate avidity for canal shares, was essentially a phenomenon of the towns of the Midlands, most notably of Leicester, Coventry, Market Harborough, and Birmingham.[3] Bristol had its own brief, localized, but characteristically extravagant, period of excitement which is best considered separately.[4] In the north substantial sums were subscribed, particularly at Manchester and its environs, to the numerous local promotions,[5] but in its character the investment of this area will not bear comparison with that of the East Midlands. For a few months in late 1792 and early 1793 the newspapers of towns such as Leicester, Oxford, and Birmingham, are filled with the advertisements of share-brokers, with the reports of crowded meetings at which enormous sums had been subscribed, and of the spectacular prices commanded by stock and scrip. Many of their readers were thus inspired aggressively to seek out investment opportunities in the most unexpected places. Behaviour of this kind is not to be found at Liverpool, Manchester, or Leeds.[6] It is probable that the inhabitants of

---

1 *Parl. Papers 1825,* v (403), 551 ff., especially 558.
2 *Parl. Papers 1830,* x (251), 719 ff.
3 Below, p. 180.
4 Below, pp. 92–4.
5 Above, pp. 55–63.
6 These statements are based upon an examination, for the relevant months, of *Aris's Birmingham Gazette, Jackson's Oxford Journal,* the *Northampton Mercury,* the *Leicester Journal, Williamson's Liverpool Advertiser,* the *Manchester Mercury,* the *Leeds Mercury,* and *Felix Farley's Bristol Journal.*

the Midlands, especially of the East Midlands, were particularly attracted to the possible advantages of inland navigation by their geographical situation, and by their familiarity with a number of local companies of the 'first generation' which had begun by this time to earn fabulous profits for their proprietors.[1]

One means by which their appetites might be fed was through the purchase of stock in established companies. Thus in the vigorous dealings in Oxford Canal shares that during 1791 and 1792 followed the completion of its line and their recovery to par, 60% were taken by persons resident outside the Oxford–Woodstock–Banbury district where the financial weight of the company lay: 118 at Coventry, 64 elsewhere in the Midlands, 45 at Liverpool, and 13 at London.[2] But investment of this kind was limited by the narrowness of the secondary market in canal stock. On the other hand, when seeking shares in the new undertakings of the 1790s, men from the principal centres of enthusiasm often collided with the exclusiveness of local promoters. Those of the Ashby-de-la-Zouch Canal, for example, invited contributions from 'all persons wishing to become subscribers and residing within five miles of some part of the intended canal'. Subscription deeds were left with solicitors at Ashby, Market Bosworth, and Hinckley only. 'The claims of land occupiers on the line of the Canal will be particularly attended to', and 'speculation shall be discouraged as much as possible and to that end strict attention shall be paid to the responsibility of the proposed subscribers.'[3]

Such restrictions were frequent, and effective. Residents of Leicester succeeded in subscribing for only 60 of the 1,500 shares in the Ashby Canal, those of Coventry only 34. In the Melton Navigation Leicester men took only 18 out of 250 shares, and in the Oakham Canal 75 out of 545.[4] The

[1] In particular the Birmingham, Erewash, and Loughborough Navigations. See p. 175.

[2] Bodleian Library, Dep. c. 102, Transfer Register. For further details of the turnover of shares in this company, see pp. 100–2.

[3] ASCH 1/1, Minutes of the Subscribers 1792–4, 23 Nov. 1792.

[4] All statements made in the following paragraphs about the geographical distribution of shares are based on the sources indicated in the accounts of individual canals given above, pp. 26–73.

inhabitants of these and other towns were therefore obliged to concentrate upon the more ambitious and speculative long-distance canals such as the Grand Junction and the Leicestershire and Northamptonshire Union to which it appears their contribution was substantial. In themselves, however, these promotions were unsatisfying: the subscription meeting for the first was held on 20 July 1792,[1] and for the second on 6 August. Thereafter the men of the East Midlands directed their attention further afield, and reports begin to appear of the journeyings of nomadic bands of would-be subscribers.

On 9 August 'a number of people from Northampton, Harborough, and various parts of Leicestershire arrived at Derby with the supposed intention of buying shares in our intended Canal; but their chagrin and disappointment were inconceivable when they found the meeting no other than a private one of the committee.'[2] They were eventually to be disabused of any expectations they might have had in this quarter. In October it was announced as the desire of the promoters of the undertaking 'that the capital sum necessary for carrying it into effect, should be subscribed and raised among such Persons as were really interested in its Completion and Future Prosperity', who were defined as the owners of land on the proposed line, and the 'gentlemen, merchants and principal tradesmen' of Derby, Nottingham, Newark, and Burton, together with the proprietors of the Trent and Mersey, Erewash, and Trent Navigations.[3]

On 1 October 1792 *Aris's Birmingham Gazette* reported from Sheffield:

At a meeting of the Proprietors of the Dun Navigation several gentlemen from Leicester, Coventry, and a few from this Town [i.e. Birmingham], attended to subscribe for the intended canal to Barnsley [i.e. the Dearne and Dove]; but the Proprietors, wishing first to give a preference to gentlemen through whose land it might pass, as was originally proposed, they were not admitted, and returned home disappointed.

After the meeting held on 23 October of the subscribers to the neighbouring Barnsley Canal, in which a similar preference to landowners was granted, Walter Spencer Stanhope, a leading promoter, noted curtly in his diary: '[£] 18,000

---

[1] *Leicester Journal*, 27 July 1792; Hadfield, *East Midlands*, p. 98.
[2] Quoted ibid., p. 67, from *Derby Mercury*, 16 Aug. 1792.
[3] *Leicester Journal*, 4 Jan. 1793.

rejected from distant Adventurers'.[1] *The Leicester Journal* of 19 October had printed a letter from Welshpool dated the 14th instant reporting on the agitation for the Montgomeryshire Canal:

It is expected that the General Meeting, which is advertised to be held at Welchpool on Tuesday 23rd Inst. to take the Navigation Scheme into Consideration will be very numerously attended, and the Subscription immediately filled by the Navigation Speculators.

If any of the speculators of Leicester rose to this bait, then the subscription contract, preponderantly local in composition, shows that they had been soundly rebuffed. In 1811 the company's Committee of Management congratulated the proprietors in its Annual Report that they had (half) built the line 'without public assistance or the intervention of strangers'.[2] At the subscription meeting for the Chelmer and Blackwater Navigation held at Chelmsford on 12 January 1793 more than fifty people from Leicester attended, but preference was given to the gentlemen of Essex, the majority of whom each obtained three shares, leaving only one at most for each of the outsiders.[3] Proprietors from Leicester and Market Harborough number about 25 among the 141 named in the navigation's Act of incorporation, so many must have attended without obtaining any shares.[4]

Such exclusiveness might be interpreted as an expression of a collective desire to keep a good thing to oneself, as a manifestation of local pride, as a precaution against the concession of economic power to outside interests, or as an amalgam of all three considerations. The reader must judge the point for himself after examining the material presented in Chapter V relating to the motives of promoters and subscribers, and that presented in Chapter VI relating to the conduct of landowners.

Whatever may have been its causes, its consequence was that the Midlands' enthusiasts, outside their own neighbourhood, were able to secure admission in large numbers to only

[1] Quoted R. M. Simpson, 'Walter Spencer Stanhope: Landlord, Business Entrepreneur, and M.P.' (Nottingham University M.A. Dissertation, 1959), p. 84.

[2] MONC 1/12, Committee Minutes 1798–1817, 1 July 1811.

[3] P. J. Cane, 'A History of the Chelmer Navigation down to 1830' (t.s. dissertation, St. John's College, York, 1961. Copy in Essex R.O.), pp. 39–40.

[4] The men of Leicester also descended upon Wisbech where they numbered 12 among the 89 subscribers to the canal of that name: House of Lords R.O., Deposited Plans, Wisbech Canal Subscription Contract, 1794. For further adventures see *Victoria County History: Leicestershire*, iii. 99–100.

two English companies, the Ellesmere and the Rochdale, both of which were exceptionally ambitious in relation to the resources of the districts which their lines were intended to serve. The evidence for the participation of capital from the Midlands in these companies has already been reviewed.[1]

A report of the meeting held in the latter part of August 1792 by the promoters of the Rochdale Canal stated that 'numbers of gentlemen who came from a distance were disappointed in being admitted to shares with the old subscribers.' Afterwards some of these held a meeting at which £60,000 was subscribed to an intended rival canal from Rochdale, Bury, and Littleborough, to Sladen, and the Leeds and Liverpool Canal. However, this scheme was refused parliamentary sanction.[2] Bury and Sladen or 'New Rochdale' scrip figures with 'Old Rochdale' in the share advertisements of contemporary Midland newspapers.[3]

The most remarkable manifestation of the enthusiasm of this region was without question the Ellesmere Canal. The company's chairman, writing in the dark days of 1805, recalled the subscription meeting of 1792:

The paroxysm of commercial ardour of the memorable tenth of September, can never be forgotten by the writer, who had the honour to be left to defend the hill near the town [Ellesmere] . . . from the excessive intrusion of too ardent speculation:- the books were opened about noon, and ere sun set a million of money was confided to the care of the Committee.[4]

Here too the 'distant adventurers' evidently became embroiled in local canal politics: the Eastern and Wirral line was promoted as a rival to that of the Ellesmere and its subscribers met at Birmingham, though in this case the dispute was resolved by a compromise.[5]

Meanwhile, on the west coast of Scotland, the promoters of the Crinan Canal across the Mull of Kintyre, a scheme which had been intermittently agitated since James Watt's favourable report of 1771, were sufficiently alert to take advantage of the excitement which was convulsing parts of

---

[1] Above, pp. 51–3, 63.

[2] *Aris's Birmingham Gazette*, 27 Aug. 1792. For the local politics of this scheme, see Tomlinson, 'Manchester, Bolton and Bury Canal', p. 240.

[3] See, for example, *Leicester Journal*, 12 Oct. 1792, 19 Oct. 1792.

[4] Quoted Hadfield, *West Midlands*, p. 168.

[5] Hadfield, loc. cit.; *Leicester Journal*, 22 Mar. 1793.

England. On 2 November 1792 an advertisement (the only one of its kind which has been noticed) solicited subscriptions to the undertaking in the *Leicester Journal*; it was addressed simply, 'TO NAVIGATION SPECULATORS'. The appeal was crude, perhaps, but unquestionably effective. By 17 January 1793, £69,200 had been subscribed, and by 31 January, £91,500. Rennie, the engineer, was consequently ordered to redesign the canal at a depth of 15 ft, increasing its estimated cost from about £63,000 to £107,512. The additional capital required had been subscribed by 21 February.[1] In December 1797 the geographical distribution of the 2,156 £50 shares in the company was as follows: Scotland 440 (20%), Leicester 450 (21%), Market Harborough 318 (15%), Coventry 131 (6%), elsewhere in the Midlands 270 (12%), London 314 (15%), elsewhere in England 170 (8%), not stated 63 (3%). It appears, however, that many of the English investors experienced difficulties in fulfilling their commitments. At this time unpaid calls totalling £34,473 were outstanding, 66% of this deficiency being accounted for by proprietors resident in the Midlands.[2] The Market Harborough draper Joseph Inkersole was one of those who asked for a delay in the payment of calls, an understandable request when the extent of his investments are considered.[3] In May 1798 Rennie reported that 'owing to bankruptcies' the capital would fall short by about £14,000 of the amount subscribed. In 1799 when the company sought a new Act as an answer to its difficulties it declared that the line 'cannot be completed by reason several of the Subscribers in England and Scotland, many of whom are Merchants and Manufacturers, have not been able to answer the calls made on their respective subscriptions.'[4] It eventually became necessary to draw on the government for financial assistance.[5]

[1] Scottish R.O., General Register House, Edinburgh: BR/CRC/1/1, Minutes of the General Meetings and Board of Directors 1793–1819, 17 Jan., 31 Jan., 14 Feb., 21 Feb. 1793.

[2] Loc. cit., BR/CRC/2/1, list of proprietors 30 Dec. 1797.

[3] 110 shares in the Crinan, 32 in the Rochdale, 25 in the Grand Junction, and subscriptions to the Ellesmere, Leicestershire and Northamptonshire Union, and Chelmer and Blackwater.

[4] *H.C.J.* xlii. 160.

[5] See in general, H. Hamilton, *An Economic History of Scotland in the Eighteenth Century* (Oxford, 1963), pp. 242–3; J. Lindsay, *The Canals of Scotland* (Newton Abbot, 1967), pp. 117–19.

The over-zealous subscriptions of 1792 must have placed a heavy burden on the trading communities of those towns where the enthusiasm had run highest. According to Throsby, writing shortly after the commercial crisis of 1793,[1]

It has been advanced, that in no town of its size (some will except none) has there been a sum, taken collectively, equal to that subscribed in Leicester to navigation-projects. Although many have gained considerably by adventures, yet we are now told that others, holders of shares, are likely to sustain considerable losses, whether from the war, or any other cause, I know not. A general opinion prevails, July 1793, that some of the schemes must fail, as the extension shares to Market Harbro [i.e. the Leicestershire and Northamptonshire Union] are now transferred for the small consideration of a bottle of wine; and others which have been some time agitated by the general shock, and still survive, are far from a state of convalescence.

However, in spite of their sufferings—many of their investments were singularly unprofitable—the subscribers of Leicester appear to have persevered. They certainly did so in the case of the Ellesmere, the only undertaking for which exact information is available as to the geographical distribution of the share capital in the early nineteenth century.[2] In 1829, when the Leicester and Swannington Railway was being promoted, difficulty was experienced in completing the subscription, 'the Leicester townspeople who had money being for the most part interested in canals'. It was therefore necessary to turn to Liverpool where about one-third of the required capital was raised.[3]

Bristol was also a centre of canal investment,[4] though on only a modest scale before the time of the canal mania. In 1776 its residents took 7 out of 200 shares in the Stroudwater Navigation.[5] In the summer of 1791 agents of the

---

[1] J. Throsby, *The History and Antiquities of the Ancient Town of Leicester* (Leicester, dated 1791, but in fact published later), p. 419. In Appendix III, below, pp. 180–2, an attempt is made to estimate the sums subscribed at different towns and the frequency of multiple subscriptions.

[2] Above, p. 53.

[3] Smiles, *Lives of the Engineers*, v. 232; *Victoria County History: Leicestershire*, iii. 110.

[4] Its importance in this respect being underestimated by W. E. Minchinton, 'Bristol, Metropolis of the West in the Eighteenth Century', *Trans. Royal Hist. Soc.*, 5th Ser., iv (1954), 85.

[5] Gloucestershire R.O., D 1180 3/1, Share Register 1774–1809.

promoters of the Herefordshire and Gloucestershire Canal attended there for the purpose of taking subscriptions, and it was reported that 'several merchants of this city, convinced of the great utility of this canal, have become subscribers to a large amount'.[1] On the evidence of the company's records Bristol men took 85 of its 750 shares.[2] In 1798 inhabitants of Bristol held 146 (8%) of the shares of the Worcester and Birmingham which had been promoted at the same time, the local attorney Samuel Worrall having acted as solicitor to the Bill in parliament.[3] In August 1793 this group succeeded in insisting that the line be constructed as a barge canal according to the original plan (the commercial crisis of the preceding months had apparently led some of the proprietors to prefer a reduced scale), a through conveyance from Birmingham to Bristol being 'a principal object of the Canal'.[4]

The period of the city's greatest excitement and most substantial investment was however that of the winter of 1792–3. The local mania began in November 1792, having apparently been inspired by the events in the Midlands, where by the end of October most of the principal promotions had been completed.[5] Perhaps in consequence of this the mania in the West was more narrowly circumscribed in form: Bristol subscribers do not appear in the speculative companies which have already been discussed, such as the Ellesmere, but were obliged to concentrate their attention on schemes centred on the city, most of them being essentially factitious and ephemeral. These included the Bristol and Worcester, the Bristol and Taunton, and the Cirencester and Westerleigh,[6] none of which received parliamentary sanction. The Bristol, Salisbury, and Southampton Canal was another local scheme and its section from Salisbury to Southampton was eventually authorized in

---

[1] *Felix Farley's Bristol Journal*, 18 June, 2 July 1791.
[2] Above, p. 53.
[3] Above, p. 47; WOBC 1/4, Committee Minutes 1791–1800, 5 Nov. 1791.
[4] Ibid., 12 Aug. 1793.
[5] For an account of the events in Bristol, see Hadfield, *Southern England*, pp. 71–8.
[6] *Felix Farley's Bristol Journal*, 8 Dec. 1792, 26 Jan. 1793.

1795, although financial and engineering difficulties prevented its completion. At the meeting for its promotion held at Southampton in December 1792, 40 of the 89 subscribers were from Bristol, but in October 1794 that city accounted, together with Bath, for only 66 of the 400 shares subscribed.[1] The financial crisis of 1793, exceptionally severe at both places, had evidently taken its toll.[2] Because of the delays incurred through local rivalries and disputes the canals of the West of England were not incorporated until the years 1794, 1795, and 1796, by which time the mania had ended. Thus the part played by Bristol was probably less than it would have been if, as elsewhere, parliamentary sanction had been obtained more promptly. Its inhabitants accounted for only 40 of the 782 shares held by subscribers to the Wilts and Berks Canal, incorporated in 1795, but a further 40 of the 228 subscriptions which had been withdrawn.[3] They number perhaps 17 among the 171 proprietors of the Somerset Coal Canal, incorporated in 1794,[4] but only one appears in the subscription contract of the ill-fated Dorset and Somerset Canal.[5] Bristol's most substantial contribution to the canal mania was therefore its promotion of the Kennet and Avon Canal; the part played by the city in this company has already been reviewed.[6] A sum in excess of £300,000 was subscribed at Bristol in the late 1780s and early 1790s to canals that secured parliamentary sanction.[7]

Bristol's part in canal finance may be compared with that of the other principal western seaport, Liverpool. Liverpool's merchants were responsible for the Sankey Navigation and took a leading role in the Leeds and Liverpool Canal, both of which were of direct interest to the town in securing its

---

[1] 35 George III *cap.* 51; Welch, *The Bankrupt Canal*, pp. 5–7.

[2] See Henry Thornton's estimate of the extent of bankruptcies, 7 Mar. 1793, printed in L. S. Pressnell, *Country Banking in the Industrial Revolution* (Oxford, 1956), p. 546.

[3] Above, p. 69.   [4] 34 George III *cap.* 86.

[5] House of Lords R.O., Deposited Plans, Dorset and Somerset Canal 1796.

[6] Above, pp. 66–8.

[7] Below p. 181. Bristol's investment in the canals of the South Wales coalfield, the only ones in the West to be really profitable, amounted to only 34 of the 2,378 subscriptions to shares which have been analysed, almost all of which may be explained in terms of personal connection: for example, the Harford family with its interests in the local iron industry.

supply of coal,[1] but beyond this its involvement was limited. In 1782, for example, it had only one proprietor, with 30 shares, in the Trent and Mersey company, although subscriptions had been sought in the town.[2] There are indications of a stirring of speculative interest in the early 1790s, most notably (I do not know why) among the local medical fraternity. As has already been mentioned,[3] in 1791, 1792, and the early months of 1793, 45 shares in the Oxford Canal were purchased by its inhabitants, 34 by Edward Alanson, and 6 by James Brown, both of whom were surgeons; James Currie, M.D., took shares in both the Peak Forest and Ashton canals; in 1798 Dr. Worthington and Dr. Lyon were requested to make application to proprietors 'and to other friends' of the Ashton Canal residing there, for the purpose of securing their subscription to the issue of promissory notes which the company was making at that time.[4] A few Liverpool inhabitants also took shares in the Lancaster Canal,[5] and they provided £1,200 of the first £3,800 subscribed for the small Ulverstone Canal, authorized in 1793.[6] In 1792 and early 1793 the merchant Cornelius Bourne bought 15 subscriptions to shares in the Rochdale Canal.[7] In 1798 an agent of the Peak Forest Canal was paid £7. 18s. 'for his Expences in going to Liverpool to procure additional Subscriptions'.[8]

In January 1793 the interest of the town's investing public was evidently sufficient to attract the attention of Phillips of Leicester, one of the most active of the Midlands' sharebrokers, who on 14 January 1793 inserted the first of two advertisements for his Navigation Office in *Williamson's Liverpool Advertiser*.[9] This was accompanied by an announcement from the publisher that 'in compliance with

[1] Above, pp. 26–7, 33–4, and references.

[2] TMC 2/2c, List of Shareholders; below, p. 97.

[3] Above, p. 87.

[4] AC 1/1, Committee Minutes 1798–1815, 2 July 1798.

[5] Above, p. 55.

[6] J. D. Marshall *Furness and the Industrial Revolution* (Barrow-in-Furness, 1958), pp. 89–90.

[7] Lancashire R.O., Dd Bo/291–2.

[8] PFC 1/1, Peak Forest Canal Committee Minutes 1794–1800, 4 July 1798; and see PFC 1/2, Committee Minutes 1800–7, 20 Mar. 1802.

[9] For Phillips and the Midland Navigation Offices, see below pp. 106–8.

repeated solicitations, he has opened a NAVIGATION OFFICE at his shop in Castle Street and that he has fixed a connection and correspondence which will enable him to serve his employees to their entire satisfaction.' The following week (21 January) he gave notice that shares in the Worcester and Birmingham, Warwick and Birmingham, and Bristol and Gloucester companies (the last an abortive promotion) were available. Thereafter nothing more is heard from him on the subject though on 18 and 25 February and 4 March J. W. Glenton, a landwaiter, advertised in the same newspaper his Canal Navigation Office, the shares offered being those of companies in the Midlands and Bristol area. Although, therefore, the canal mania reached Liverpool, it did so in a very attenuated form; its subscriptions during the early 1790s probably did not exceed £20,000. Only the faintest premonition is given of the part which the town was to play in railway finance.[1]

While Liverpool at an early date took an active interest in projects for inland navigation which could be expected to serve directly its local economic interests,[2] it was relatively indifferent to later, more speculative, manifestations. At Bristol, on the other hand, an enthusiasm for canals did not appear before the early 1790s, when it was extravagantly directed towards undertakings which were without exception ultimately unprofitable and probably of little economic value to the city. All this raises questions as to the expectations and motives of investors which will be considered elsewhere.[3]

[1] Cf. S. A. Broadbridge, 'The Early Capital Market: The Lancashire and Yorkshire Railway', *Econ. Hist. Rev.,* 2nd Ser., vol viii, no. 1 (1955), pp. 209–11.

[2] Cf. Barker, 'Lancashire Coal, Cheshire Salt . . .'; Harris, 'Liverpool Canal Controversies . . .'.

[3] Below, pp. 138–42.

IV

THE ORGANIZATION OF CANAL FINANCE

As their needs were generally modest and the sources of funds upon which they drew were essentially local, the financial organization of most canal companies was rudimentary. Their histories, unlike those of the government debt and the railway promotions, do not occupy an important place in the development of a formally organized market for capital. Share lists were filled by the opening of subscription books; the attention of investors was attracted by the publicity generated by the activities of the promoters. Often the promoters themselves took a large proportion of the shares and the need to look much further afield was obviated. Thus at the meeting held in Banbury on 25 October 1768, where Brindley's report and survey of the proposed Oxford Canal were received, £50,000 was subscribed.[1] Books for the most ambitious of the early canals were opened at quite widely separated places, for example, in the case of the Trent and Mersey, at Stafford, Lichfield, Newcastle under Lyne, Liverpool, Manchester, Congleton, Birmingham, Wolverhampton, Walsall, Burton on Trent, Tamworth, Derby, Nottingham, Newark, Gainsborough, Hull, and Bristol,[2] and in that of the Leeds and Liverpool, at Leeds, Bradford, Ottley, Keighley, Riddlesden, Skipton, Settle, Colne, Liverpool, York, Hull, Pontefract, Wakefield, Barnsley, Doncaster, Sheffield, and Chesterfield.[3] It has been noticed, however, that residents of the more distant towns were reluctant to participate and that with the exception, in the case of the Trent and Mersey, of some support from London the subscription lists were filled locally, although the proprietors of the Leeds and Liverpool succeeded later in distributing their shares more widely.[4]

---

[1] Hadfield, *East Midlands*, p. 17.
[2] *History of Inland Navigation* (1766) edn.), p. 86.
[3] LLC 1/1, Subscribers' Minutes 1766–70, 9 Jan. 1769, 18 Apr. 1770.
[4] Above, pp. 28–36.

The persons with whom subscription books were left included the occasional banker (for example, Abel Smith of Nottingham for the Trent and Mersey), or attorney (for example, John Moorhouse of Keighley for the Leeds and Liverpool), but were for the most part shopkeepers and merchants. They do not appear to have been paid for this service and, although they may have urged the advantages of their employers' schemes informally, there is no reason to suppose that the part which they played was anything other than passive. Underwriters or other financial intermediaries were not used to fill subscription lists. In 1768 William Marsden of Barnsley, gentleman, made a declaration of trust that the £500 which he had invested in the Calder and Hebble Navigation was the proper money of Thomas Beaumont of Nottingham, clerk,[1] and in 1770 it was represented to the committee of the Leeds and Liverpool Canal that 'many Persons have entered their Names in the Subscription Books for this Undertaking as Subscribers for other Persons . . .' and that the persons so subscribed for wished to be entered in their own names.[2] However, an examination of transfer books and later lists of proprietors in conjunction with original subscription lists makes it clear that arrangements of this kind were rare: where they occur they probably represent in most cases no more than one of the ways in which the handful of distant proprietors investing through personal connection, which appears in many companies, could make their subscriptions, the use of the declared proxy being the other.[3] In particular, there is no evidence that attorneys took shares on behalf of their clients. Many invested substantially,[4] but many were rich men in their own right, with a taste for speculation as well as the fees which private bill legislation and land purchase entailed: a hostile writer at the time of the canal mania termed navigation

[1] Halifax Public Library, Parker Collection no 2264.
[2] LLC 1/2, Minutes of the Committee and General Assembly 1770–82, 30 Aug. 1770.
[3] The proxy was also useful for Persons of Quality who found attendance at the rough and tumble of a subscription meeting uncongenial. See Oxfordshire R.O., CH/III/9, Oxford Canal subscription deed, for subscriptions on behalf of the Duke of Marlborough and other peers.
[4] Some examples are given by Hadfield, *Canal Age*, pp. 40–1.

schemes 'the empty and *interested* professions of *Solicitors*, Engineers and the whole tribe of BUYING AND SELLING ADVENTURERS'.[1]

In the circumstances of the early 1790s it ceased to be necessary for the promoters of even the most ambitious lines to cast about for subscribers: they congregated of their own accord, often in embarrassing numbers.

GRAND MERE CANAL

A few well-dressed *Sharps*, observing the *Navigation Mania* so prevalent among all classes of men, determined to make JOHN BULL pay for the frenzy of the moment. They in consequence took a room, and laying a map of *Botany Bay* (as the proposed line) upon the table, stiled themselves *Proprietors* in the intended *Grand Mere Canal*, and resolved that no person should subscribe for more than ten shares, nor less than one, and that an immediate deposit of one-half per cent should entitle the subscriber to be a proprietor. It was no sooner whispered abroad, than the FLATS flocked to the standard, and the SHARPS moved off with about 1500£.

In real life, of course, a proportion of the shares would have been reserved for the owners of land on the proposed line,[2] and navigation meetings were usually too numerously attended to be held in the intimacy of a room at an inn (they were held in a field,[3] on a hill,[4] or, in one case, in the parish church[5]), but otherwise this report[6] is probably a passable vignette of their procedure.

Thereafter, during the war years, few new canals were promoted. For the projections of the period of the joint-stock mania subscription books were opened locally and in London, and in the case of the Grand Union brokers were employed for a commission of £1 per share,[7] while scrip was traded on the Stock Exchange. However, there seems to be no reason why special importance should be attached to this: it has already been argued that the developments of 1807–11

---

[1] *Leicester Journal* 1 Mar. 1793. Italics as in the original.

[2] Below, pp. 153–7.

[3] Hadfield, *East Midlands*, p. 98. (Leicestershire and Northamptonshire Union).

[4] Hadfield, *West Midlands*, p. 168 (Ellesmere).

[5] *Jackson's Oxford Journal*, 28 July 1792 (Grand Junction).

[6] *Leicester Journal*, 14 Sept. 1792. The satire presumably alluded to the Ellesmere Canal, subscribed for on 10 Sept.

[7] Hadfield, *Canal Age*, p. 43.

were peculiar and short-lived.[1] As the primary market for canal stock in the post-war years remained local in extent, it may be supposed that it remained local and unsophisticated in organization.

The character of the secondary market for canal stock was similar.[2] Here are some statistics for the turnover of shares in the Birmingham, Oxford, and Leeds and Liverpool companies during their early years:[3]

	Birmingham	Oxford	Leeds and Liverpool
1768	101 (20·2%)		
1769	93 (18·6%)	67 (5·5%)	
1770	122 (24·4%)	95 (7·8%)	63 (3·2%)
1771	82 (16·4%)	29 (2·4%)	382 (19·1%)
1772	82 (16·4%)	84 (6·9%)	344 (17·2%)
1773	47 (9·4%)	22 (1·8%)	208 (10·4%)
1774	56 (11·2%)	80 (5·7%)	112 (5·6%)
1775	43 (8·6%)	96 (6·8%)	98 (4·9%)
1776	58 (11·6%)	65 (4·6%)	127 (6·4%)
1777	83 (16·6%)	59 (4·2%)	155 (7·8%)
1778	47 (9·4%)	23 (1·6%)	165 (8·3%)
1779	56 (11·2%)	30 (2·1%)	74 (3·7%)
1780	59 (11·8%)	3 (0·2%)	30 (1·5%)
1781	38 (7·6%)	0 —	17 (0·9%)
1782	28 (5·6%)	24 (1·7%)	82 (4·1%)
1783	25 (5·0%)	42 (3·0%)	41 (2·1%)

[1] Above, pp. 82–6.

[2] The usual method of transfer, stipulated in the Acts of incorporation, was a short form of the deed of bargain and sale, a duplicate of which had to be deposited with the clerk of the company and copied into a book of transfers. In most cases the proprietor's title was constituted by the record of his stock in the company's books, although some of the later incorporations began to issue share certificates. For details, see A. B. Dubois, *The English Business Company after the Bubble Act* (New York, 1938), pp. 358–62, notes 97, 98 101.

[3] Calculated from Bodleian Library Dep. c. 102–3, Oxford Canal Transfer Registers 1769–1800; BCN 2/26, Birmingham Canal Transfer Ledger 1768–1835; LLC 2/1, Leeds and Liverpool Canal Transfer Ledger 1770–1819. The bracketed percentages indicate the rate of turnover. There were 1,223 shares in the Oxford Canal 1769–73 and 1,412 thereafter, 500 in the Birmingham, and 2,000 in the Leeds and Liverpool. Some Oxford Canal shares had arrears of unpaid interest added to their par value, others did not. All have been regarded as equal. Transfers for a nominal consideration, e.g. from executors to heirs, have been ignored. The first figure in each column relates to part of a year only.

1784	8 (1·6%)	23 (1·6%)	66 (3·3%)
1785	25 (5·0%)	16 (1·1%)	72 (3·6%)
1786	28 (5·6%)	29 (2·1%)	159 (8·0%)
1787	30 (6·0%)	43 (3·0%)	93 (4·7%)
1788	41 (8·2%)	23 (1·6%)	183 (9·2%)
1789	33 (6·6%)	37 (2·6%)	152 (7·6%)
1790	13 (2·6%)	26 (1·8%)	190 (9·5%)
1791	23 (4·6%)	184 (13·0%)	117 (5·9%)
1792	37 (7·4%)	275 (19·5%)	91 (4·6%)
1793	76 (15·2%)	195 (13·8%)	329 (16·5%)

The annual rate of turnover averaged about 10% for the Birmingham Canal, 4% for the Oxford, and 7% for the Leeds and Liverpool. The differences between them may be attributed to the differing circumstances of the three companies.

From the first, Birmingham stock stood at a premium in anticipation of the company's prospects (£26 to £29 per share was given in December 1768);[1] the high rate of turnover in the company's first five years must reflect a certain amount of speculative dealing by its largely urban proprietary, which seems to have been curtailed by the commercial crisis of 1772. However, the main line was completed in the same year and the regular payment of dividends began two years later.[2]

The proprietary of the Oxford Canal, on the other hand, being less commercial in character, is likely to have been less volatile, and its shares seem at first to have been traded at par. The payment of the last call in 1775 saw the line only half built and the stock fell almost immediately to a discount of about £10. During the worst years of the American war its marketability suffered severely; when dealings were resumed in 1782 it stood at about £80 per share, falling rapidly to a nadir of £50 in 1786. The completion of the line in 1790, and the commencement of regular dividend payments in 1791, led to a flood of transactions and a rise of the share price from £75 to £200 by the early months of 1793. With the termination of the canal mania it relapsed to par, and the rate of turnover was very much reduced: 60 shares changed hands in 1794, 26 in 1795, 34 in 1796, 62 in 1797, 33 in

[1] BCN 1/1, Committee Minutes 1767-71, 9 Dec. 1768.
[2] Hadfield, *West Midlands*, p. 68.

1798, 45 in 1799, but in 1800 a recovery to 178 occurred.[1] It is not clear why the response of the market in Birmingham stock to the canal mania was comparatively so muted; perhaps the resources of the town's investors were being absorbed by the many other local navigations which they were financing at this time.[2] The company had not in any case experienced the dramatic recovery from misfortune enjoyed by the Oxford.

The history of the Leeds and Liverpool includes elements of those of the other two companies. As with the Birmingham there was brisk early dealing among its mercantile proprietors; like the Oxford it suffered during the American war from the failure to complete its line. In the 1780s regular, if modest, dividend payments restored a degree of marketability to its shares. It was only slightly affected by the canal mania: Lancashire and the West Riding lay outside the areas of most intense enthusiasm, and, in any case, much remained to be done towards the completion of its works.

Unfortunately, few records survive with which the extent of dealings in the shares of the new companies of the early 1790s might be measured: it would be interesting to know the volume of speculative transactions. For the Kennet and Avon Canal a 'Public Register Book' was opened in February 1793 to record transfers of script,[3] but no document of this kind has been found. Some transfer registers of smaller companies have survived, but they usually date only from 1793, or later, when most were incorporated, by which time the main period of excitement had passed. Three illustrations of the rate of turnover will suffice:[4]

---

[1] These details and the price date have been taken from the Transfer Registers. For details about dividend payments by the companies discussed here, see Appendix I.

[2] See Appendix III.

[3] *Felix Farley's Bristol Journal*, 16 Feb. 1793. At that time its scrip was sold at premia of as much as £50 per share: P.R.O., Order Book of the Court of Bankruptcy, B. 1/86, f. 243.

[4] Melton Navigation (incorporated 1791): Shareholders' Register, cited above, p. 40, n. 5. Derby Canal (1793): Transfer Book, cited above, p. 42, n.l. Wilts and Berks Canal (1795): Subscription Ledger, cited above, p. 69 n.l.

	Melton Mowbray	Derby	Wilts and Berks
1791	36		
1792	34		
1793	8	34	
1794	2	146	
1795	1	28	5
1796	5	36	31
1797	1	2	27
1798	2	20	2
1799	0	55	2
1800	0	43	6
1801	0	21	10
1802	1	40	n.a.
1803	8	66	n.a.
1804	10	55	n.a.
1805	3	51	n.a.

The capital of the Melton Navigation comprised 250 shares, that of the Derby Canal 600, and that of the Wilts and Berks Canal 782, declining to 642. The average annual rate of turnover was therefore 3% for the first company, 8% for the second, and 1·5% for the third.

Once again it appears that the marketability of a company's stock was determined by the circumstances of the time and its own prospects. Of these three, the situation of the Derby was best, although even so it suffered severely in the difficult year of 1797, and the rate of turnover during the years covered averaged less than 10%. The recovery of dealings from 1798 probably reflects the commencement of dividend payments, the first of which was proposed in that year.[1] The turnover of Melton and Wilts and Berks shares was negligible: both were 'agricultural' lines whose proprietors might tend to be unusually stable (though the promoters of the Derby Canal had professed to eschew speculation),[2] but it also seems likely that the stability of their holdings was at

[1] Derby Central Library, Derby Canal Coll., Committee Minutes 1793–1820, 4 June 1798. For the Company's dividend history, see Hadfield, East Midlands, p. 70.
[2] Above, p. 88.

least in part involuntary, for no dividend was paid by the first until 1804[1] or by the second until 1812.[2]

It appears that these companies were not alone in their misfortunes. In 1797 the committee of the Grand Junction Canal was attacked by a pamphleteer who alleged mismanagement and extravagance ('not a few sumptuous entertainments have been had and the particulars held back from the Company') and remarked unfavourably on the fall in price of the stock from a premium of £90[3] to a discount of £30. The committee replied:[4]

It is difficult to account for the capricious prices which in times of profound peace and rage for adventure have been given for canal stock upon speculation, and the depreciation arising from the times can hardly be brought in charge against the Company or its Committee, but even the prices given for shares in this undertaking were exceeded by the prices given for shares in several other Canals then [i.e. 1792-3] depending, and this concern will be found to have felt less depression from the times than any other canal unexecuted. In proof of this fact the shares of this Company are almost the only ones now marketable and at the last public sale they were (from the progress made) rising in price and considerably above the discount so injuriously and fallaciously stated in the pamphlet.

As the transfer records of the Grand Junction do not survive, it is impossible to verify this statement, but it seems plausible. In November 1802 Phillips reported: 'The Grand Junction Canal fluctuates as usual. The Shares of £100 have been as high as £210 and as low as £65. They are now at £150.'[5] No other stock is described as 'fluctuating' in this way. The statement therefore suggests that the Grand Junction's stock enjoyed a regular market, and that in this it was unusual, at least among the newer companies.[6]

[1] Hadfield, op. cit., p. 93.

[2] Swindon Public Library, Wilts and Berks Canal Coll., vol. 32, Ledger 1810-17, f. 5; and above, pp. 70-1.

[3] *Jackson's Oxford Journal*, 11 May 1793, a premium of 90 guineas asked for Grand Junction Canal stock.

[4] GJC 1/39, General Assembly and General Committee Minutes 1793-8, 15 Nov. 1797.

[5] Phillips, *General History* . . . (1803 edn.), p. 310.

[6] Shares in the completed, well-established lines may have been readily marketable, though the evidence relating to the Oxford and Birmingham companies does not suggest that they were traded very briskly. However, as by this time they rarely needed to raise additional capital, the advantages which they might derive from this fact were limited.

The implications of this for canal finance are obvious: most undertakings, when faced with the inevitable need to enlarge their capital, were obliged to rely almost exclusively on their proprietaries, employing devices which in many cases amounted to no more than inducements to throw good money after bad.[1] The Grand Junction, on the other hand, appears in consequence of its size, financial prospects,[2] geographical situation, and access to the London capital market, to have been alone in its ability to recruit additional funds in a careful, orderly, and even sophisticated manner.[3]

Finally, mention may be made here of the turnover of shares in the Grand Union Canal, the only promotion of the period of the joint-stock mania for which the data are available:[4]

1810	797	(35%)
1811	467	(21%)
1812	152	(7%)
1813	89	(4%)
1814	104	(5%)
1815	49	(2%)
1816	32	(2%)
1817	46	(2%)

A brief period of speculative trading was succeeded by a market as dull as that for any of the earlier promotions.

How was the market in canal shares organized? Some information about the London agents who took part in it has already been given,[5] but they could have accounted for only a small proportion of dealings. It appears that in the provinces the market, or rather markets, were informal, localized, and based mainly on personal connections, supplemented by newspaper advertisements and the part-time activities of a few jobbers and brokers. The dealings of John Hustler, the Bradford woolstapler, in the shares of the Leeds

[1] See below, pp. 116-23.
[2] For the history of its dividends, which began in 1806, see Hadfield, *British Canals*, pp. 175-7, and below, p. 176.
[3] Described below, pp. 123-5.
[4] GJC 2/2, Share Register 1809-37. There were 2,250 shares.
[5] See above, pp. 81-2.

and Liverpool Canal have already been mentioned.[1] During the early years of the Oxford Canal the Banbury auctioneer Joseph Hawtyn and the Oxford attorney John Walker bought and sold many of its shares, while in January 1792 James Dunsford, the company's clerk-accomptant, announced that he would undertake purchases and sales of loan or stock 'at the usual allowance of ⅛ per cent', 'it having been found from Experience, that it would be a general Accommodation, if an Office were opened where Persons who have any Business to transact in this Concern might readily apply'.[2] Although the service offered here was apparently that of a broker, Dunsford also emerged in the later 1790s as the most extensive buyer and seller of Oxford stock.[3] During the same period the clerk of the Lancaster Canal was acting as a broker in transfers of the company's shares, though in November 1796 he wrote to Christopher Rollestone, the proprietor of a London 'Inland Navigation Office' that as 'there is not any sale of shares in this part of the country, of course I cannot advise anything concerning the price of them.'[4] The Birmingham attorney Matthias Mogeridge dealt in shares in the Worcester and Birmingham,[5] and Warwick and Birmingham[6] Canals. Among the so-called 'canal agency' papers[7] of the Banbury innkeeper William Pratt (his business seems to have consisted mainly in the payment of calls on behalf of a few local shareholders in the Warwickshire canals of 1793–4) is a letter of the year 1800 from an Edward Smith of Birmingham[8] reporting that Grand Junction shares stand at 100 guineas, Stratford shares at a discount of 50%, and that he is offered many 'Naptons' (i.e. Warwick and Napton shares) at par.

During the canal mania some of these local dealers were inspired to transmogrify themselves briefly into 'Navigation

[1] See above, p. 35.

[2] Bodleian Library, Dep. c. 102; *Jackson's Oxford Journal*, 7 Jan. 1792.

[3] Bodleian Library, Dep. c. 102–3, Transfer Registers 1769–1800.

[4] LC 8/2, Letter Book 1792–7, ff. 593, 622.

[5] WOBC 1/4, Committee Minutes 1791–1800, 7 July, 22 Aug. 1792.

[6] See, e.g., WBC 1/1, General Assembly Minutes 1793–1812, list of shareholdings, 29 Sept. 1795.

[7] Warwickshire R.O., CR 580 Box 50.

[8] There are three residents of that name in the *Universal British Directory* of 1792, including an innkeeper.

Offices'. The first of these short-lived phenomena to appear was that of Richard Phillips, a Leicester publisher and bookseller, in November 1791.[1] With the widening of the perspectives of his fellow-townsmen in the later summer of 1792 he advertised[2] that he was

induced from the central situation of Leicester, to offer his Services to the Publick as Agent in the Purchase of SHARES in all the NAVI-GATIONS in ENGLAND, and having been for some Time engaged in such a Business respecting the Navigations more immediately connected with Leicestershire, he conceives he shall be able to render himself more useful to the Publick, by extending his scheme to Navigations in general.

Others who followed his example were the Banbury auctioneer Joseph Hawtyn,[3] and J. Wilkinson of Leicester who styled himself a 'canal broker',[4] while Stephen Seagar of Birmingham (grocer),[5] James Boott of Loughborough (auctioneer),[6] and William Heyrick of Leicester (attorney)[7] were active traders who did not aspire to give their dealings institutional form. The stocks usually advertised were those of the recent Midland promotions with a few from further afield, such as the 'Old' and 'New Rochdale', resulting from the excursions of local investors. The sources with which the volume of activity at the Offices might be measured do not exist, but it seems that their economic importance was slight. The impression given by an advertisement such as this:[8]

Several Gentlemen have agreed to meet at [the] Lion and Dolphin Dining Room, every Monday, Wednesday, and Friday Evenings, at Six o'Clock, to buy, sell, transfer &c. . . .

is that even at Leicester, when the excitement was at its height, share dealing was treated as an essentially frivolous activity. The offices resembled gambling schools more than capital markets, however rudimentary, and were immediately extinguished by the collapse of the canal mania. While they

[1] A. T. Patterson, *Radical Leicester* (Leicester, 1954). pp. 67 ff.

[2] *Jackson's Oxford Journal*, 18 Aug. 1792.

[3] *Jackson's Oxford Journal*, 24 Nov., 1 Dec., 15 Dec. 1792.

[4] *Leicester Journal*, 1 Mar. 1793. Either Joshua Wilkinson, a grocer and cheesemonger, or John, a tailor.

[5] *Leicester Journal*, 2 Nov. 1792.

[6] Ibid., 6 Apr., 25 May, 29 June 1792, etc.

[7] Ibid., 17 Feb., 15 June 1792.

[8] Ibid., 16 Nov. 1792.

lasted they were, like the mania itself, a phenomenon of the Midlands, though at Bristol in December 1792 Mr. Thomas (not identified) 'next door to the Rimmer Tavern' offered his services in the purchase and sale of shares,[1] and the following month Phillips of Leicester briefly advertised in that city.[2] The short-lived Navigation Offices of Liverpool (apparently the only examples to occur in a northern town in the years 1792-3) have already been mentioned.[3] One 'Canal Agency Office' of a data subsequent to the mania has been noticed: that of John Thompson 'Canal Broker, Law Stationer, Auctioneer and Commissioner' at 10 Bridge Street, Manchester. Though in his advertisements Grand Junction and 'Manchester Theatre' shares are mentioned once, he seems to have dealt almost exclusively in the stock, optional notes, and mortgages, of the Lancashire and Yorkshire lines.[4]

Although intermediaries were not employed to activate the primary market in canal stock, in the recruitment of loan capital the professional expertise of attorneys could be drawn upon to supplement appeals to the proprietors and public advertisements.[5] In 1775 the undertakers of the Aire and Calder Navigation decided to raise £60,000 on mortgage of the tolls to finance improvements.[6] The Leeds attorneys Charles Barnard and Charles Buck are recorded as creditors on their own account for £3,000 and £3,500 respectively. In addition a letter to the company's clerk of May 1775 refers to the security that 'is supposed to be given to Mr. Barnard's clients for the money to be advanced by them'. A year later Barnard himself wrote to the clerk:

Mr Barnard has sent to Mr Hebden [the clerk] the 17 mortgages which he will please to examine with Mr Barnard's clerks and get executed as soon as possible. Mr Barnard is exceedingly hurt that these Securities

[1] Felix Farley's Bristol Journal, 22 Dec. 1792.
[2] Ibid., 12 Jan. 1973.
[3] Above, pp. 95-6.
[4] Halifax Journal, 20 June, 24 Oct. 1801, 9 Jan., 16 Jan. 1802 etc.
[5] For an example of the latter, see Leeds Mercury, 14 July 1792 (Leeds and Liverpool Canal); for the former, below pp. 116-7.
[6] This and the following details from B.T.H.R. (York), ACN 1/5, Minutes of General Assembly 1774-87, 1 Feb. 1775; ACN 2/14 list of creditors 1775; ACN 4/112/5, File of Letters, Russell to Hebden, 31 May 1775, Barnard to Hebden, 23 May 1776. The creditors were mostly the trustees, widows, and daughters of Leeds merchants.

have not been executed long ago, especially as above £10,000 of the Money lies without any security from the Proprietors or their trustees.

Further examples of procuration or attempted procuration of this kind by attorneys (often the clerks of the companies involved) might be given: Mr. Derbyshire for the Chester[1] and Anthony Lax for the Chesterfield[2] in 1776, John Eagle of Bradford for the Leeds and Liverpool in 1778,[3] Hebden himself for the Aire and Calder in 1779 and 1780,[4] and the Nottingham attorneys Francis Evans and Charles Twells for, respectively, the Cromford in 1792[5] and the Grantham in 1796,[6] while the Bristol attorney (and building speculator) Isaac Cooke lent his firm's money to the Bridgwater and Taunton, and the Chard Canals of which he was clerk.[7]

The part played by banks in the finance of canals was modest. As is well known, the banking system in England developed primarily for the purpose of effecting commercial payments, and extending commercial credit, and it was not suited to underwrite investment projects of a long-term character. Bankers frequently occur as subscribers to shares in newly promoted canals, sometimes for substantial amounts,[8] but they never represented more than a small minority among investors as a whole, and, as in the case of attorneys, there is no reason to suppose that their investments represented anything other than their personal wealth. In the only substantial departure which has been noticed from this rule both canal and bank failed.[9] In late 1792 and early 1793 William Morgan, a member of the Chepstow banking firm of Lewis, Stoughton, Buckle, and Co., engaged

[1] CC 1/3, Committee Minutes 1775–9, 8 Mar. 1776.

[2] CHC 1/1, Committee and General Assembly Minutes 1771–80, 27 Sept. 1776 30 Nov. 1778.

[3] LLC 1/2, Committee and General Assembly Minutes 1770–82, 25 Sept. 1778.

[4] ACN 1/5, 9 Apr. 1779, 11 Jan. 1780.

[5] CRC 1/1, Committee and General Assembly Minutes 1789–99, 10 Dec. 1792.

[6] GCN 1/1, Committee and General Assembly Minutes 1793–1809, 5 May 1796.

[7] Hadfield, *Canal Age*, p. 41.

[8] For examples, see Hadfield, op. cit., pp. 47–8, L. S. Pressnell, *Country Banking in the Industrial Revolution* (Oxford, 1956), pp. 389–98.

[9] *Felix Farley's Bristol Journal*, 8 Feb. 1794: notice by the assignees of the Bath City Bank for the sale of 160 shares in the Salisbury and Southampton Canal.

in speculative purchases of canal stock at Bristol (100 shares are mentioned, in all cases being scrip in ephemeral promotions which never received parliamentary sanction). He alleged that these purchases were on account of the bank, but this was denied by his partners and he was ejected from the firm in consequence of his failure to contribute his quota towards an enlargement of the capital needed to cover the damage wrought by the commercial crisis of 1793.[1]

Dr. Pressnell[2] quotes a 'knowledgeable pamphleteer' of 1804 on the services which might be rendered by banks:

A line of canal is projected to pass through this part of the country; it is considered advantageous, the subscription fills, the bank itself takes a few shares, their friends take many more; the stated periods for payment come round, the shares are pledged, the notes are received for it, and the business of the bankers increases rapidly.

No convincing example has been noticed of a bank assisting subscribers in this way. In March 1773 the Oxford brewer Henry Drought mortgaged his ten shares in the Oxford Canal (which were not fully paid up until 1775) to William and Thomas Fuller of Lombard Street, bankers, as security for bills of exchange to the amount of £600,[3] but this seems most likely to have been a precaution demanded by the commercial crisis of 1772. In 1781 John Hustler mortgaged[4] his 27 shares in the Leeds and Liverpool and one share in the Bradford Canal to Daniel Mildred, banker, and Jonathon Hoare, merchant, both of London, but the payment of calls had been completed long before this date.[5]

The most valuable service provided by banks to canals was their execution of the role of company treasurer, an office which they usually filled, especially from the 1780s. Its first aspect was the purely mechanical one, the provision of a

[1] P.R.O., Chancery Bills and Answers, C. 12/239/15.

[2] Op. cit., p. 393.

[3] Bodleian Library, Dep. c. 102, Transfer Register 1769–93.

[4] Prior's Kitchen, Durham, Backhouse MSS., nos. 247–8.

[5] This perhaps suggests that some West Riding merchants found their canal investments burdensome during the wartime depression. See also William Cudworth, 'The First Bradford Bank', *The Bradford Antiquary*, n.s. (1903), 235: In 1781 the Bradford banking partnership of Thomas Leach of Riddlesden, William Pollard of Halifax, and William Hardcastle of Bradford, formed in 1777, was declared bankrupt on the petition of Nathaniel Jowett of Clockhouse who had lent it £800 on the security of 4 shares in the Leeds and Liverpool Canal. Leach and Hardcastle had been among the original subscribers to the canal.

means by which moneys might be received and disbursed, but they were also able to provide financial assistance by means of loans and overdrafts. Cases in which they did so are listed in Appendix IV; it will be seen that most canal companies at one time or another borrowed from banks. It must be noted, however, that the references relate to widely scattered dates and are in most cases taken from company minute books. The most common occasion for a debt due to a treasurer to be recorded here was a crisis in his relations with the proprietors. Thus notice of a company's indebtedness is most likely to be available when it has reached its worst stage; but where, less frequently, consecutive series of treasurers' accounts survive, positive balances are found considerably to outnumber negative ones. Canals may in this way have furthered the development of English banking.

Advances from banks rarely assumed very considerable proportions either absolutely or in relation to the total capital outlay required by a company's works. However, they may sometimes have cushioned companies from delays by their proprietors in the payment of calls and allowed expenditure to proceed in a regular manner. For example, at their General Assembly of 1 July 1793, the proprietors of the Leicester Navigation accepted the recommendation by the committee of what appears to have been a supplementary subscription on the shares, 'in order to provide an extraordinary supply of Money for carrying on the Works in the expeditious manner in which they are now carrying on' and also resolved that 'in case a sufficient sum cannot be raised by such Means that the Committee be enabled to borrow of the Treasurers or otherwise at any time at their discretion such Sum or Sums of Money not exceeding Three Thousand Pounds for a space of Time not exceeding Six Months'. On the fifth of the same month letters were sent to all the proprietors asking them to pay their subscriptions promptly, but in October it was found necessary to borrow £3,000 from the treasurers in pursuance of the resolution of the General Assembly. The following month it was reported that arrears of £1,605 on the calls were outstanding.[1]

[1] LCN 1/2, Committee and General Assembly Minutes 1791–5, 1 July 1793, 5 July, 11 Oct., 22 Nov. 1793.

Unfortunately it was just when properties found most difficulty in paying their calls that bankers were least likely to be willing to extend their advances. The later 1790s, when a large proportion of the canal network was built, were financially difficult years for everyone. Thus in July 1794 the treasurers of the Leicester Navigation declined to extend their advances.[1] In the same year a request for an additional loan by the committee of the Horncastle Navigation to the Lincoln Bank, in which one of their number was a partner, received the chilling reply that the partners 'wish not only to decline advancing any more money for the Company, but on the contrary express a desire to receive again what has already been advanced.'[2]

1797 was a year of particular stringency. In the spring the committee of the Lancaster Canal tried to arrange finance to complete before the following winter their line as far as Preston, the point at which it would start to yield revenue. This would require expenditure in anticipation of the calls. The sum of £10,000 was sought without success from five different banks in Lancaster, Kendal, and Preston. The company's treasurer, Thomas Worswick of Lancaster, was at first prepared to lend only £15,000 in advance of the call of 1 July 1797, a sum which the committee demanded be increased to £20,000 and extended to the call of 1 January 1798. Although as late as May the company, 'having yet some difficulty with the Treasurer in regard to his advances', was considering a curtailment of the works, Worswick eventually seems to have relented, perhaps in consequence of the threat made to offer the treasurership to someone else. At least, the crucial Preston–Tewitfield connection was completed by the following November.[3]

The Kennet and Avon company was less fortunate. In April of the same year its General Committee, faced with arrears in the payments on more than 800 shares, asked the treasurer Samuel Worrall of the Bristol banking firm Worrall, Blatchley, and Co., for further accommodation. He answered: 'he could not, on account of the pressure of the

[1] Ibid., 7 July 1794.
[2] Lincolnshire A.O., T.L.E. I/1/1, Committee Minutes 1792–1803, 9 Dec. 1794. How much was due is not clear. £1,000 had been sought on 29 July 1794.
[3] LC 8/2, Letter Book 1792–7, ff. 672, 679, 696–7.

times and being then £6,000 cash in advance for the company', a reply which the committee found 'unsatisfactory'.
But he prepared for its consideration a programme of
retrenchment as an answer to the company's difficulties. One
of his suggestions was that the labourers on its works be paid
with 21-day notes which shopkeepers should be personally
urged by committee members to accept, and 'that such Notes
be prepared from Copper Plates, with a slight Device descriptive of the Canal Work, in order to give them a better
appearance than Letter Press and in Consequence thereof a
Currency . . .' However the committee was evidently un-
impressed by this gratuitous insight into the craft of country
banking and Worrall was deprived of the treasurership.[1] It is
recorded that when the bank of Worrall and his partners
failed in 1820 there was 'an extensive circulation of their
notes, principally for small sums, in the hands of the lower
classes'.[2]

It would be tedious to chronicle at length every passage of
arms which took place between canal companies and their
bankers. It may merely be reiterated that, because of the
circumstances in which most lines were built, the assistance
which they could derive from this quarter was strictly
limited. Only three instances have been noticed where a
company came to rely on bank finance more or less to the
exclusion of other sources, those of the Brecknock and
Abergavenny, the Kennet and Avon, and the Worcester and
Birmingham Canals. It may be significant that each dates
from the period of exceptional and perhaps unhealthy credit
expansion of the last years of the Napoleonic wars, and that
the more austere conditions of the peace brought a rapid
curtailment of the advances.[3]

The most frequently recurrent and most intractable problem of canal finance was that of raising additional funds to
cover an increase in the cost of the works over the original
estimate. Such an increase appears to have occurred, with
only one exception, in the case of every line successfully

[1] KAC 1/9, Minutes of the Committee of Management 1794–1805, 22 June,
20 July 1796, 10 Apr., 11 Apr. 1797.
[2] J. W. Buck, *Cases in Bankruptcy* (1820) i. 531.
[3] Below, pp. 187–8, 190.

completed during the period covered by this study.[1] As is mentioned elsewhere,[2] the scarcity of detailed costings precludes an exact analysis of the causes of this escalation. In general blame may be ascribed to the original incompetence of the engineers in making their estimates (they had, of course, no incentive to take a pessimistic view of the costs likely to be incurred), the rising prices of labour and materials while the works were in progress, and inefficiency in their execution. An aggravating but, except for some of the 'second generation' companies, relatively minor problem to be faced was that of defalcations among the proprietors in the payment of calls.[3]

Additional funds might be raised by an enlargement of the capital (either through further calls on the old shares, or the creation of new ones), by borrowing, or out of toll income. A summary review of the financial histories of the principal canals has already been given,[4] and here it is only necessary to indicate certain salient features.

By its Act of incorporation a canal company was empowered to raise a sum equivalent to the estimated cost of its line by the creation of shares, usually of £100.[5] In addition, provision was made for a supplementary capital,[6] amounting in general to between one-quarter and one-half of the original, to be raised, if need should arise (as it almost invariably did), by the creation of additional shares, by making further calls on the old ones, or by borrowing on security of the tolls. For the 'first generation' of canals this formula proved, on the whole, perfectly adequate, though in most cases the supplementary provision was found to be insufficient, and it was necessary to obtain a further Act or Acts to enlarge it. Some of these companies, especially the

---

[1] The exception is the Shropshire Canal. The Pocklington Canal was built between 1815 and 1819 within its original estimate thanks to the postwar deflation. The original line of the Warwick and Braunston (later Warwick and Napton 1794–1800: £80,000) was shortened.

[2] pp. 148–9.   [3] See, for example, pp. 52, 61, 67.

[4] Above, pp. 26–73.

[5] £200 in the case of the Trent and Mersey (6 George III *cap.* 96), and £50 in those of the Crinan and Ulverstone (33 George III *caps.* 104, 105).

[6] Except in the case of the Stourbridge (16 George III *cap.* 28). See Evans, *British Corporation Finance*, pp. 39–61, for a useful review of developments in the legislative provision for supplementary capital, though their economic background is not made sufficiently clear.

smaller ones,[1] raised the additional capital which they required among themselves, while others[2] called only £100 on their shares but borrowed substantial sums on mortgage. It is only among a few of the most impecunious companies[3] that suggestions were entertained of financial procedures any more elaborate or exotic than these.

The same formula was applied in the series of Acts of the early 1790s which incorporated the promotions of that period. In the circumstances of the war years which followed, however, it became generally unworkable as companies found themselves ground between the upper and nether millstones: on the one hand, an inflation of costs at a rate which often made the original estimates of engineers appear ridiculous,[4] and on the other, heavy government borrowing and years of bad trade which depreciated and made virtually unmarketable their shares,[5] precluding any resort to the public at large for additional funds. A few companies[6] were fortunate in being able to complete their works quickly, financing excesses over the estimates in the 'traditional' manner by supplementary calls on the shares and borrowing on mortgage, but these were shorter lines which in many cases were already well on the way to completion by 1793 when the difficult period began. Among the rest even the strongest companies, those such as the Birmingham, and the Leeds and Liverpool, which had established themselves at an earlier date, which could offer substantial revenues as security, and which paid dividends on their shares, experienced acute difficulties.

Under its Act of 1784[7] the Birmingham company borrowed £114,300 (£115,000 had been authorized) to build

[1] e.g. the Staffordshire and Worcestershire, Stourbridge, Stroudwater, Loughborough. The proprietors of smaller companies perhaps found it easier to agree among themselves to pay additional calls.

[2] Trent and Mersey, Oxford, Coventry, Birmingham, Chesterfield.

[3] In particular, the Chester and the Coventry. See pp. 120-1.

[4] The classic case being Rennie's 1794 estimate of £377,364. 19s⁻6d. for the Kennet and Avon. By 1812 £979,314. 17s. 9d. had been spent, though this included the cost of buying the Kennet Navigation and a controlling interest in the Avon: Hadfield, *Southern England*, p. 148.

[5] Above, pp. 103-4.

[6] The Leicester, Melton, Nottingham, Cromford, Derby, Wyrley and Essington.

[7] 24 George III *cap.* 4.

the line to Fazeley. In 1794 a further Act[1] was obtained authorizing an increase of the mortgage debt by a further £45,000 but during the next five years only £7,100 was raised on this account. In March 1797 the committee of management was compelled to recommend a reduction of the half-yearly dividend from 18 to 10 guineas per share so that expenditure on the works might be financed, 'the present scarcity of money preventing them from borrowing'.[2] In 1806 it was thought necessary to obtain an Act authorizing the sale of annuities in order to discharge mortgage debts totalling £100,000 (repayment had begun in 1800), although there is no evidence that the power thus granted was ever used. The mortgage debt was finally liquidated in 1819.[3] In 1794 the Leeds and Liverpool Canal was obliged to obtain parliamentary authority for the admission of new proprietors so that the £101,394 of the £200,000 borrowed under the Act of 1790 which had been apparently called in by the lenders might be repaid. For this purpose additional shares were issued, though the company was eventually able to resume borrowing (the debt reached a maximum of £442,154 in 1822) and was the only one which succeeded in raising capital in this way to any great extent during the war years.[4]

The situation of the newer companies with little or no revenue of their own was of course much less favourable and the history of canal finance during this period is largely that of the search for means by which additional funds might be wrung from reluctant shareholders to complete the undertakings which they had so optimistically and lightheartedly embarked upon in the years of peace. The methods which came to be generally employed for this purpose were of three kinds: borrowing within the company from proprietors anxious to see their previous investments brought to fruition, compulsory calls on the proprietors under Acts obtained especially for the purpose, and the issue of depreciated shares. These will be considered in turn.

The point was often put to proprietors, as by the committee of the Basingstoke Canal company in May 1794, that

[1] 34 George III *cap*. 87.
[2] Birmingham Ref. Lib., 568603, f. 17.
[3] 46 George III *cap*. 92; BCN 4/17, Loan Ledger, ff. 90–1, 140–1.
[4] 30 George III *cap*. 65, 34 George III *cap*. 94, above p. 35.

until the works were completed they could expect no benefit from their shares, and that as the payment of loan interest had the first claim on the profits, it would be advantageous for them to subscribe towards it. No useful purpose would be served by an appeal to the general public, 'especially as in times like the present, it is much to be doubted whether money could be raised by public advertisements, a mode that, it is submitted, should and must be reserved as a dernier resort . . .'[1] It is not clear what the outcome of this appeal was. The argument of the committee of the Horncastle Navigation in 1795, faced with debts of £1,600 and the need to raise £6,400 in excess of the share capital to complete the line, was similar. The Act of incorporation authorized a supplementary capital of £10,000 to be raised on mortage of the tolls, yet they could not advise a resort to the open market, as

in the present state of money matters, they fear no indifferent person will advance the money, but recommend each subscriber to advance such sum as may be convenient . . . [otherwise] . . . the prospect of interest for the subscribers is very distant.

In this case, however, stronger measures were required and the additional sum was eventually raised by the issue of preference shares.[2] In 1797 it was admitted by the clerk of the Lancaster Canal with respect to an appeal for a voluntary advance of £15 on each share (which seems to have been fairly successful), that 'it cannot be expected that any but proprietors will aid this Loan in the present state of the Concern'.[3] The Thames and Severn was another company which borrowed money in the same way.[4]

The second method of supplementary finance was that of additional calls on the shares. This was of course an expedient which had been widely used by the first generation of companies, and by a few of the more favourably situated concerns of the 1790s, but the novelty which affected its use during the war years was the introduction of an element of compulsion in response to the increased recalcitrance of proprietaries.

[1] Birmingham Ref. Lib., 568603, f. 45.

[2] Lincolnshire A.O., T.L.E. I/1/1, Minutes 1792–1803, 14 Jan. 1795; below, p. 122.

[3] LC 8/2, Letter Book 1792–7, f. 642. In March 1797 it was reported that the proprietors of 2,108 of the 4,141 shares had agreed to the advance, ibid., f. 663.

[4] Above p. 66.

Here it may be apposite to describe the legal obligations of shareholders. Acts of incorporation usually authorized companies to take action in law or equity to recover arrears of unpaid calls on shares. However, as Dubois has remarked 'it is difficult to find proof of the actual bringing of actions as distinct from the threat of litigation',[1] although a few examples have been noticed in minute books of orders to the company's clerk to begin prosecutions.[2] It appears that in many cases such orders, or the threat of such orders, were sufficient in themselves, perhaps because proprietors, in particular those actively engaged in trade, feared the damage which might be done to their personal credit by the prolongation of an action for debt. Thus in September 1796 the committee of management of the Kennet and Avon Canal ordered that the owners of 129 shares be informed that they would suffer forfeiture if the arrears due on them were not paid up; the owners of $161\frac{1}{2}$ other shares were to be prosecuted at law. No explanation was given for the different treatments thus accorded. Three months later the clerk, reporting on the progress of the actions, declared that of the 37 proprietors directed to be prosecuted almost all had submitted to paying or giving notes, drafts, or other securities for payment. The prosecutions against those who had not done so were to be continued. However, in March 1797 it was necessary to order the forfeiture of $404\frac{1}{2}$ shares.[3]

It appears that the victims of such forfeitures were usually either dead, insolvent, or bankrupt, conditions which put them in law or in fact beyond the reach of the most remorseless of companies.[4] No prosecution leading to a recovery of damages awarded by the court, as prescribed by

[1] Dubois, *English Business Company*, pp. 368–9, notes 179–87. He instances many 'cajolements, threats, entreaties and prayers' from the harassed committees.

[2] e.g. ASCH 1/2, 14 Nov. 1797 (Ashby Canal); SHRC 1/1, 15 May 1797 (Shrewsbury Canal).

[3] KAC 1/9, 1 Sept., 6 Dec. 1796, 8 Mar. 1797.

[4] Only one instance has been noticed in which a company proved a debt under a commission of bankruptcy against a proprietor in arrears: after the canal mania the Leicestershire and Northamptonshire Union Canal company made a claim of £1,400 for shares subscribed against Edward Harrison of Leicester, money scrivener (i.e. attorney): P.R.O., Court of Bankruptcy Order Book, B. 1/91, ff. 313–15. In 1814 it was ruled in the case of the Weald of Kent Canal, an abortive promotion of 1811, that the administrators of a decedant's estate were not liable to pay calls which he had owed: *English Reports*, cxxviii. 907–10.

the Acts, has been noticed. The Huddersfield, however, which was perhaps plagued more than any other company by defaulters, in 1797 went so far as to order the arrest of one of their number, although it is not known whether the order was implemented.[1] The previous year this company had also attempted to challenge in the courts the right, clearly enunciated in its Act, of a subscriber to end his liability to answer calls by transferring his shares. In the case in point the transferee had since become insolvent, 'it appearing to this committee that there are several other instances of defaulters in payment of calls now due under the like circumstances'. But its argument was emphatically dismissed by Lord Kenyon, the judge, 'as it is a matter of infinite moment to the great mass of property embarked in this kind of speculation' that the right to effect transfers be upheld.[2]

If this aspect of company law was clear enough, there were others which were not. Companies were authorized by their Acts of incorporation to raise additional funds by borrowing, the admission of new proprietors, or further calls on the shares. But these Acts did not say what was to be done if proprietors disagreed among themselves about the exercise of this last option as, in the circumstances of the 1790s and early 1800s, they often did. The general opinion was that supplementary calls could not be compulsory.[3] Several Acts were therefore passed to enforce the will of majorities over recalcitrant minorities: for the Grantham Canal in 1797, to raise a further £20,000 by calling £50 on each share,[4] for the Stainforth and Keadby in 1798,[5] for the Oakham in 1800 (£15,000 by £30 per share),[6] and for the Barnsley in 1808 (£43,200 by £60 per share).[7] This last Act is said to have caused many of the Barnsley's proprietors to dispose of their shares (on which £100 had already been paid) at the price of £5 each.[8] In 1800 the Huddersfield had sought a similar authority, with the right to order the forfeiture of those

[1] HUC 1/2, 2 Nov. 1797.

[2] *English Reports*, ci. 842–6, Huddersfield Canal Company *versus* Buckley; HUC 1/2, 31 Mar. 1796.

[3] Dubois, *English Business Company*, p. 100.

[4] 37 George III *cap*. 30.   [5] 38 George III *cap*. 47.

[6] 40 George III *cap*. 56.   [7] 48 George III *cap*. 13.

[8] Priestley, *Historical Account*, p. 59.

shares whose proprietors failed to pay the necessary calls. Petitions were received in parliament from dissident stockholders protesting at the harshness of the proposals to those who from their status as legatees or trustees, or who 'from the Pressure of the Times, and a Want of pecuniary Resources, are not enabled to advance or subscribe any more Money to the said concern than they have already subscribed'.[1] The company was however authorized to call a further £20 on each share, and also to issue additional ones at depreciated rates.[2]

This last procedure was the third and most commonly employed expedient resorted to by companies at this time. The principle of such issues is obvious: shares newly created, to be acceptable, must carry the market price of the old, which in the case of the unfinished canals of the 1790s and 1800s was with few exceptions less than par.[3] The first company to consider this course was apparently that of the Coventry Canal in 1782. It was proposed that the £30,000 necessary for the completion of the line to Coleshill be raised by the creation of 750 shares at £40 each 'being the present market price of the stock'. But the suggestion evidently met with disfavour, and £40,000 was eventually borrowed on mortgage of the tolls.[4] Later, however, when large-scale loans of this kind had become out of the question for most companies, proprietaries were obliged to entertain this distasteful procedure (involving as it did a devaluation of the dividend and voting rights of previous investments) with increasing frequency. Because it was held that the terms of the Acts of incorporation prohibited issues at less than par,[5] they required explicit parliamentary sanction, for which purpose supplementary Acts began to be sought in 1800, the first to be passed being that for the Peak Forest company.[6] A

[1] *H.C.J.* lv. 305–6, 339.   [2] 39, 40 George III *cap.* 39.

[3] Exceptions include the Leeds and Liverpool, above, p. 35, and the Grand Junction below, p. 124.

[4] CVC 1/3, 30 June 1782; above p. 31.

[5] Cf. Dubois, op cit., p. 395, n. 69, opinion of J. Mansfield of the Inner Temple, 1797, in the case of the Barnsley Canal, that in the event of an increase of the capital the original proprietors would have a valid ground for objection if the proposed new shares were sold at the market price of £80 each (£100 having been paid on the old), even if they were allowed the right of pre-emption.

[6] 39, 40 George III *cap.* 38; followed by the Lancaster, Huddersfield, Kennet and Avon, Wilts and Berks, Worcester and Birmingham; above, pp. 47, 56, 61, 67, 70.

variant of this method of finance was the issue of interest-bearing notes carrying the option of conversion into shares at a stipulated rate; scrip privileged in this way could be disposed of at a higher price.[1] Proprietors were given first refusal of new shares (the right of pre-emption), usually in proportion to their holdings of the old, and the evidence available suggests that in most cases this right was exercised fully, or almost to the full.[2] The depreciated share was therefore in practice less a means of attracting new investors than one of raising further capital from an existing proprietary. Its advantage over other means of accomplishing this, such as the additional call, lay in its flexibility. The recalcitrant shareholder could decline to exercise his right of pre-emption (at the cost to himself of seeing his share of the company's future profits reduced) and his entitlement would, if the issue had been priced realistically, be acceptable to others. Against the refusal to pay a call, on the other hand, only the drastic remedy of forfeiture, with its attendant odium, was available. For this reason, the companies which issued new shares were the largest ones, those least likely to be able to reach unanimous agreement as to the means of raising further capital.

Finally, mention may be made of two infrequently adopted and essentially unimportant methods of company finance, the preference share and the annuity. In 1777 the Chester Canal, the least successful of the promotions of the 1760s and 1770s (in 1779 its shares on which £100 had been paid were selling for one shilling each), obtained an Act under which it was authorized to raise 60% on its capital of £42,000 by voluntary loan subscriptions which were to be entitled to receive an interest of 5% preferentially, and be convertible into stock when it became possible to pay a dividend in excess of this rate. Additionally, the subscribers to this loan were to be preferred in the payment of dividends on the original stock. This scheme did not meet with success and in 1778 it was necessary to obtain a further Act under which compulsory calls were made on the shares.[3] In 1796 it

---

[1] e.g. the Kennet and Avon, Ellesmere, Grand Junction, Ashton, pp. 45, 52, 57, 67.

[2] Above, pp. 53, 61-2, 71.

[3] 17 George III *cap.* 67; 18 George III *cap.* 21, CC 1/3, Committee Minutes 1775–9, 30 Apr., 20 June 1777, 4 Jan. 1779.

was proposed to the proprietors of the Herefordshire and Gloucestershire Canal that an Act be obtained under which additional shares might be issued 'allowing subscribers a Preference on the Dividends to the amount of 6 or 7 per cent' (this preference was to be limited to a certain number of years). They however resolved 'that the mode of raising any preference beyond legal interest will be prejudicial to the Company and ought not to be adopted', and merely proposed that £5,000 be borrowed among the proprietors. In 1798 funds were exhausted and work on the half-completed line was abandoned, not to be resumed until 1839.[1] The Horncastle Navigation under its Act of 1800 devised a complicated formula by which to raise the £8,200 necessary for the completion of the line. All new subscribers, and all holders of original stock who were prepared to double their investments, were to receive dividends of up to 6% on a preferred basis, then 5% was to be paid to the proprietors who had not doubled their holdings, then 2% to those who had, then a further 3% to those who had not. Thereafter all dividends were to be made equally. In spite of these optimistic projections the most that was ever paid was 4% on the preferred stock (in the 1840s).[2] In 1806 the Rochdale Canal received parliamentary authority for the issue of preference shares, but it is not known whether it was exercised.[3] In 1809 the Thames and Severn Canal issued preferred stock but this was a reconstitution of its loan capital, not a means of raising additional funds.[4]

The evasion of the Usury Laws by the sale of annuities (the ultimate financial degradation for corporations as well as individuals)[5] was rarely attempted. A number of companies obtained parliamentary authority for such a course, the Chester in 1772, the Leicester in 1797, the Worcester and Birmingham in 1798, the Stratford in 1799, the Rochdale in 1800, the Birmingham in 1806, and the Grand Surrey and

[1] HGN 1/1, Minutes of the General Assembly 1791–1882, 10 Nov., 15 Dec. 1796, Hadfield, *South Wales and the Border*, pp. 202–5, above, pp. 53–4.

[2] 39, 40 George III *cap.* 109; Lincolnshire A.O., T.L.E. I/1/1, 30 Apr. 1800, I/1/7, Dividend Book 1813–61.

[3] Above, pp. 63–4.   [4] Above. p. 66.

[5] Cf. Sybil Campbell, 'The Economic and Social Effect of the Usury Laws in the Eighteenth Century', *Trans. Royal Hist. Soc.*, 4th Ser. (1933), 197–210.

the Croydon in 1811,[1] but only two instances have been noticed of it being exercised, by the Stratford between 1809 and 1816, and the Worcester and Birmingham after 1815.[2]

The display of financial expertise by canal companies in the procuring of additional capital is distressingly rare. In 1789, when the proprietors of the Leeds and Liverpool decided to resume work on their line, the committee was charged to find what were the lowest terms on which money might be raised on security of the tonnage. The following year it was reported that 'frequent meetings were held with some of the principal proprietors in and about London who it is assumed were the best informed on the subject as to the mode of borrowing the money which will be necessary for compleating the Canal, whose unanimous opinion was the borrowing it in different sums as it might be wanted and so as not to put it in the power of any combination to demand payment in such a manner as to distress the Company would be the most preferable.' In consequence of this advice it was decided to raise the money half-yearly, according to need, on bonds of not less than £500, six months' notice being required for repayment. The available evidence suggests that the sources of capital drawn upon in this way were in the main local.[3]

From 1793 most companies lived from hand to mouth, relying in the main upon their long-suffering proprietaries. Mention may be made here, however, of an unusual, if not unique, example of a properly considered marketing operation, that of the Grand Junction Canal. It has already been suggested that this concern, in common with a few others of Southern England, came to rely to an increasing degree upon London investors as construction proceeded.[4] The care which it gave to the enlargement of its stock was possibly both a cause and an effect of this. In 1798 it was decided to raise £150,000 by the issue of interest-bearing notes carrying

[1] 12 George III *cap.* 75; 37 George III *cap.* 51; 39 George III *cap.* 31; 39 George III *cap.* 60; 40 George III *cap.* 36, 46 George III *cap.* 92; 51 George III *caps.* 11, 170.

[2] Above, pp. 48-9. In 1805 this mode was considered by the Rochdale Canal proprietors but apparently rejected (*Halifax Journal*, 8 June 1805).

[3] LLC 1/3, General Assembly and Committee Minutes 1782-90, 9 Oct. 1789, 2 July 1790; above pp. 35-6.

[4] Above, pp. 46, 81-2.

the option of conversion into stock at the rate of £100 per share before 25 March 1803, and the order was given:[1]

> That Scrip Sheets assimilated as near as circumstances will admit to Government Loan Scrip Sheets be provided in sufficient Number and for the proper Gradations of Scrip from Five Hundred Pounds to Twelve Pounds ten shillings.

In January 1800 consideration was given to the raising of additional funds, either by the disposition of some unsubscribed shares, or by a further issue of optional notes. Thomas Homer, the company's auditor, was appointed to report on the merits of these alternatives. He found that while its shares had recently been selling at a premium of about 2·5%, the subscriptions to the optional notes stood at 10% above par. Therefore, he considered,[2]

> the introducing any considerable Number of Shares to Sale over and above those which casually come onto the market from Individuals to answer their private views and necessities, would probably tend to depreciate the value of the shares, and that an increased subscription to the Loan or optional notes would be less likely to produce such effect, and at the same time raise for the Company's use more immediate money for the same quantity of stock . . .

In the following month £7,000 was raised in the way thus recommended. In May of the same year Homer was prompted by an increase in the market price of the company's shares[3] to offer proposals for the financing of work on the tunnel at Blisworth. Whereas a year ago it had seemed that capital could only be raised by the disposal of shares at a discount, and a railway had therefore been recommended as a temporary expedient, they would now fetch a premium of 60%, or, better still, 150% if issued in the form of optional notes. It was decided to raise £100,000 by the latter.[4] In 1801 a further £108,920 was raised by similar issues convertible into shares at the rate of £280, and 'as upon former occasions much Jealousy has arisen upon the right of subscribing to the sums that have already been borrowed', stock

---

[1] GJC 1/39, General Assembly and General Committee Minutes, 1793–8, 5 June 1798.

[2] GJC 1/40, 29 Jan. 1800.

[3] In April 1800 premia of £11 to £25 were reported, in May of 43–4 guineas, in June of £60 to £70 (GJC 1/40, 15 Apr. 20 May, 17–18 June 1800).

[4] GJC 1/40, 14 Mar., 20 May 1800.

and loan-holders were to be given a right of pre-emption (which they had not apparently been allowed before).[1] However, economic depression and the return of war in 1803 evidently depreciated the shares and precluded further issues on such favourable terms. In November 1802 it was decided to dispose of 2,345 shares of £100 among the company's proprietors and loan-holders.[2] In May 1805 it was reported that the shares stood at a discount of 2%.[3] In these circumstances the rates at which the issues of 1800–1 had been priced proved to be excessive and a Sinking Fund was set up to provide for their redemption.[4] In 1812 the ingenious Thomas Homer was appointed Superintendent to the newly-constituted Regent's Canal Company. In 1815 he was charged with and convicted for the embezzlement of its funds and sentenced to seven years' transportation.[5]

Because their economic positions were weaker, marketing methods of the kind employed by the Grand Junction were out of the question for most companies. However, their share prices may have benefited similarly from the comparative prosperity of 1800–2;[6] this would account for the succession of Acts passed in those years for the enlargement of capitals.

[1] GJC 1/40, 4 Nov. 1801.

[2] GJC 1/41, 2 Nov. 1802.

[3] House of Lords R.O., Committee Book no. 50 (1805), f. 324.

[4] Above, pp. 45–6. The option to convert the issue of £250 to stock ran until 25 Mar. 1812, and the option to convert that of £280 ran until 25 Mar. 1808.

[5] H. Spencer, *London's Canal. The History of the Regent's Canal* (1961), pp. 21, 37, 43, 46. Its line ran from the Grand Junction's basin at Paddington to the docks at Limehouse. Homer had been the first to promote the scheme in 1802.

[6] A. D. Gayer, W. W. Rostow, and A. J. Schwartz, *The Growth and Fluctuation of the British Economy 1790–1850* (Oxford, 1953), i. 8–9, 58 ff. For the recovery of dealings in Oxford Canal stock in 1800, see above, p. 102.

V

THE MOTIVES OF INVESTORS

WHY did men, and women, invest in canals? It seems likely that they usually did so for selfish rather than altruistic reasons; therefore two possible motives may be distinguished: on the one hand, the desire to reduce transport costs, and, on the other, the expectation of financial advantage through the receipt of dividends, interest payments, or the appreciation of the capital value of shares. For the sake of brevity, in the following pages the first will be referred to as the 'economic' motive and the second as the 'financial' motive. It is also useful to distinguish between those who promoted canal schemes and those who financed them. Having made these distinctions, it must be acknowledged that although they may be clear in principle they were rarely so in practice: promoters and financiers were often the same men, and with both proprietaries as a whole and individual shareholders motives might be mixed. It is, nevertheless, useful to maintain them, subject to this caveat, for the purposes of analysis.

In considering the question of motive we are faced with a problem which did not arise in the previous chapters devoted to matters of fact: although documentation of the history of canals is abundant, most is either formal or polemical in character. There is, for example, an extensive pamphlet literature ostensibly devoted to the statement by promoters of their aims, but, because this was directed as much to the members of parliament whose legislative sanction was sought as to potential investors, the eloquent protestations of disinterested concern for the public welfare of which it largely consists cannot be usefully brought to bear upon the problem under consideration here. Material giving a candid and authentic view of the aspirations of canal proprietors is scarce; most, such as it is, probably lies in personal and business papers outside the company records upon which this study is principally based.

It may be supposed that the investor subscribing for 'economic' reasons is someone directly concerned with efficiency in the means of communication, for example, a landowner, manufacturer, or trader in bulk commodities such as coal, timber, or corn; that in the locally circumscribed business-world of the eighteenth century he usually lives near the canal which he finances; and that in its management he requires that the tolls levied upon its traffic be low rather than that its profits and dividends be high. The investor whose motives are 'financial', on the other hand, may be of any or no occupation, so long as he has the means with which to pay his calls; he may be resident far from the enterprise which he underwrites; his principal concern will be for the amount and security of his dividend and for the capital value of his shares on the open market; as for rates of tonnage, he is content that they be whatever the traffic will bear.

The paradigm of the canal builder moved by 'economic' considerations is perhaps the author of the first true English canal, the Duke of Bridgewater. The Worsley Canal connected his mines with the town of Manchester and his remuneration came through the increased volume and increased profitability of the sale of his coal there. But the case of the Duke's second undertaking, the Manchester-Runcorn Navigation, is less clear. He certainly had a direct or 'economic' interest in Manchester's general prosperity, and the canal might also have been expected to extend the market for the output of his mines, but these possible benefits could not in themselves have provided a sufficient return on the expenditure of a quarter of a million pounds. He must therefore have expected to profit from the passage of other men's goods, his motives thus being 'financial' as well.

The example suggests some of the ambiguities which are to be met with in the consideration of this problem, particularly in the history of the 'first generation' of canals. The initiative for these undertakings came typically from men with a local, 'economic', interest in their completion: Birmingham manufacturers in the case of the Birmingham Canal,[1]

---

[1] Hadfield, *West Midlands*, pp. 63-64.

Bradford merchants in that of the Leeds and Liverpool,[1] while the campaign for the Trent and Mersey was led by Josiah Wedgwood, on behalf of the potters of Staffordshire, in conjunction with some of the principal local landowners;[2] and such men usually took many shares in their own promotions. But individuals with a direct interest in the reduction of transport costs account for only a part, and by no means the greater part, of the capital subscribed; and the pricing policies of completed canals do not seem to have been dictated by the interests of potential shippers.

We may begin by considering the Trent and Mersey Canal company, incorporated in 1766.[3] This concern was of crucial importance for the development of the Staffordshire pottery industry, and yet potters accounted for only 5% of its share and loan capital. The most notable sources of support were landowners (£141,100), London (£56,000), and the city of Lichfield (£46,500). It might be held that the landowners had an 'economic' interest, but of their contribution £46,750 was provided by one man, Samuel Egerton of Tatton Park and, however substantial a proprietor he may have been, it is difficult to suppose that he could have expected to be reimbursed for an outlay of this magnitude solely through the improvement of his estate. The same must be true of the Londoners; some may have had local interests but many were trades- and professional men apparently drawn in through the propaganda of the promoters. Finally there is the investment of the inhabitants of Lichfield, a city of genteel rentiers rather than of active industry for which much advantage could be expected from improved communications. This is how Boswell saw it in 1776:[4]

Very little business appeared to be going forward at Lichfield. I found however two strange manufactures for so inland a place, sail-cloth and streamers for ships; and I observed them making some saddle-cloths and dressing sheepskins: but upon the whole of the busy hand of industry seemed to be quite slackened. 'Surely, Sir, (said I) you are an idle set of

[1] Above, pp. 33–4; below, p. 151.

[2] Meteyard, *Life of Wedgwood*, i. 345 ff.

[3] Above, p. 29, for details.

[4] See H. Thorpe, 'Lichfield: A study of its growth and function', *Collections for a History of Staffordshire 1950–1* (1954), pp. 139–211, where the following passage from Boswell's *Life of Johnson* is quoted. The city was not, in fact, directly on the line of the canal.

people'. 'Sir, (said Johnson) we are a city of philosophers, we work with our heads, and make the boobies of Birmingham work for us with their hands.'

The city of Oxford might, perhaps, be similarly described, and during the 1770s and 1780s it was a notable source of support, to the amount of about £100,000, for the Oxford Canal, rather more than half of this sum being accounted for by the members of its colleges.[1] It seems likely that the motives of investors such as these were for the most part 'financial'.

This conclusion, based upon generalities, is confirmed if we proceed to particulars and examine the personal fortunes of some of the individuals who subscribed to stock or loan in the earlier canals. In many cases their occupations and the distribution of their assets are such as to suggest most strongly that they did so for the sake of the dividend or interest payments which were in prospect. Here are some details taken from the wills of proprietors or creditors of the Oxford Canal.[2] In 1787 Walter Ruding, Doctor of Physic and fellow of Merton College, left fourteen shares of £100 in this company and £200 in its loan. His other specific bequests included books, silverware, and £1,200 due to him on bonds from various relatives.[3] In the will of Henry Turner of Blenheim Park, gentleman, apparently a steward of the Duke of Marlborough, proved in 1785, the only specific bequest made is that of £700 worth of shares to two sons. Two other sons are mentioned, one of whom had been provided for at an earlier date.[4] In 1797 Joseph Parsons of Oxford, barber, left houses in St. Ebbes' and St. Aldate's, £700 in the company's loan, £150 standing in the Funds in his own name though in fact the property of his daughter, and £15.[5] John Jackson of Oxford, printer, had taken seven shares. His bequests in 1775 comprised £3,050 and annuities of £102.[6]

[1] Above, pp. 32–3.

[2] It is of course hazardous to attempt to assess a man's worth from his will, but most of those cited here are of bachelors or widowers, who are likely to have disposed of a large proportion of their estates by specific bequest.

[3] Bodleian Library, Dep. c. 103, ff. 73–4.

[4] Bodleian Library, MS. Wills Oxon. 100, Oxford Diocese Register of Wills, 1784–96, f. 48.

[5] Bodleian Library, Dep. c. 103, f. 117.

[6] Ibid., ff. 96–8. His second will of 1795 mentions £12,500, lands, three houses at Oxford, and new-built premises at Headington.

Joshua Green of Banbury, shag-manufacturer, had taken three shares. In 1777 he left £1,100 in trust for one of his three sons, a minor, to be invested in the Funds, on mortgage, or in the Oxford Canal, and a further £1,180.[1] An incomplete account of the will of Sir Charles Nourse of Oxford, surgeon, which was made and proved in 1789, mentions £19,000 in the Funds (par values), £1,300 in the stock and £8,000 in the loan of the Oxford Canal, £1,100 secured on the tolls of the Oxford Market (built in the 1770s), and £2,500 on the tolls of the Kidlington–Deddington Turnpike trust. His estate totalled about £50,000.[2]

Two shareholders in other canal companies may be mentioned. The note-books of Edward Sneyd of Lichfield, Esquire, whom I have classified as a 'capitalist', record that in 1777 he held 21 shares of £200 in the Trent and Mersey Canal, 10 of £145 in the Staffordshire and Worcestershire, and 5 of £140 in the Birmingham, a total investment of £6,350. The only other investment mentioned is that of £908 in the Funds, though between 1779 and 1782 a further £11,000 (par values) of such securities were added.[3] The will of Jeremiah Lowe of Coventry, silk-manufacturer, proved in 1794,[4] mentions £28,400 in trust moneys, legacies, and recent gifts, and also 30 shares in the Coventry Canal, 27 in the Oxford, 54 in the Grand Junction, 4 in the Leicestershire and Northamptonshire, 3 in the Wyrley and Essington, and 25 subscriptions to shares in the Rochdale, the last four companies being promotions of the 'second generation'. Thus roughly one third of that part of his not insubstantial estate which he specifically bequeathed was in canals. Unless the investment behaviour of these men is to be considered highly

[1] P.R.O., PROB 2, Prerogative Court of Canterbury Wills, 1777/266. For an early example of canal stock being used as a trust fund see P.R.O., Chancery Proceedings, C. 12/1418/12: John Gibbons of Birmingham, japanner, by his will of 1772 leaves four shares in the Birmingham Canal, their produce to be applied to the education of the children of Clement Pane also of Birmingham, japanner, until they reach the age of 21 years.

[2] *English Reports*, xxix. 872–3; xxx. 377; P.R.O., Chancery Proceedings, C. 12/457/19.

[3] William Salt Library, Stafford, H.M. 37/40.

[4] P.R.O., PROB 2, Prerogative Court of Canterbury Wills, 1794/317.

irrational, the canal companies of which they were members must have been expected to yield a 'financial' return.

It is possible that persons who lived near the line of a proposed canal might have supported it from a general interest in the improvement of their neighbourhood and without an expectation of immediate personal advantage, whether 'economic' or 'financial'. Such motives may have been important in particular cases, but it must be noticed that the average individual investment, although it varied considerably in size, was about four shares of £100. By contemporary standards the sum involved was considerable; the annual income of Colquhoun's 'average' shopkeeper was, for example, £200.[1] Thus most subscriptions towards canals cannot have been made, as towards an infirmary or a set of assembly rooms, merely out of a generalized local patriotism or sense of social duty. They were investments made by persons who expected a reasonably secure and profitable employment for their money. As was argued by a pamphleteer writing in 1788 about the proposed Kennet and Avon Canal,[2] the prospects of a sufficient subscription

must depend on the opinion of the public, as to the returns that are likely to be made by the canal. It is not the subscriptions that may be expected from the spirit of patriotism, or from the individuals through whose neighbourhood the canal may be carried, that will be sufficient to complete a work of this magnitude: but if the public is satisfied that the canal will answer the expectations of the projectors, that besides the country traffic, and marketing from place to place, there will be a considerable traffic between London and Bristol, that the shares will remain at par, and the dividends to be made to the proprietors of the produce arising from the canal, will pay more interest than can be made of money by any other means; people of all denominations will be glad to place their money to so good advantage, and to embrace an opportunity which offers them such considerable emolument . . .

But subscribers, although they may have been concerned for their dividends, were by no means 'blind', at least not in the first phase of canal building. The supply of information as to the quality of investments was imperfect and individuals were therefore obliged to exercise their personal judgement, which

[1] Colquhoun, *Treatise on the . . . British Empire* (1814), p. 125.
[2] *Observations on a Scheme for extending the Navigation of the Rivers Kennett and Avon . . . by a Canal from Newbury to Bath*, p. 12.

was necessarily based upon local knowledge. Many investors continued to act in this way until a much later date, as a witness before a parliamentary committee of inquiry in the mid-nineteenth century remarked:[1]

Take, for instance, turnpike bonds, it is within the county, a man sees the road, and judges of the probability of profit; and there is five per cent usually paid upon turnpike bonds . . .

Considerations such as these are apparently reflected in an early report on the promotion of the Leeds and Liverpool Canal:[2]

Though inland navigations have in general been deemed precarious undertakings, it is very remarkable that this canal meets with the approbation of persons of all denominations resident on its borders, and who best know the populous trading country through which it is to pass, in so much that as we are credibly informed the admission to become a proprietor is now solicited as a favour.

Thus the fact that most, though not all, of the shareholders in the 'first generation' of canals lived near the lines whose construction they financed cannot be taken to show that their motives as investors were 'economic' rather than 'financial'.

Canal companies usually preferred the payment of high dividends to their members to the imposition of low tolls on their traffic. The promoters of the Trent and Mersey, for example, had offered the prospective subscriber the satis-faction both of lending his assistance 'to so public a good' and also 'of receiving yearly 20£ interest for his 100£ so lent';[3] the proposal made by the Birmingham manufacturer Samuel Garbett, that a statutory limitation be imposed upon the company's dividends, was rejected. In 1767 Wedgwood, having received news from an M.P. sitting on the committee for the Forth and Clyde Canal bill, with which Garbett was also concerned as a proprietor of the Carron Iron Company, wrote gleefully to a correspondent:[4]

[1] Parl. Papers 1850, xix, Report from the Select Committee on Investments for the Savings of the Middle and Working Classes, Q. 673.

[2] York Courant, 26 June 1770, quoted Killick, 'Leeds and Liverpool Canal', p. 206.

[3] Phillips, Hist. Inland Navigation, p. 158.

[4] K. E. Farrer (ed.), Letters of Josiah Wedgwood 1762 to 1770 (n.d., n.p.), pp. 134–5. In 1768 a similar proposal was made to the promoters of the

You remember what plague & trouble our good frd. Mr Garbett gave us with his limitation scheme of 10 per ct. int. on the Navn. Capital. That very plan is now urged urged upon him & the intended proprietors of the Navigation sorely against their wills, & he is now reduced to the dilemma of proposing & defending a plan which he was before so vigorous in opposing and depreciating.

The Forth and Clyde Company was in fact the only one of the 'first generation' of promotions to be incorporated with a dividend limitation.[1]

It is, therefore, not at all surprising that from the very earliest years of canal navigation the stock of each company was traded at prices which reflected its financial prospects: Birmingham, and Staffordshire and Worcestershire commanded premia, Trent and Mersey remained at par, while Chester, Chesterfield, Coventry, and Oxford fell to discounts;[2] and the successful few attracted unfavourable comment:[3]

Subscribers are always looking after their private gain instead of the improvement of the Navigation; this is the Case att present upon the Birmingham Canal, for it is cramp'd in many particulars on account of the Expence, although att this time tho' only just finished, every £100 [recte £140] share sells for £170. If this additional value had been expended upon the Canal instead of falling into private pocketts, it would have been much more noble than it is.

With the subscribers to the 'first generation' of canals, therefore, 'financial' motives were powerful. It might nevertheless be conjectured that the motives of promoters are to be distinguished from those of investors along the following lines: promoters, typically merchants, manufacturers, landowners, etc., had an obvious 'economic' interest but were obliged, in order to ensure success for their costly and novel undertakings, to call upon the support of a wider investing public by offering 'financial' advantages. This supposition is in principle a reasonable one. For example, it is difficult to

Birmingham Canal, and was similarly opposed: Hadfield, *West Midlands*, p. 64. The promoters claimed that they were not expecting any return greater than 6% p.a.

[1] 8 George III *cap.* 63.

[2] Farrer (ed.), *Wedgwood Letters*, p. 129; Hopkinson, 'Inland Navigation in South Yorkshire and North Derbyshire', p. 239; above, pp. 101, 120–1.

[3] James Sharp, London Common Councillor to George III, 1770. Quoted Hadfield, *West Midlands*, p. 69.

see what 'financial' interest Wedgwood could have had in the Trent and Mersey—he took no shares in it—but he nevertheless opposed any limitation of the dividend, perhaps because he recognized that the resources of those with an 'economic' interest did not permit them to build the canal on their own account. As the sums required were large, outside support was needed and, as the enterprise was hazardous,[1] a return in excess of the legal rate of interest had to be offered. Thus all canals were financed in the first instance by equity rather than by loan capital.[2]

However, having postulated such a distinction between the motives of promoters and investors, we must notice that there are rarely any signs of it in the later history of canal companies; conflicts between 'economic' and 'financial' objectives in their management are few, even when the more favourably situated undertakings of the 'first generation' settled down to earn spectacular dividends for their shareholders at the expense of their customers.[3] Nor can this apparently unchallenged primacy of 'financial' interests be attributed to alterations in the character of proprietaries

[1] For the contemporary remarks about the promotion of the Leeds and Liverpool Canal, see above, p. 132.

[2] This may be contrasted with the financial organization of the less adventurous river works of the period, which usually relied upon mortgage finance, particularly when they entailed the improvement of an existing navigation rather than the creation of a new one. Thus the improvement of the river Lee navigation in Hertfordshire, undertaken in 1767 at the instigation of the brewers, maltsters, etc., who controlled it and are known to have had 'economic' interests at stake (P. Mathias, *The Brewing Industry in England, 1700–1830*, (Cambridge, 1959), pp. 441–7), was financed by borrowing £35,000 at 4% from persons who had no connection with the river's trade and whose interest could only have been 'financial'. For the details about these creditors, see B.T.H.R., Lee 2/6, Register of Assignments of Four per cent Securities 1768–1846.

[3] See below, pp. 175–8. See also Hadfield, *West Midlands*, p. 69, for Samuel Garbett's quarrel with the Birmingham Canal company in 1769, when he alleged that it ignored the public interest by not supplying coal as cheaply as possible. On the other hand, the men controlling the Carlisle Canal company, incorporated in 1819, are said to have reduced tolls to benefit their own businesses at the expense of the dividends of the general body of proprietors: W. T. Jackman, *The Development of Transportation in Modern England* (2nd edn., 1962), p. 418, n.l. This is the only case which I have noticed of a complaint of this kind. The company's subscription contract shows an exceptionally large number of small shareholders who were perhaps unable to uphold their own interests: House of Lords R.O., Deposited Plans, Carlisle Canal Subscription Contract, 1819.

through changes in shareholdings and the consequent super-
session of the influence of the original promoters: the rate of
turnover in the secondary market for canal shares was low,
such transactions as there were did not significantly alter the
occupational character of proprietaries within our period,
and most of the original members of committees of management held office for several years.[1] Therefore, all that can be
said of the 'economic' motive of promoters is that from the
first, through inclination and expediency, it coexisted with
the 'financial'; the fact that it was compromised or forgotten
with so little obvious difficulty suggests also that from the
first its strength *vis-à-vis* its alternative was limited.

The preceding discussion has been confined to canals of
the 'first generation' because it is with these that ambiguities
of motive are most troublesome. During the canal mania, on
the other hand, the situation is clearer. There is little direct
evidence as to the motives of the new lines' promoters—they
were still usually local commercial men and agriculturalists—
but it is noteworthy that with only eight of more than fifty
companies was the dividend formally limited,[2] although at
this time any subscription list could be filled with ease. As
for the general body of subscribers, what it wanted is clear:
'the subscribers to these new canals are inspirited by the
enormous profits (30 and 40 per cent) made by the proprietors of the old canals . . .'[3] The expectation of such
returns fuelled the brief frenzy of speculation. Thus early in
1793 Edward Webb, a Leicester tallow-chandler, took some
shares in the Caistor Canal, a short 'agricultural' line in North
Lincolnshire.[4] He did so, on his own admission, in the belief
that 'the said Canal was likely to be one of the most
advantageous Canals in the Country and would pay the
Subscribers thereto Twenty Pounds per Cent and that the
Article of Wool alone would pay five per Cent . . .' The
subscribers to the Leicester Navigation negatived a motion
that the dividend be limited to 15% and adopted as the

---

[1] See below, pp. 183-5.
[2] Below, p. 137.
[3] *The Universal British Directory of Trade, Commerce and Manufacture . . .*, ii
(1793), 204.
[4] P.R.O., Chancery Proceedings, C.12/652/27, C.12/659/17.

motto of their company a line from Horace: *Liquidus Fortuna Rivus Inauret.*[1]

A further guide to the new companies' aims is provided by their reaction to the proposal made by Pitt in 1796 that, as a measure of war finance, a tax be imposed upon the carriage of goods by inland navigation. The management committee of the Cromford Canal complained that 'the proposed augmentation of the rates of tonnage will operate so far in favour of the land carriage as to be likely to be injurious to the interest of the Canal Company, whose speculation has been already detrimental to themselves and useful to the public.'[2] It requested exemption for their company, at least until the proprietors had received 'a reasonable interest . . . for the capital expended and the risque incurred'. Between February and June 1797 many companies sent delegates to a conference at London in order to put pressure on the prime minister against the bill (he eventually dropped it).[3] The statement of objection to the tax upon which they agreed was as follows:[4]

That as the highest Rates of Tonnage consistent with the Interest of the Proprietors of Navigations are already taken any addition must therefore lessen the trade unless such addition be paid out of the Pockets of the Proprietors.

That any parliamentary Charge tending to diminish the Income of the Proprietors will operate as a tax upon them and therefore be contrary to the express provisions contained in most of the Acts for making the respective Navigations.

That such diminution will further reduce the value of Navigation Stock which has already in many instances fallen below its original Cost and lessen the Security of Mortgages of such Navigations.

That a tax or Charge so circumstanced will tend to prevent compleating Navigations now executing and the undertaking of new ones.

That Mortgagees of Navigation Interests who may be regarded as equitable Proprietors will receive a dividend in the shape of Interest much greater than the original Proprietors (as very few receive 5 pr.cent upon their Capital) and yet the latter will bear the tax for both.

[1] 'May the liquid stream of fortune cover you with gold.' LCN 1/1, 24 Jan. 1791.

[2] CRC 1/1, 22 Dec. 1796.

[3] LLC 1/50, Minutes of the Delegates of the Proprietors of Inland Navigations 1797. Representatives of 28 companies made an appearance, 20 of these being promotions of the 1790s and 2 (the Leeds and Liverpool, and Dudley) older companies which were still building.   [4] Ibid., 9 Feb. 1797.

That the tax by whomsoever paid will be unequal not only with respect to the value of the Articles but also with respect to the distance such Articles may be conveyed.

That it will in many Cases tend to give a preference to Land Carriage.

That discouraging the making of navigable Canals will tend to prevent the great public Advantages expected to arise from lessening the number of Draught Horses and also the free conveyance of heavy Articles which may be necessary for the improvement of Agriculture in General and of Waste Lands in particular and the carrying on of Manufactures.

That it is presumed the produce of any other public Undertaking however lucrative hath not yet been taxed and it is conceived that Navigations are objects of national support particularly as they very much promote the improvement of Agriculture, the convenience of trade, the reduction of the price of the necessaries of Life, and the increase of Revenue in various Ways.

That from all the information which has yet been obtained there is great reason to apprehend the tax (were it politic) will not be effective.

The primary concern of the canal companies is the financial interests of their own proprietors. The more general effects which the tax would have had upon transport costs and the interests of producers are referred to only as an afterthought.

It is true that in a minority of undertakings such interests may have assumed greater weight; the only companies to be subjected by their Acts of incorporation to a limitation of the dividend all date from the period of the canal mania.[1] But in all of these the involvement of persons with direct interests[2] was greater than usual and that of members of the general investing public was less. Of one of their number, the Montgomeryshire, it was alleged:[3]

This Canal was not undertaken with the view of large profit accruing from the Tolls; for there is not even a Probability that any such can arise; and therefore the Subscribers were the Noblemen and Gentlemen either possessed of estates in this County, or resident therein, who had for their Object the Extension of Agriculture, the Reduction of

[1] They were the Nottingham, Derby, Grantham, Sleaford, Horncastle, Chelmer and Blackwater, Montgomeryshire, and Glamorganshire Navigations. The limitation was 10% in the case of the Montgomeryshire, and 8% for the remainder, any surplus remaining after these had been paid to be applied to the reduction of tolls, Priestley, *Historical Account* . . . For the circumstances of the Nottinghamshire Canal limitation, see p. 154.

[2] Ironmasters in the case of the Glamorganshire, agriculturalists or coal owners in the remainder.

[3] Quoted Hadfield, *West Midlands*, p. 190.

Horses . . . the increase of Horned Cattle, and the Preservation of the
Roads; with the consequent Advantage to the Public.

Nevertheless, even here investors from the urban middle class
appear,[1] and the company abandoned work on the line in
1797, before it had been completed, because of 'the present
scarcity of money'. The payment of dividends began in 1805,
considerably sooner than with many of the 'commercial
projects' which it affected to scorn.[2]

It is therefore to be concluded that the motives of many
promoters and most investors were more 'financial' than
'economic'.

At this point we may recall the difference which has been
noticed between the history of canal finance at Liverpool and
at Bristol.[3] It may be explained as follows: Liverpool
promoted and financed some early local navigations for
primarily 'economic' reasons; Bristol did not because its
geographical situation made such enterprises unfeasible. Later
Bristol invested extensively in canals for 'financial' reasons,
because it possessed large balances of surplus capital; Liverpool did not because it was not similarly burdened with idle
assets in search of employment.

The canal mania at Bristol coincided with a similar local
enthusiasm for the speculative building of upper-class houses.
It, too, was terminated by the commercial crisis of 1793,
after several thousands of pounds, most of which belonged to
local men and women, had been sunk in bricks and mortar;
the principal terraces and crescents of Clifton date from this
time.[4] Bristol's building boom was the local manifestation of
a national trend[5] but it was distinctive in its extravagance
and, once again, the contrast with Liverpool is marked.
There, at a rather earlier date, a local observer had remarked
upon the narrowness and lack of uniformity of the streets
and offered as an explanation 'that spirit of frugality which

---

[1] Above, p. 53.

[2] Hadfield, *West Midlands,* pp. 192–3; MONC 1/12, reports for 1798 and
1809.

[3] Above, pp. 92–6.

[4] W. Ison, *The Georgian Buildings of Bristol* (1952), especially pp. 24–8; J.
Latimer, *Annals of Bristol in the Eighteenth Century* (Frome, 1893), pp. 493–5.

[5] T. S. Ashton, *Economic Fluctuations in England, 1700–1800* (Oxford,
1959), pp. 100–3, 164–9; H. A. Shannon, 'Bricks—A Trade Index, 1785–1849',
Economica, n.s., no. 3 (Aug. 1934), pp. 316–7.

always prevails among a people who are beginning the career of commerce'.[1] Liverpool's inhabitants could not be so described by the 1790s, but their building schemes remained modest. Kent Square (formed *c.* 1783), for example, 'like many other similar attempts in Liverpool . . . was never completed. A few good houses were built, and in the course of time, the remainder of the land not being taken up, was converted into cooperages and yards'.[2]

The reason for the two ports' differing propensities for speculative investment is probably to be sought in their respective economic circumstances. The principal trade in which they were engaged, the West Indian, required in its expansionary phases very considerable investments or credits, but could otherwise be made to yield a comfortable surplus. Bristol in the later eighteenth century was in relative decline as a port and active trading centre, while Liverpool continued to enjoy a rapid growth which is known to have stretched the resources of its merchants.[3] John Pinney is Bristol's best-documented West Indian. After returing to England in 1783 his main business objective was the contraction of overseas interests and the repatriation of the greater part of his fortune; he must be a good representative of his city for this unheroic chapter in its commercial history. Pinney rapidly accumulated surplus capital: by February 1793 he was considering investment in the American Funds. In the previous month his firm had subscribed for ten shares in the Bristol and Cirencester Canal, and Pinney personally took one share in the Dorset and Somerset Canal of 1795.[4] In the event the commercial crisis put an end to his plans for North American investment, the Bristol and Cirencester Canal was

[1] William Enfield, *An Essay Towards the History of Liverpool* (1774 edn.), p. 20.

[2] J. A. Picton, *Memorials of Liverpool, Historical and Topographical* (1873), ii. 328.

[3] R. Pares, *Merchants and Planters*, Econ. Hist. Rev. Supplement no. 4 (Cambridge, 1960), Chapter 4; S. G. Checkland, 'Finance for the West Indies, 1780–1815', *Econ. Hist. Rev.*, 2nd Ser., x (1957–8), 461–9. For shipping and trade statistics see A. F. Williams, 'Bristol Port Plans and Improvement Schemes in the 18th Century', *Trans. Bristol and Gloucs. Arch. Soc.* lxxxi (1962), and C. N. Parkinson, *The Rise of the Port of Liverpool* (Liverpool, 1952).

[4] R. Pares, *A. West-India Fortune* (1950), especially chapters 8, 12, 13; Bristol University Library, Pinney MSS., Letter Book no. 11: John Pinney 1792–6, ff. 39, 55, and Ledger no. 11: John Pinney 1789–1800, ff. 70, 95–6.

never executed, and it appears that he took no part in speculative building; most of the growing family fortune was put into green acres. But there must have been other local men and women, directly or indirectly sharing in the returning stream of imperial tribute, who were more adventurous in their choice of investments.[1]

At Bristol, a stagnant or slowly growing economy yielded surplus capital, and the desire to employ this capital as profitably as possible led to speculative investment in canals. This sequence of cause and effect recurs: in the 1770s the Quakers of Norwich assisted their industrially more successful co-religionists through their contribution to the Leeds and Liverpool Canal;[2] in 1782, when their trades were prejudiced by the American War of Independence, London slave- and colonial merchants subscribed to the Thames and Severn Canal;[3] in the early 1790s Coventry, with its sluggish silk industry, and many of the quiet market towns of the East Midlands were, together with Bristol, among the most notable centres of the canal mania.[4]

This line of reasoning may be reinforced by a consideration of the various propensities of the counties of England for investment in the public Funds. The following statistics are derived from an analysis of the geographical distribution of stockholders between 1780 and 1793 in the Four Per Cent Consolidated Annuities for Twenty Eight Years.[5] A comparison has been made with the distribution of population as reported in the census of 1801.

---

[1] For a further indication of surplus capital at Bristol, see the contemporary newspaper advertisements by attorneys of money to be lent. Thus, in *Felix Farley's Bristol Journal*, 30 July 1791, Messrs. Hughes and Anderdon offered on behalf of their clients the sums of £35,000, £20,000, £10,000, £10,000, and £5,000, at 4.5%. For J. P. Anderdon's later connections, as a partner of London merchants, with West-India Finance, see *Caribbeana*, i. 290; iii. 304; iv. 100.

[2] Above, p. 35.

[3] Above, pp. 64–6.

[4] Above, pp. 86–92; below, pp. 180–2.

[5] The analysis is based upon the index to the ledgers for that Stock in the custody of Bank of England. I am grateful to the Bank of England for permission to undertake this research, and for assistance rendered.

	Number of Stockholders	Number of Stockholders per 100,000 population
London and Home Counties		
Middlesex and Surrey	11,765	1,082
Berkshire	167	153
Hertfordshire	129	132
Kent	406	132
Essex	207	91
Buckinghamshire	91	85
Sussex	41	26
West		
Gloucestershire	176	70
Hampshire	148	67
Wiltshire	124	67
Somerset	181	66
Dorset	43	37
Devon	85	25
Cornwall	18	10
East		
Suffolk	98	47
Bedfordshire	25	39
Cambridgeshire	32	36
Norfolk	97	35
Huntingdonshire	10	27
Lincolnshire	39	19
Midlands		
Worcestershire	88	63
Oxfordshire	63	57
Northamptonshire	46	35
Warwickshire	59	28
Nottinghamshire	36	26
Herefordshire	21	24
Shropshire	41	24
Rutland	4	24
Staffordshire	41	17
Leicestershire	21	16
Derbyshire	23	14
North		
Yorkshire	160	19
Durham	27	17
Northumberland	16	14
Cumberland	16	14
Westmoreland	6	14
Cheshire	20	10
Lancashire	60	9

Wales and Monmouthshire	49	8
Scotland	57	4

It will be seen that the propensity of counties to invest in this stock is an inverse function of their distance from London and also of the vigour of their economies. Thus the number of stockholders as a proportion of the population is lower in Lancashire and Cheshire than in the counties immediately adjacent, and it is lower in such counties as Warwickshire, Staffordshire, Nottinghamshire, and Leicestershire than in, say, Norfolk, Worcestershire, Gloucestershire, and Somerset.

It is useful to consider separately the investments of certain provincial towns.

	Number of Stockholders	Number of Stockholders per 100,000 population
Bath	138	429
Bristol	99	156
Liverpool	46	59
Birmingham	19	26
Manchester	8	10

Bath, a city of rentiers, is perhaps a case apart, but Bristol's high participation rate is especially to be noted. Relative economic decline is accompanied by the export of capital.

VI

LANDOWNERS AND CANALS

IT is sometimes asserted that eighteenth-century English landowners played a distinguished, perhaps even a principal part in the promotion and finance of canal building. In England, the argument runs, proprietors commonly took an active and intelligent interest in the improvement of their estates as agricultural enterprises and also in the exploitation of any mineral assets, particularly coal measures, that lay beneath them. Therefore they placed their political and economic resources in support of the development of necessary facilities for communication; manufacturing industry, as it was widely dispersed about the countryside, stood to benefit both directly and indirectly from such a disposition. The progress of industrialization here thus enjoyed an advantage unknown in the countries of continental Europe where, for various reasons, the concerns of landowners and manufacturers were not interrelated to the same degree.[1] There is some truth in all this, though perhaps not as much as is often thought. An attempt is made here to put the contribution of landowners to the extension of canal navigation into proper perspective.

In Chapter II an estimate was made of the parts taken by the different occupational classes in the finance of canals; this was compared with contemporary accounts of the distribution of the nation's larger incomes. The investments of landowners (Class I, Peers, and Class II, Landed Gentlemen) appear to have been no more than proportionate to their incomes.[2] It therefore cannot be argued convincingly that in this respect the contribution of landowners to the development of canals was in any way distinctive.

[1] For versions of this argument see H. J. Habakkuk, 'Economic Functions of English Landowners in the Seventeenth and Eighteenth Centuries', *Explorations in Entrepreneurial History*, vi (1953), 92–102; E. J. Hobsbawm, *Industry and Empire* (1968), p. 16; H. Perkin, *The Origins of Modern English Society, 1780–1880* (1969), pp. 75–7.

[2] Above, pp. 74–6.

The matter cannot, however, be adequately dealt with in a merely statistical fashion, and the remainder of this chapter is devoted to the consideration of 'qualitative' factors. First, it is necessary to consider briefly the problem of land purchase.

A canal, according to its width and the extent of its wharfs, reservoirs, and other ancillary works, usually required between five and eight acres of land per mile, the purchase price of which appears in general to have accounted for about a tenth of its cost, though this proportion varied considerably.[1] By their Acts of incorporation the canal companies were given powers to acquire by compulsory purchase the land they required. Irreconcilable disputes over the price to be paid were referable in the first instance to a body of named Commissioners (usually the principal local landowners), and in the second, if their verdict failed to satisfy, to a jury appointed by the magistrates at Quarter Session.[2] It has been suggested, though this is a matter of some debate,[3] that in the nineteenth century landowners took advantage of the needs of railway companies by demanding excessive prices for the land which they required. To what extent were eighteenth-century canal companies liable to similar exactions?

In cases where it was necessary to make special payments to buy off opposition it can perhaps be assumed that a price substantially above the market rate was effectively being paid. The Duke of Bridgewater was obliged to pay Sir Richard Brooke £1,900 for permission to take his navigation through the latter's estate;[4] the Coventry Canal paid the Hon. Charles Finch £500 for the right to go through his garden;[5] the Grand Junction Canal paid the Earl of Clarendon £5,000 'for the accommodation of carrying the canal through his Lordship's Park and Grounds' (this course was necessary to avoid tunnelling), and a similar payment of £15,000 was made to the Earl of Essex;[6] the Brecknock and

---

[1] See below, pp. 146-9.
[2] Hadfield, *British Canals*, p. 45.
[3] H. Pollins, 'A Note on Railway Constructional Costs 1825-1850', *Economica*, xix (1952), 395-406; J. R. Kellett, *The Impact of Railways on Victorian Cities*, (1969), pp. 427-31.
[4] Northamptonshire R.O., E.B. 1460, f. 66.
[5] CVC 1/3, Minutes 1777-90, 5 Sept. 1787.
[6] GJC 1/39, Minutes 1793-8, 4 Mar. 1795.

Abergavenny Canal paid Mr. William Morgan £1,500 in addition to the usual price of the land for the right to cut through his estate at Mamhilad.[1] Similarly, the canal companies usually appear to have been the aggrieved parties in those cases where disputes over valuations were sufficiently serious to be recorded in their minute books. According to the committee of the Leeds and Liverpool Canal in 1773, 30 years' purchase was the usual rate in the parts of Yorkshire through which their line ran, but in some cases it was necessary to give more than this. The landowners of Bingley were especially troublesome. The commissioners, some of them acting as judges in their own cause, made what were considered to be exorbitant awards of up to £160 per acre, although a jury later reduced these to an average of about £70 per acre. As rents ranged from about 20 shillings to 45 shillings per acre these would seem to be generous.[2] A few years later the Earl of Stamford created difficulties over the purchase of his land by the Stourbridge Canal, in which he held shares, and succeeded in eliciting offers of £100 and 100 guineas per acre, almost certainly excessive prices for land in the Pensnett Chase area through which the canal ran (Lord Dudley, another shareholder, accepted £12. 10s. per acre for some of his land on the Chase which was required for a reservoir).[3]

One example has been noticed of an individual, probably not a 'gentleman', who made speculative purchases in advance of a canal in order to profit on the resale. In 1793 a Mr. Dobbs demanded of the Worcester and Birmingham Canal £90 per acre for land which he had bought eleven months earlier at the rate of £25 (the company offered £60 per acre).[4] By 1810 the stakes had been raised. In that year Dobbs took before the commissioners his claim for £300 per acre on ten and a half acres of water-meadow which he admitted to having bought three years before for £1,000, knowing that it was designed by the canal company as the site for a reservoir. The company itself offered Dobbs £135

---

1 BAC 1/4, Minutes 1802–10, 29 May 1810.
2 Killick, 'Leeds and Liverpool Canal', pp. 210–6; LLC 1/2, Minutes 1770–82, 1 Feb. 1773.
3 STN 1/3, Minutes 1776–83, 28 Oct. 1777, 21 Apr. 1778, 9 May 1780.
4 WOBC 1/4, Committee Minutes 1791–1800, 2 Jan. 1793.

per acre (£4. 10s. at thirty years' purchase).[1] Unfortunately in neither case is the outcome of these disputes known.

Nevertheless, extravagant demands of this kind were not common; usually negotiations with proprietors went smoothly. Sometimes these were begun before the Act of incorporation was sought, in order to obviate opposition.[2] Between 1788 and 1827 the commissioners were called only nine times by the Thames and Severn Canal, though the infrequency with which this procedure was used may have been due in part to the fact the company thought there was little advantage to be derived from it: in 1827 a leading member of the company alleged that commissioners almost always decided against canals in disputes with landowners.[3] The prices commonly paid by this company were 27 to 30 years' purchase on rentals of 14 to 60 shillings per acre. In the late 1760s and early 1770s the Droitwich Canal paid an average of about £60 per acre on its purchases.[4] In 1770 Sir Roger Newdigate asked £950 for $12\frac{1}{2}$ acres (i.e. £76 per acre) required by the Coventry Canal.[5] By 20 August 1778, $63\frac{3}{4}$ miles of the Oxford Canal had been completed, at a cost of £205,148, £26,414 (13%) of which had been spent on land, suggesting, at 7 acres per mile, an average of about £60 per acre.[6]

Prices paid during the second phase of canal building were of a similar order. In Leicestershire during the 1790s and 1800s they averaged about £75 per acre.[7] In 1798 the engineer of the Oakham Canal included 80 acres of land at £60 per acre as part (19%) of his estimate of £24,979 as the cost of completing the line.[8] In a notebook kept in the latter part of 1794 by agents of the Warwick and Birmingham Canal employed to negotiate with landowners on behalf of

---

[1] Birmingham Reference Library, Jewel Baillie MSS., 83 b/10.

[2] For example, the Rochdale Canal promoters in 1793. *H.C.J.* lv. 533; P.R.O., Chancery Proceedings, C. 12/1417/19, C./1421/18.

[3] Household, 'Thames and Severn', pp. 173–5.

[4] Calculated from Worcestershire R.O., 614/56, Droitwich Borough Records, bundle of agreements by Droitwich Canal with landowners for purchases.

[5] Warwickshire R.O., C.R. 136A/7, Newdigate Diary, 31 May 1770.

[6] Bodleian Library, Dep. a. 16, Oxford Canal Accounts.

[7] Calculated from Leicestershire R.O., Q.S. 50/1, Enrolments of Bargains and Sales to the Companies of Proprietors of Navigations, Vol. i, 1792–1808.

[8] Tew, *Oakham Canal*, p. 36.

the company, prices of about £40, £45, or £60 per acre are common. The annual rental of arable land was usually assessed at roughly 30 shillings per acre, of meadow land from 2 to 3 guineas.[1] By 1816 the Wilts and Berks Canal company had spent £283,101 on capital account, of which £50,669 (18%) was for 'Land, Damages, and Expences of settling for the same'.[2] The average price given had been £80 per acre.[3] By 18 August 1795 £296,402 had been spent on the works of the Grand Junction Canal,[4] and by March 1796, £55,569 had been spent on land.[5] The figures are perhaps too widely separated in time to be considered together, but they do suggest that this company was finding it necessary to devote an unusually large proportion of its resources to the purchase of land (it is perhaps for this reason that a report was prepared on the subject). This may be accounted for by the substantial sums paid to the Earls of Clarendon and Essex[6] which are included in this total, and by the high property values obtaining in Middlesex where work had begun. Meadow land near Uxbridge had been valued at £4 to £5 per acre rental and 33 to 35 years' purchase (i.e. £132 to £175 per acre).[7]

These data may be compared with contemporary estimates of land values, for which the most convenient source is the series of *County Reports* submitted to the Board of Agriculture: 18 shillings per acre per annum was considered a usual rate in Warwickshire, though from 15 to 35 shillings for inclosed pasture in the southern and eastern parts of the county;[8] 20 shillings for inclosed land in Northamptonshire;[9] 30 shillings in Leicestershire, but from £3 to £5 or more for 'water meadow land and good grass and other land near

[1] Birmingham Ref. Lib., Jewel Baillie MSS. 308.

[2] Swindon Public Lib., Wilts and Berks Canal Coll., no. 32, Ledger 1810–17, f. 107.

[3] Calculated from loc. cit., no. 1, Copy Book of Conveyances 1798–1816.

[4] Buckinghamshire R.O., Way MSS. D/W, 96/12.

[5] GJC 1/39, Minutes 1793–98, 15 Mar. 1796.

[6] See above, p. 144.

[7] Buckinghamshire R.O., D/W 94.

[8] John Wedge, *General View of the Agriculture of Warwick* (1794), pp. 12, 21.

[9] James Donaldson, *General View of the Agriculture of the County of Northampton* (Edinburgh, 1794), p. 14.

towns';[1] 30 shillings for arable and pasture in the Vale of the White Horse, 40 to 50 shillings for meadow, though as much as £3. 10s. at Abingdon;[2] in Middlesex 'for several miles East, North and West of London . . . from four to six pounds an acre'.[3] According to Arthur Young[4] the number of years' purchase current for land was as follows:

1768–1773	32
1778–1789	$23\frac{1}{4}$
1792–1799	27
1805–1811	28

Rates such as these accord fairly well with those paid by the canal companies, although I have made no attempt to take into account variations in time and place.

Another possible procedure might be to compare the rates which, in their estimates of expense, the companies had anticipated they would have to give for land, with those which the proprietors in fact secured. However the results yielded by this line of inquiry are both limited and equivocal. Although it was often the misfortune of committees of management to have to explain to their shareholders that estimates had been exceeded and that additional funds would be required, attempts to state the reasons for this in lucid, quantitative terms are notably few. Indeed it was only from 1794 that canal promoters were required to submit detailed accounts of anticipated expenses to parliament[5] and before that date such accounts were rarely published, even if they were prepared. Thus both the Trent and Mersey and the Staffordshire and Worcestershire companies spoke vaguely of 'the great Increase in the Value of Land, and Wages of Artists and Labourers, and . . . other unforeseen circumstances and expences' as the circumstances which required an increase of

[1] William Pitt, *General View of the Agriculture of the County of Leicester* (1813), pp. 45–6.

[2] William Mavor, *General View of the Agriculture of Berkshire* (1813), pp. 83–4.

[3] Thomas Baird, *General View of the Agriculture of the County of Middlesex* (1793), pp. 11–12.

[4] A Young, *An Enquiry into the Progressive Value of Money in England* (1812), p. 99. See also Norton, Trist, and Gilbert, 'A Century of Land Values: England and Wales', *Journal of the Royal Statistical Society*, liv (1891), reprinted in E. M. Carus-Wilson (ed.), *Essays in Economic History*, iii (1962), 128–31.

[5] *H.C.J.* xlix. 473–5.

their authorized capital in 1770,[1] but in neither case do the records survive with which these generalities might be put upon a statistical footing. The necessary information does survive for a few later companies. In May 1792 the committee of the Cromford Canal prepared an account to explain an anticipated increase of £10,022 over the £49,973 originally estimated in the cost of completing their line: £1,000 of the excess costs were attributed to the 'extraordinary expence' of land purchased from Sir Richard Arkwright.[2] On the other hand, in a similar statement prepared in 1795 by the engineer of the Nottingham Canal, expenditure on land was not a cause of the escalation of costs: it had accounted for £6,270 (13%) in the original estimate of £45,985 and £6,270 (9%) in the revised total of £67,303. The discrepancy was accounted for entirely by increases in the costs of the works.[3]

On the whole it appears that the canal companies were not held to ransom by the owners of the properties through which they ran. Those obviously unreasonable demands to which they were obliged to submit reflect the obstructiveness or greed of individuals and not the general opposition of local landed society.[4] If the prices given were perhaps rather generous, account must be taken of the fact that from their nature canals often took their course through valuable meadow land and that their needs were peculiar, sometimes causing inconvenience to owners and occupiers,[5] although they were required by their Acts to make accommodation bridges and to purchase small plots severed by the works,

[1] Preambles to 10 George III *caps.* 102 and 103.

[2] CRC 1/1, Minutes 1789–99, 29 May 1792.

[3] NC 1/2, Minutes 1792–7, 4 May 1792. Similarly, Rennie's account of why the Kennet and Avon had exceeded its estimates in 1801 makes no mention of the price of land, House of Lords R.O., House of Lords Committee Book no. 46 (1801), f. 111.

[4] One exception must be noticed to this rule. The Gloucester and Berkeley was required under the terms of its Act of incorporation to give 38 years' purchase for all land taken by its line, a rate which the engineer in his report of January 1796 described as '10 or 12 years in my opinion too much in the present value of land and money'. But this stipulation was, as the committee justly remarked, 'unprecedented': 33 George III *cap.* 97; GBC 1/1, Minutes 1793–1823, 31 Mar. 1794, 8 Jan. 1796; and see below, p. 156.

[5] For example, the damage done to adjacent farms by the 'irregular heaps' of earth left by the works of the Grand Junction Canal: John Middleton, *View of the Agriculture of Middlesex* (1807), p. 533.

and separate payments were usually made for damages. Furthermore, sympathetic proprietors sometimes afforded relief to a hardpressed company by allowing the purchase money due to them to remain out at interest until a more convenient time,[1] or to take the form of a perpetual rent charge. One case has been noticed where payment was accepted in the form of shares which were of little intrinsic value.[2] It may thus be concluded that landowners usually accepted fair prices for their property.

The most plausible argument which has been adduced in favour of English landowners as the patrons of canal building is that their financial contribution, although in statistical terms relatively modest, was strategically important and was accompanied by equally valuable, though less tangible, assistance in the field of public relations. It was the Duke of Bridgewater who in the 1760s was the first to demonstrate on a large scale the potentialities of the new means of communication and it was the Trent and Mersey Canal company, very largely financed by other landholders, many of them his relatives, which was the first to follow his example. Thereafter, it is argued, when the utility and profitability of canal navigation had been established beyond doubt, its extension could be based upon an investing public which was socially more diverse, but due credit must be given to the pioneers.[3] However this argument, although correct in many respects, requires some qualification.

There can be no doubt that the Duke of Bridgewater through his remarkable enterprises, the Worsley (1759–1765) and Manchester–Runcorn (1762–1780) Navigations, gave a powerful impetus to the extension of canal building and that effectively, if not literally, he was its pioneer in this country. Dr. Barker, it is true, has demonstrated in great detail that Smiles's cursory but widely credited dismissal of Brindley's

---

[1] For example, Lord Spencer and the Oxford Canal, for land at Wormleighton taken at £65 per acre: OXC 1/4, Committee Minutes 1787–97, 9 July 1787.

[2] Lincolnshire A.O., T.L.E. I/1/9 (Horncastle Navigation). Canals were commonly obliged by their Acts to serve the interests of agriculture by providing free passage for manures and roadstone. This, however, is a factor which defies quantification.

[3] See, for example, G. E. Mingay, *English Landed Society in the Eighteenth Century* (1962), pp. 189–201. Professor Mingay's account of landlord enterprise in canals is more exhaustive than illustrative.

engineering predecessors and of all navigation schemes of an earlier date than 1759 was unwarrantable. The Newry Canal in Ireland had preceded Bridgewater's undertaking by almost a generation and the Sankey Navigation had done so by four years.[1] Furthermore, in 1754 a bill had been introduced in Parliament for making a canal from Salford to the coalfield at Leigh, but was defeated by the strength of vested interests, including landowners and turnpike trustees.[2] In 1755 a survey is said to have been made at the expense of the Corporation of Liverpool for a canal from the Trent to the Mersey, and in late 1758 and early 1759 Brindley was definitely engaged on a similar undertaking at the expense of Lords Gower and Anson.[3] With precursors as numerous as these the inference might be made that Bridgewater's example was superfluous. It must however be recalled that his first canal, which crossed watersheds and entailed spectacular engineering work (the underground tunnelling, the Barton aqueduct, etc.), enjoyed a considerable éclat, which the Sankey Navigation, for instance, did not. The latter followed its river valley, and contemporaries may be pardoned for being unable to distinguish it from navigation works of the more traditional kind such as, for example, the Kennet Navigation of the 1720s which had more than eleven miles of artificial cuts.[4] But men came to the banks of the Mersey to see and wonder, and they recorded for posterity the effect which their visits had upon them. In the case of the Leeds and Liverpool Canal it was through the report on the Bridgewater navigations, brought back in about 1766 by the Halifax engineer John Longbottom, that the merchants and woolstaplers of Bradford were finally induced to undertake a canal over the Pennines via the valleys of the Aire and Ribble, a scheme which had·been agitated in general terms for many years but which only 'the late improvements in canal naviga-

[1] T. C. Barker, 'The Beginnings of the Canal Age in the British Isles', in L. S. Pressnell (ed.), *Studies in the Industrial Revolution* (Manchester, 1960), pp. 1–22; *idem*, 'The Sankey Navigation'.

[2] V. I. Tomlinson, 'Salford Activities connected with the Bridgewater Navigation', *Transactions of the Lancs. and Chesh. Antiq. Soc.* lxvi (1956–7), 57–9.

[3] Hadfield, *West Midlands*, p. 19 and references.

[4] Thacker, *Kennet Country*, pp. 309 ff.

tion made by a noble lord' had shown to be practicable.[1]
Elsewhere it was acknowledged that[2]

When the utility of Canal navigations had been manifested by a noble
Duke who was their original promoter in this country, a grand design
was formed by two distinct Companies in the year 1766 [i.e. the Trent
and Mersey, and the Staffordshire and Worcestershire], to open a
communication between the ports of Bristol, Liverpool and Hull, by a
general Inland Navigation, which would connect those seaports with the
large manufacturing towns of the midland Counties ...

Once again this was a project conceived and canvassed many
years before[3] which was set on foot under the inspiration of
Bridgewater's example.

But although his enterprise is historically important it does
not provide, in itself, a sufficient basis for generalization
about the economic functions of the eighteenth-century
English landowner. Contemporaries wondered not merely
that the Worsley Navigation should have been built at all, but
also that it should have been built by a peer: 'When the
influence of exalted rank, and the power of large possessions,
are thus nobly and usefully exerted, they confer additional
lustre on the possessor: and such a laudable application of
the gifts of fortune is so rare that it ought not to pass
unnoticed.'[4] They were perhaps aware that the part which
the aristocracy had played in the earlier history of river
navigation had not been distinguished;[5] their judgement was
certainly confirmed by the later history of canal building.

To take the 'first generation' of canal promotions,
although local landowners offered substantial support to the

---

[1] Killick, 'Leeds and Liverpool Canal', pp. 175–6, 198–9; Priestley, *Historical Account* . . ., p. 418; *The History of Inland Navigations, Particularly those of the Duke of Bridgewater in Lancashire and Cheshire* (3rd edn., 1779), p. 93. The first edition of this work appeared in 1766. In the British Museum *Catalogue of Printed Books* it is attributed to James Brindley, but this attribution is open to doubt according to Dr. W. H. Chaloner, 'The Cheshire Activities of Matthew Boulton and James Watt of Soho, near Birmingham 1776–1817', *Transactions of the Lancs. and Chesh. Antiq. Soc.* lxi (1949), 124, n. 9.

[2] *An Address to the Public on the New Intended Canal from Stourbridge to Worcester with the Case of the Staffordshire and Worcestershire Canal Company* (n.p., 1786), p. 3.

[3] Thomas Congreve, *A Scheme or proposal for making a navigable Communication between the Rivers of Trent and Severn in the County of Stafford* (1753).

[4] *Hist. Inland Navigation* (1766 edn.), p. 46.

[5] See above, Chapter I.

Trent and Mersey Canal, which was rapidly completed, their counterparts in Oxfordshire, Warwickshire, and Yorkshire were less generously inclined to the Oxford, Coventry, and Leeds and Liverpool companies, and these suffered from financial difficulties which seriously delayed the completion of their lines.[1] The Duke's example was not enough, in itself, to assure the smooth progress of inland navigation under the patronage of a broader investing public.

It is also instructive to consider the varying attitudes of landowners to the 'second generation' of promotions. In the company records and Acts of incorporation of the 1790s there begins to appear, for the first time, the stipulation that a certain proportion of the share capital be reserved for the proprietors of land to be crossed by the line of the canal. It is to be met with both in the case of the new undertakings, and in that of old ones which were labouring to complete their works, or embarking upon substantial extensions. In April 1791 the committee of the Leeds and Liverpool Canal received a request from landowners seeking admission as proprietors in right of their land which was to be taken;[2] of a new issue of 900 shares decided upon by the Dudley Canal in 1792, 330 were to be reserved for the landowners.[3] In the reports and records of subscription meetings for new companies held during this and the following years such a reservation occurs regularly: £100,000 out of £350,000 of the capital in the Grand Junction Canal,[4] £50,000 out of £150,000 in the Ashby-de-la-Zouch,[5] £26,000 out of £80,000 in the Leicestershire and Northamptonshire Union,[6] 25% in the Wilts and Berks, and the Salisbury and Southampton,[7] and so on.

Fortunately, in the case of one canal, the Nottingham, a record of the political background to a reservation of this

---

[1] Above, pp. 28–36.

[2] LLC 1/4, Minutes 1790–3, 8 Apr. 1791.

[3] DDC 1/2, Minutes 1776–1846, 24 Sept. 1792.

[4] *Leicester Journal,* 27 July 1792.

[5] ASCH 1/1, Minutes of the Subscribers 1792–4, 8 Nov. 1792.

[6] LNC 1/1, Minutes of the Committee 1792–3, 6 Aug. 1792.

[7] *Jackson's Oxford Journal,* 22 Dec. 1792, 1 Feb. 1794. For other examples, see pp. 87–8.

kind has survived.[1] The list of signatories to the minutes of the first meeting for the promotion of this scheme shows that the initiative came from the inhabitants of the town of Nottingham. In their proceedings they appear to have made considerable efforts to show deference to the interests of the landowners through whose property the navigation was intended to pass: they were to have the first opportunity to sign the subscription contract, in proportion to the amount of their land which was to be taken; dividends were to be limited to 10%; and the rates of tonnage were to be set unusually low. Of the 45 eligible proprietors, 36 took up the option thus accorded them. At the same time the committee of the Nottingham promoters noted that it was impossible to accept more than a small proportion of the applications which had been made for the 25 shares remaining after the original Nottingham subscribers had received their allotment of four shares each. The landowners then appear to have taken advantage of the conditions created by this mania for canal shares to raise their terms. Following a meeting with Lord Middleton, one of their number, the Nottingham committee 'inferred' that the only means of obtaining their assent to the scheme was to admit them to a share of £20,000 in the subscription of £50,000, to reduce the tonnage on bricks, and to limit the dividend payable to 8%[2] in order to 'destroy speculations in shares that have been sold at large premiums [sic] to the great prejudice of the principal landowners and coalowners who are liable to pay them out of their property'. These stipulations were met. Lesser landowners, including some residents of Nottingham, received one or two shares each, the Duke of Newcastle took 20 (10 for himself and 10 for his steward), and Lord Middleton 40 (10 for himself and 30 for his friends). The remainder were shared out among the original promoters of Nottingham who received two or three each.

Behaviour of this kind might be condoned on the grounds that it was the legitimate concern of landowners that the

---

[1] The following paragraph is based on NC 1/1, Minutes of the Committee of Subscribers 1790–2, 5 Nov. 1790, 24 Oct., 28 Oct., 31 Oct., 16 Nov., 14 Dec. 1791, 19 Jan. 1792.

[2] For other examples of such a limitation, see p. 137.

development of communications in the areas where their property lay be undertaken by persons with a 'stake in the country', and not by mere speculators seeking quick gains through the promotion of bubble companies or the levy of excessive tolls on their traffic. Thus the reason given by the promoters of the Dorset and Somerset Canal for granting a preference in the subscription to local landowners was 'to avoid any improper Speculation and to render the Navigation as beneficial as possible to the Proprietors of the Lands through which the same will pass . . .'[1] However, although many such protestations may have been sincere, there is no doubt that in the early 1790s landowners were as alive as the members of any other class to the prospects of financial advantage which the development of inland navigation appeared to offer. Furthermore, their conduct on a number of occasions was such as to show that they made no scruple to use their political and social power to secure for themselves allotments of scrip which stood at high premia. Capital, of course, is capital, and a subscription to shares upon which it is advanced must be acknowledged no matter what may have been the motives of the subscriber. However, in the experience of a number of companies, investors under the terms of a parliamentary reservation could prove to be false friends. With the collapse of share prices following the commercial crisis of 1793 and the termination of the canal mania the enthusiasm of many landowners waned. So did that of other subscribers, but against the latter, if they should be tempted to default, the companies had a legal remedy; against the former, whose subscriptions were optional, they did not.[2] For a number of undertakings this raised considerable problems.

---

[1] *Felix Farley's Bristol Journal*, 19 Jan. 1793. But the terms of this announcement are ambiguous. The promoters emphasized the profits which they hoped to derive from the carriage of potters' clay from Poole to Bristol, as much as the benefits which they expected to accrue from the canal to local agriculture.

[2] For the legal position of the general body of subscribers, see above, pp. 118-9. No record has been noticed of an attempted prosecution in a case of default by a subscriber in right of land taken, even where, as in the case of the Ellesmere Canal, above, p. 52, the option had been exercised. Landowners subscribing in their personal capacity were of course liable to make good their subscriptions in the usual way.

The company most seriously affected was perhaps that of the Gloucester and Berkeley Canal. As the committee of management remarked bitterly in its report to the proprietors of March 1794:

It is hardly necessary to remind this meeting that among the variety of stipulations with which this undertaking was fettered in the outset, by the jealousy of the landowners, a reservation of one fifth of the number of Shares was insisted upon and acquiesced in, leaving it optional in each individual landowner to take or decline them . . .

Many had since failed to exercise their option, and an attempt had been made to distribute among the other proprietors the shares which were thus left outstanding. However, because of the 'tardiness of some subscribers in fulfilling their engagements' a deficiency of £22,400 in the authorized capital of £140,000 remained. In 1796 the company's engineer anticipated the cost of completing the line as £169,440.[1]

A petition was prepared in 1807 for the consumption of the House of Lords, although it was never submitted, which set out the unfortunate circumstances of the company's early history in more measured terms and at greater length:[2]

That the line of the intended Canal passing through the Lands of several respectable Landholders, your Memorialists to obtain their Consents were obliged to submit to the Conditions of reserving one fifth part of the Shares into which the Stock of your Memorialists was to be divided for their option, to be taken or refused by such Landholders.

That at the Period of such Stipulation Shares bore a very large Premium, but that soon after obtaining the Act, War broke out, and the Value of these Shares in common with all other Kinds of public Adventures, being considerably diminished, the Landholders in general declined taking the Shares reserved for them as aforesaid, and by the Time they had so formally signified their Determination to relinquish the same, the Shares had fallen very much below par, and your Memorialists being restrained by the Provisions of the said Act from admitting new Subscribers at less than par, nearly 300 Shares remained undisposed of . . .

Similar defalcations on the part of landholders, for similar

[1] GBC 1/1, General Assembly Minutes 1793–1823, 30 Sept. 1793, 31 Mar. 1794, 8 Jan. 1796. For the stipulation as to the price of land, see above, p. 140, n. 4. Additionally, £5,000 had to be invested in government stock as a fund for the security of the landholders.

[2] GBC 1/1, 11 Mar. 1807.

reasons, have been noticed in the case of the Ellesmere, and the Kennet and Avon Canals.[1]

This unique privilege enjoyed by landowners, the right to have second thoughts, affected the distribution of their investments. Proportionately they were greatest in the short agricultural[2] and mineral[3] lines, which touched their economic concerns immediately, and the latter offered as an additional attraction the probability of financial success.[4] They were proportionately least in the long-distance navigations which provided the framework of the canal system as it developed in England. They had, it is true, fewer direct interests in such undertakings but their relative indifference may also be attributed in part to the prospects of a respectable return on their capital. Where these were good, as was the case with the ultimately prosperous Grand Junction Canal, landowners had few qualms about subscribing to a 'commercial' project: half of those entitled by their property to take shares in this concern did so.[5] But where prospects were doubtful, as was usual with the more ambitious lines, then they were circumspect: the equivalent proportion for the Kennet and Avon is less than one-tenth.[6] It was the long-distance canals whose completion was most frequently delayed by financial difficulties; it was in those cases where it would have been most valuable that assistance from landowners was least likely to be forthcoming.

Such considerations must qualify any tributes rendered to eighteenth-century landowners as patrons of inland navigation. In particular instances their assistance was of great importance, but these were few and might be matched by those equally rare occasions on which they were conspicuously hostile or obstructive. It is true that if they had wished they could have seriously delayed the progress of the canals, as they had earlier delayed the making navigable of

[1] Above, pp. 52, 67.

[2] e.g. the Montgomery, Grantham, and Oakham Canals.

[3] e.g. the Dearne and Dove, Barnsley, and Nottingham Canals.

[4] For the concern of landowners that they receive shares in the Barnsley and Nottingham Canals, see pp. 88, 154.

[5] Above, p. 44. Above, p. 104, for the financial prospects of this company in the 1790s; below, p. 176, for its later achievements.

[6] Calculated from House of Lords R.O., Deposited Plans, Kennet and Avon Canal, Subscription Contract and Book of Reference.

rivers, but the fact that they did not do so, it seems largely because of the evolution of public opinion in favour of 'improvement', cannot reasonably be used as a positive argument in their favour. Most landowners were indifferent, or they invested—if at all—merely as one class among many. When they participated they did so to serve their own interests, which were not so extensive as to embrace all other areas of economic activity. Manufacturing industry in England may have been widely dispersed but it did not exist merely in the interstices of the great landed estates. Over large areas of the Midlands, the West Riding, and Lancashire, the interests of commerce and manufactures were already concentrated and self-consciously differentiated from their agricultural environment. If these interests wished to improve the facilities for communication at their disposal then they were obliged to act on their own behalf, and this is what they did. England's canal system was essentially their achievement; it may be suggested, though it cannot be proven, that in this field of endeavour the landed interest received more benefit from the town dwellers than they from it.

Nor is this conclusion surprising, for, whether or not a particular navigation served the immediate interests of the local landlords, constraints were imposed by their peculiar style of life limiting the extent to which their income might be devoted to economically productive ends. One of these was suggested by the Duke of Bedford in correspondence with Samuel Whitbread about the subscription for a new bridge at Bedford: 'it strikes me that Tavistock [his son] ought to subscribe, but as I believe the Hounds run away with all his *superfluous Cash* I must pay the Money for him.'[1] Many members of the landowning class were in debt and much of this indebtedness originated in their characteristically improvident expenditure. But perhaps even more was inherited or involuntary and represented the means by which, under a system of primogeniture, younger children battened on the family estate. As J. S. Mill observed: 'It is a natural effect of primogeniture to make the landlords a needy

---

[1] Bedfordshire R.O., Correspondence of Samuel Whitbread, WI/75, Duke of Bedford to S.W., 12 Sept. 1810.

class.'[1] Their accumulated wealth was held in a highly illiquid form and there were many competing demands upon current income.

There is no systematic study of the finances of eighteenth-century landowners with which this point might be demonstrated and thus it is necessary to resort to impressionism by taking a brief excursion through the countryside crossed by the Coventry and Oxford Canals, two undertakings whose completion was interrupted by financial problems. Sir Roger Newdigate of Arbury subscribed £500 to the first and £3,000 to the second. In 1778 he was indebted to his London banker, Robert Child, for £20,000 and to a Miss M.C. for £8,000.[2] Francis Cartwright of Aynho subscribed £800 to the Oxford Canal. In 1770 Thomas Cartwright, the head of the family, obtained a private Act of Parliament enabling him to sell part of his estates in order to raise £15,000 for portions.[3] Between 1767 and 1792 at least seven parishes in which he held land were subjected to Acts for their inclosure and more than £4,000 was borrowed specifically to meet the expense of this.[4] Sir James Dashwood of Kirtlington took twenty shares of £100 in the Oxford Canal. In 1791 his heir, Sir Henry Dashwood, sold ten of these[5] and between 1794 and 1796 £3,778 was borrowed to finance inclosure in five parishes where the family held lands.[6] It is true that the sums advanced to this company by the Duke of Marlborough (£21,900) do not suggest that his finances were in any way precarious during the time in which its line was built, though he was selling annuities by 1799,[7] but mention should

[1] J. S. Mill, *Principles of Political Economy* (1848), Book V, Chapter IX, Section 2.

[2] Warwickshire R.O., Newdigate Diaries, C 136A/6, 18 June 1778. For the Coventry and Oxford Canals, undertaken 1768–9, see above, pp. 31–3.

[3] 10 George III (Private) *cap.* 77.

[4] Northamptonshire R.O., Cartwright (Aynho) MSS., nos. 3408–3487.

[5] Bodleian Library, Dep. c. 102.

[6] Oxfordshire R.O., Dashwood MSS., IX/iii/16/1, X/ii/xx/1, X/ii/xxi/1, XIII/i/27, XVIII/ii/13. Examples of borrowing to finance inclosure by other local landowners who did not invest in the canal might be given: ibid., Stockton and Fortescue Coll., Box 33, bundles B and I (W. H. Wykeham, Sulgrave, Northants., 1767, £1,034; Swalcliffe, Oxon., 1772, £120); DIL/II/c/5d–g, (Viscount Dillon, Spelsbury, Oxon., 1806, £4,500); Buckinghamshire R.O., D/LE 1/732, 734 (Sir William Lee, Hartwell, Bucks., 1781–2, £1,500).

[7] Oxfordshire R.O., J. II/a/33.

perhaps be made of his neighbour, the Hon. Charles Dillon-Lee, who following his inheritance of the Ditchley estate in 1776 ran up debts of at least £70,000 and was obliged to live for many years at Brussels, a refugee from his creditors.[1]

A final problem may be briefly considered here: the extent to which the quest for interest in parliament affected the distribution of shares. According to a correspondent of Matthew Boulton, writing in March 1793 about the proposed Netherton extension of the Dudley Navigation,[2] 'To my certain Knowledge many Gentlemen who are using their greatest Interest in favour of the Bill were not original Subscribers but have been induced to take a Part in it by having Shares given to them altho' they have a premium.' In November 1792 the promoters of the Ashby-de-la-Zouch Canal carefully reserved £15,000 worth of shares (one-tenth of the total) 'to be distributed or disposed of as occasion may require during the progress of the Bill in Parliament'.[3] However, the evidence which is available does not suggest that precautions of this kind were widely employed. M.P.s or peers do not appear with any special frequency in shareholders' lists, either of the Dudley and Ashby in particular, or of canals in general. It might in fact be inferred from the case of the Ashby that navigation stock was not welcome in either house: 117 (8%) of its shares were taken by Londoners, a rather higher proportion than was usual for canals of its time and place, suggesting, perhaps, that the promoters had been obliged to dispose among the inhabitants of the metropolis scrip which was unwanted by the members of parliament. But, as has been shown,[4] the enthusiasm for canal shares at the time of the canal mania was confined to certain localities and it is perhaps not to be expected that it should find very marked expression in a national assembly.

---

[1] Introduction to the National Register of Archives report on the Dillon MSS. (t.s., 1959).

[2] Quoted in A. B. Dubois, *English Business Company*, p. 393, n. 65.

[3] ASCH 1/1, 8 Nov. 1792.

[4] Above, pp. 86–96.

VII

CANAL FINANCE AND ENGLISH ECONOMIC DEVELOPMENT

WE may now widen our perspectives and consider more generally what can be learnt from the study of canal finance about England's economic development. At this point it seems desirable to bring back the earlier river navigations within our terms of reference.

Clearly the extension of inland navigation during the seventeenth and eighteenth centuries is to be seen above all as an effect of the concurrent growth and commercialization of the English economy. It begins in the South and East towards the end of the sixteenth century in conjunction with that revolutionary transformation of agricultural technique and expansion of agricultural output made familiar to us by the work of Dr. Kerridge.[1] From the 1690s the centre of activity tends to shift towards the North with the rise to prominence of its industries. From the 1750s canal building is intimately associated with the Industrial Revolution.

All this is obvious enough. It remains to consider whether, apart from the increased demand for transport facilities inevitably consequent upon economic growth, a second factor, the supply of capital, in any sense conditioned or determined inland navigation's progress. I have in mind here the argument of the late T. S. Ashton that the quickening of economic development during the course of the eighteenth century may to some extent be explained by the marked fall of interest rates which had occurred in the preceding period. This fall, he contended, brought for the first time within the bounds of financial viability many costly undertakings whose execution had earlier been inhibited by a scarcity of investible funds and the consequent high cost of credit.[2]

---

[1] E. Kerridge, *The Agricultural Revolution* (1967).
[2] T. S. Ashton, *The Industrial Revolution 1760–1830* (rev. edn., Oxford, 1968), pp. 7-11.

Is this hypothesis confirmed by the history of the navigations? It must first be noticed that among their records I have seen no mention of the rate of interest as a determinant of investment activity, but, considering that these records are largely formal, such references are perhaps not to be expected; certainly their absence proves nothing. As before in the analysis of investors' motives we must resort to circumstantial evidence. We may begin by placing in juxtaposition statistics of the chronology of navigation investment with those of the two variables, traffic growth and interest-rate movements, which might have determined it. I have supplemented the data for navigations by some relating to the coasting trade and to turnpike trusts.

My information is not sufficient to yield continuous series before the 1660s. Four navigation projects have been noticed in the 1600s, three in the 1610s, two in the 1620s, six in the 1630s, none in the 1640s, and two in the 1650s.[1] As for interest rates, it may be recalled that the legal maximum was reduced from 10% to 8% in 1625, and from 8% to 6% in 1651. The following statistics of coastal shipping have been obtained for four ports serving districts where river improvement was attempted at this time.[2]

Hull		*King's Lynn*		*Bridgwater*		*Minehead*	
1600	385	1601	541	1600	39	1615	61
1602	363	1603	597	1604	52	1616	38
1625	421	1616	735	1613	28	1629	30
1627	406	1621	509	1615	18	1632	34
1634	456	1631	749	1630	37	1634	82
1636	484	1634	970	1632	106	1635	106
1645	484	1639	949	1640	201	1636	96
1655	621	1642	776	1646	96	1638	165
1664	790	1645	766	1647	68	1639	136
1667	451	1646	774	1662	502	1640	106
		1647	911			1662	427
		1662	1,225				
		1664	1,436				

[1] These statistics are derived principally from Willan, *River Navigation*.

[2] From P.R.O., E. 190, Exchequer Port Books. The figures give the number of ships moving in and out of each port.

The high level of activity attained in the early 1660s is to be noted. It appears to have constituted a short-term peak followed by a marked recession. At ten ports for which data have been collected the average number of shipping movements fell by 16% between 1660-9 and 1670-4.[1] Tables II-IV provide a conspectus of the main trends after 1651, 1660, or 1675.

The following chronology of traffic growth is suggested by the data. The first three decades of the seventeenth century saw a modest increase, followed in the 1630s by a marked and general acceleration. The 1640s and 1650s are poorly documented and mysterious but, to judge by the level of shipments attained in the 1660s, the trend of the 1630s must have been sustained, at least after the conclusion of the Civil War in 1648. The late 1660s brought recession with recovery, but little more, in the 1670s and 1680s. The onset of war in 1689 brought recession again, though the intermission of peace 1697-1702 was very prosperous. Growth was resumed with the peace in the 1710s and continued until the later 1720s. Thereafter the several indices of traffic growth agree in confirming the course of progress made familiar by the work of Hoffman, Ashton, Deane, and Cole on the contemporary fiscal data:[2] relative stagnation in the 1730s and early 1740s; rapid growth from the late 1740s—briefly interrupted by the Seven Years War, 1756-63—until the commencement of hostilities with the American colonies in the late 1770s; then a brief intermission of depressed trade followed by the unparalleled prosperity of the later 1780s and early 1790s associated with the onset of rapid industrialization; and further progress, briefly interrupted by the commercial crisis of 1793 and the outbreak of war, proceeding more or less unchecked until the dislocation of overseas trade by the Continental System and Orders in Council.

---

[1] These ports are: Hull, King's Lynn, Southampton, Portsmouth, Cowes, Minehead, Bridgwater, Gloucester, Beaumaris, and Liverpool.

[2] W. G. Hoffmann, *British Industry 1700-1950* translated by W. O. Henderson and W. H. Chaloner (Oxford, 1955); Ashton, *Economic Fluctuations*; P. Deane and W. A. Cole, *British Economic Growth 1688-1959* (Cambridge, 1962).

TABLE II

Transport Investment

Key: (1) Acts for River Navigations and Canals
     (2) Acts for Harbour Improvement
     (3) Acts establishing Turnpike Trusts

	(1)	(2)	(3)
1660–4	3	2	1
1665–9	4	—	—
1670–4	3	1	—
1675–9	1	—	—
1680–4	—	—	—
1685–9	—	—	—
1690–4	—	—	—
1695–9	6	2	4
1700–4	3	2	2
1705–9	1	4	8
1710–14	2	—	12
1715–19	1	1	11
1720–4	7	2	10
1725–9	2	2	35
1730–4	1	4	12
1735–9	2	—	13
1740–4	—	—	16
1745–9	—	3	21
1750–4	3	1	79
1755–9	7	1	91
1760–4	3	1	83
1765–9	13	2	87
1770–4	7	1	55
1775–9	5	1	20
1780–4	4	1	13
1785–9	6	1	21
1790–4	51	7	47
1795–9	9	4	24
1800–4	6	11	30
1805–9	3	6	29
1810–14	8	9	47

Note: The sources of this table are: for navigation and harbour improvement Acts, O. Ruffhead (ed.), *The Statutes at Large* vols. iii–xviii (1763–1800), and T. E. Tomlins and J. Raithby (eds.), *The Statutes of the United Kingdom of Great Britain and Ireland,* vols. i–v (1804–14); for turnpike Acts, the list given by W. I. Albert, *The Turnpike Road System in England* (Cambridge, 1972), pp. 202–23. Notice is taken only of Acts affecting a navigation, harbour, or road, for the first

TABLE III

Traffic Growth

Per cent change (+ or −) on previous quinquennium

Key: (1) Coasting Trade
(2) Navigations: Southern and Midland Counties
(3) Navigations: Northern Counties
(4) Turnpike Trusts: Southern and Midland Counties
(5) Turnpike Trusts: West Riding of Yorkshire
(6) Average of (1), (2), (3), (4), and (5)

	(1)	(2)	(3)	(4)	(5)	(6)
1675–9	+ 15·3					+ 15·3
1680–4	+ 9·9					+ 9·9
1685–9	+ 5·4					+ 5·4
1690–4	−12·1					−12·1
1695–9	+ 14·1					+ 14·1
1700–4	+ 1·3					+ 1·3
1705–9	+ 1·5					+ 1·5
1710–14	+ 13·5		+ 11·1			+ 12·3
1714–19	+ 5·1	+ 11·9	+ 26·7			+ 14·6
1720–4	+ 5·0	+ 3·2	+ 15·8			+ 8·0
1725–9	+ 4·4	+ 4·4	+ 13·6			+ 7·5
1730–4	−2·2	−2·7	+ 30·0	+ 3·0		+ 7·0
1735–9	+ 2·2	+ 5·0	+ 13·9	+ 0·8		+ 5·5
1740–4	−11·7	−6·9	+ 14·5	−2·5		−1·7
1745–9	+ 1·6	+ 5·3	+ 12·6	+ 5·6		+ 6·3
1750–4	+ 19·7	+ 10·9	+ 16·0	+ 2·6		+ 12·3
1755–9	+ 11·8	+ 0·7	+ 21·8	+ 0·8	+ 9·4	+ 8·9
1760–4	−2·2	+ 7·6	+ 21·7	+ 8·5	+ 3·1	+ 7·7
1765–9	+ 22·6	+ 30·8	+ 10·0	+ 10·5	+ 4·0	+ 15·6
1770–4	+ 9·2	+ 7·3	+ 32·2	+ 7·4	+ 5·9	+ 12·4
1775–9	+ 1·0	−3·0	n.a.	+ 23·1	+ 4·1	+ 6·3
1780–4	+ 0·3	−12·8	+ 15·9	+ 8·3	+ 3·2	+ 3·0
1785–9	+ 15·7	+ 13·2	+ 39·1	+ 3·1	+ 10·0	+ 16·2
1790–4	+ 14·9	+ 18·1	+ 27·0	+ 11·2	+ 11·4	+ 16·5
1795–9		−7·8	+ 26·2	+ 8·8	+ 12·7	+ 10·0
1800–4		+ 20·5	+ 67·6	+ 9·8	+ 3·0	+ 25·2
1804–9		+ 10·7	−2·7	+ 0·3	+ 7·4	+ 3·9
1810–14		+ 22·3	+ 3·2	+ 9·5	−2·2	+ 8·2

time. The statistics of Acts passed provides a useful guide to the chronology of fluctuations in navigation investment, though not to its long-term growth. On average about £10,000 was spent on each navigation enterprise between 1600 and 1750, and about £140,000 between 1750 and 1815.

Note: For the sources on which this table is based see Appendix VI.

TABLE IV

Interest Rates

	Percentage of Mortgages Contracted at the Rate of:							Number in sample	Average Yield on 3% Consols (Per Cent)
	6%	5·5%	5%	4·5%	4%	3·5%	3%		
1651–9	100							7	
1660–4	100							8	
1665–9	100							9	
1670–4	100							12	
1675–9	67	11	22					9	
1680–4	67	8	25					12	
1685–9	22		50	17	11			18	
1690–4	30		67		4			27	
1695–9	43		50		7			14	
1700–4	10	5	86					21	
1705–9	42		58					24	
1710–14	45		55					29	
1714–19			100					12	
1720–4			95	5				20	
1725–9			96		4			24	
1730–4			72	16	13			32	3·1
1735–9			42	12	45			33	3·0
1740–4			47	31	22			32	3·0
1745–9			44	44	11			18	3·5
1750–4			14	30	47	7	2	43	2·9
1755–9			28	33	38	3		40	3·3
1760–4			55	21	24			42	3·8
1765–9			24	46	29			41	3·4
1770–4			39	33	27			33	3·5
1775–9			63	23	14			35	4·0
1780–4			89	3	8			36	5·1
1785–9			83	17				23	4·2
1790–4			63	30	7			27	3·8
1795–9			95		5			19	5·2
1800–4			83	8	8			12	4·8
1805–9			70	20	10			10	4·8
1810–14			88		13			8	4·8

This chronology accords well with our current understanding of the nature of England's economic development.[1] Its course was determined in the first instance by demographic circumstances. The growth of population added to demand, thus inducing technical innovations and increases of

Note: The sources of this table are: mortgage deeds principally from the MSS. collections at the Oxfordshire R.O., Bedfordshire R.O., and the Sheffield Central Library Archives Department, supplemented with the interest rates paid by turnpike trusts listed by Albert, *Turnpike Road System*, pp. 247–59; annual average yields on 3% Consols given by T. S. Ashton, *Economic Fluctuations in England 1700–1800* (Oxford, 1959), p. 187, and B. R. Mitchell and P. Deane, *Abstract of British Historical Statistics* (Cambridge, 1962), p. 455. A similar table printed by G. S. L. Tucker, *Progress and Profits in British Economic Thought 1650–1850* (Cambridge, 1960), p. 31, suggests a very similar chronology.

[1] For the most authoritative treatments of the issue of long-term development, see Kerridge, *Agricultural Revolution*; J. D. Chambers, *The Vale of Trent 1670–1800*, Econ. Hist. Rev. Supplement No. 3, n.d.; Deane and Cole, op. cit.

output within agriculture and also redistributing income to landowners and capitalist tenant farmers, whose propensity to buy manufactures and other traded goods was high, from wage labourers, with whom this propensity was low. Therefore when rapid population growth occurred agricultural prices rose or at least remained firm in the face of a rapidly increasing volume of output, landlords' rents and farmers' profits rose, the real wages of labourers stagnated or fell, and trade flourished. When it did not, then the opposite conditions held. This mechanism operated in a manner favourable to the growth of output during most of the first seven decades of the seventeenth century, from the 1690s to the later 1720s, and from the 1750s onwards without any further serious interruption.

The basic, demographically-induced fluctuations were in some measure overlaid by exogenous developments in overseas trade. Thus while agriculture and provincial trade were relatively depressed during the late 1660s, 1670s, and 1680s, at the same time London's entrepôt trade flourished. The city does not appear to have suffered from the recession of the late 1660s and the average number of shipments in its coasting trade increased by about 50% between the early 1670s and the late 1680s, as against little more than 30% for the provincial ports which have been studied.[1] The statistics of the sea-borne coal trade suggest a similar dichotomy.[2] Contemporaries recognized the phenomenon in their frequent complaints that London was growing at the expense of the provinces.[3] From the 1690s the depressing and purely adventitious influence of war upon the whole national economy was often felt.

To return to the subject of this inquiry, how should the statistical evidence be interpreted? The main problem is to decide what perspective to take. Between the beginning of the seventeenth century and the middle of the eighteenth the

[1] Details from P.R.O., E. 190, Exchequer Port Books.

[2] Compare the statistics of shipments from Newcastle and Sunderland with those for London's imports given by J. U. Nef, *The Rise of the British Coal Industry* (1932), ii. 380–1.

[3] See, for example, 'An Essay Concerning the Decay of Rents, & their Remedys, written by Sir William Coventry abt. the year 1670', Bodleian Library, MS. Eng. Misc. c. 144.

rate of interest fell markedly[1] and the level of investment in navigations rose, but the volume of traffic rose also and when taking such a long view it is in practice impossible to distinguish the relative importance of the two movements.

Over the short and medium term it appears that the progress of inland navigation was more closely correlated with the growth of traffic than with movements in the rate of interest. Thus when trade flourished, as in the early 1660s, later 1690s, 1710s, 1720s, 1750s, 1760s, early 1770s, and early 1790s, then navigation projects were numerous, although the rate of interest at those times as measured against current trends was in many cases not especially low. On the other hand, a fall in the rate of interest without any concomitant acceleration of traffic flows, as in the 1670s and 1680s, or 1730s, had no effect. Furthermore, much even of that measure of correlation which can be discerned between navigation investment and interest rates probably reflects no causal connection. For in the eighteenth century short-term increases of interest rates usually originated with government borrowing for war, and war through its disruption of trade relations often tended to depress economic activity. Therefore while it lasted navigation schemes were less likely to be attractive for reasons independent of the increased cost of credit. Although both forces operated concurrently and to distinguish their relative strength is difficult, my judgement is that trade disruption, rather than war finance, was the more powerful deterrent to investment activity. Thus while the American War of Independence, which both depressed trade and raised interest rates, effectively stopped canal building for its duration, the war against revolutionary France from 1793, which raised rates to comparable levels but which was accompanied by vigorous economic development, did not have the same result. Any canal company offering a reasonable prospect of profit was willing and able to raise money, at a price. Although most promoters and shareholders sought

---

[1] Part of this fall must be attributed to the effects of the transition from a period of rising prices to one in which they were stable or falling. Similarly the late eighteenth-century rise of interest rates must have been due in part to the return of price inflation. But in spite of this there is no doubt that the trend of nominal rates is a useful index.

the most profitable employment for their assets, it is probable that their calculations were made principally with reference to the revenue likely to accrue, that is, to the anticipated level of traffic, rather than to the current rate of interest. When the return on investment hoped for was of the order of 10% or 20%, a difference between, say, 4% and 4·5% in the yield on Consols is not likely to have determined whether a particular project was feasible and advantageous.

It therefore seems that traffic growth was the main determinant of the rate of extension of inland navigation; the supply of capital, in so far as it is satisfactorily measured by the course of interest rates, was not a strategic variable in its history. Although capital accumulation was obviously a necessary precondition for the great increase in the level of investment associated with the canals, it was a precondition which had been largely fulfilled long before their commencement, and was not their proximate cause as Ashton implied. Nevertheless, I am inclined to believe that there remains an important element of truth to his theory which an analysis concentrating solely upon short- and medium-term fluctuations is likely to overlook. In some ways a longer perspective might be more fruitful.

It has been noticed that in the seventeenth century successful navigation schemes were few, limited in scale, and subject to long delays in their completion. In the eighteenth century river improvements and canals were both more numerous and more ambitious; it became rarer for works to be abandoned uncompleted. However, the length of time required for their execution often remained considerable, although this may be attributed in part to the recurrence of war; certainly even the most powerful of the eighteenth-century canal companies could not aspire to that comparative facility with which the nineteenth-century railway companies built their lines.[1] Thus the impression is conveyed that in

---

[1] 46 years were required for the completion of the Leeds and Liverpool Canal, more than 30 for the Gloucester and Berkeley, and more than 20 for the Oxford, Coventry, Stratford-upon-Avon, Worcester and Birmingham, and Lancaster. During peacetime the Trent and Mersey was built in 11 years and the Thames and Severn in 6. For comparison: of the early trunk railways, the Grand Junction was built in 4 years (1833–7), the London and Birmingham in 5 (1833–8), the Great Western (1835–41) and the London and Southampton (1834–40) in 6.

moving from the seventeenth century through the eighteenth century to the nineteenth century we pass from an age in which capital for the finance of transport investments was relatively scarce into one in which it was relatively abundant, that in the early history of such undertakings problems of finance operated as a constraint and that gradually, with the course of time, this constraint was relaxed or removed.

The objection might be made that the difficulties experienced by the earlier navigations originated not in a scarcity of capital but in the more generally unfavourable conditions of the time in which they were conceived, that is, in a low level of economic activity which did not yet warrant such costly provision of means of communication; as these conditions improved with economic growth, then inland navigation was extended more rapidly. But while an insufficient level of economic activity might explain why in any particular period less capital was invested than later, it cannot explain why projects once begun were drawn out in their execution over many years, if they succeeded at all, so that investments once made came only slowly, if at all, to fruition. For the objection to hold it would be necessary to assume that the navigations were in their original conception entrepreneurial errors, but that some were corrected by further years of growth in the volume of potential traffic. However, as a number of even the early navigations appear once completed to have yielded profits which compared favourably with those obtained concurrently in other areas of economic activity, this assumption does not seem reasonable.[1]

Thus we may postulate a shortage of capital that did in fact inhibit the progress of inland navigation. How might it have done so? Two possibilities are to be distinguished: firstly, a scarcity of real resources, of men and materials and techniques with which the navigations could be built; and secondly, a deficiency in the instruments available for their recruitment, perhaps through institutional imperfections in the market for credit, or through attitudes on the part of holders of wealth hostile to its economically most effective deployment.

[1] See above, p. 16, and R. Grassby, 'The Rate of Profit in Seventeenth-Century England', *English Historical Review*, lxxxiv (1969).

The first possibility does not seem probable. Although eighteenth-century canal building could perhaps at times have inflationary effects, these effects were never serious or long-lasting. Thus in 1793 a bill introduced in the Commons to restrict canal cutting at harvest time was rejected. Speakers pointed out that there were 'vast numbers' of labourers coming from Scotland and Ireland to undertake these works. In Burke's words: 'The Harvest never yet was injured by the Waste of People in the most devouring Wars; and there was nothing to be suffered from slumbering, drowsy Canals.'[1] The much more modest river undertakings of the seventeenth century are even less likely to have placed a strain upon resources, for the main input, unskilled labour, was then cheaper than in the eighteenth century, and contemporary engineers lacked no important technical knowledge possessed by their successors.

The second possibility is more attractive. There were unquestionably imperfections in the market for capital which are likely to have limited its recruitment to investment of this kind. These arose principally from the irregularities in its social and geographical distribution. In pre-industrial England the richest men were the landowners and the merchants. We have already seen how landowners were as a rule indifferent or hostile to river improvement. As for merchant capital, it was concentrated in London; while it might easily be employed by governments to finance their wars, the factor of distance impeded its use by the provincial navigations.[2] Although in their early history the London undertaker, London shareholder, or London creditor, is a common figure, such financial connections were probably difficult to initiate and difficult to sustain because appropriate capital market

[1] Williamson's Liverpool Advertiser, Apr. 1793.

[2] Thus P. G. M. Dickson, *The Financial Revolution* (1967), Chapters 6, 11, has shown that in the first half of the eighteenth century ownership of the Funds was concentrated almost wholly in London and the Home Counties. In a sample analysis for 1717 only 6% of the holders of one stock were resident outside London (ibid., p. 276). It was a commonplace among contemporary writers on economic subjects that Londoners held a disproportionate share of the nation's financial assets: see, for example, C. Davenant, 'A Memorial Concerning Credit', in A. P. Usher (ed.), *Two Manuscripts by Charles Davenant* (Baltimore, 1942), p. 74; E. H., *Reasons for the Abatement of Interest to Four in the Hundred* (1692), p. 49; W. Allen, *Ways and Means to Raise the Value of Land* (1735), p. 9.

institutions did not exist and the scale of investment was insufficient to support the cost of their creation.

The only important group of possible investors remaining were the inhabitants of the provincial towns which the navigations served. As the later history of canal finance was to show, it was essentially upon the growth of their financial capabilities that the progress of inland navigation depended. And it is important to remember how limited, until a relatively late date, these capabilities were. Thus at Kidderminster about the time of the Civil War,[1]

there were none of the Tradesmen very rich, seeing their trade was poor, that would find them Food and Raiment. The Magistrates of the Town were few of them worth 40£ *per. An.* and most not half so much. Three or four of the Richest thriving Masters of the Trade [the linsey-woolsey manufacture] got about 500£ or 600£ in twenty years, and it may be lose 100£ of it at once by an ill Debtor.

Even in the mid-eighteenth century it was necessary for a Sheffield patriot, writing about a proposed turnpike road into the Derbyshire countryside, to recommend that 'qualifications for Commissioners be no more than Fifty Pounds per Annum or One Thousand Pounds Personalty or realty and personalty jointly. If a greater qualification be required Sheffield and the Country about it will have very few Persons qualifyed to Act and the Derbyshire People would carry everything as they pleased.' The prospective Sheffield commissioners were described as 'dayly employed in Business'.[2] Such statements are confirmed by the inventories made of personal estates at death. For a sample of 247 inventories of provincial townsmen and townswomen whose wills were proved at the Prerogative Court of Canterbury between 1660 and 1689 the average value was £699; for 684 such inventories of the years 1720–49 the average value was £1,237.[3]

[1] Richard Baxter, quoted in *Victoria County History: Worcestershire*, ii (1906), 293. In the 1660s Kidderminster was the scene of an unsuccessful navigation project; see above, pp. 3–5.

[2] Sheffield Central Library, T. C. 362, Considerations respecting a proposed Sheffield–Derbyshire turnpike (n.d. but *c.* 1758).

[3] These figures have been calculated from inventories in the collections, P.R.O., PROB 3 and PROB 4. Inventories do not record real estate, but neither usually do they deduct liabilities. As a rule only the richest members of provincial society would have their wills proved at the Prerogative Court of Canterbury. See

Most provincial townsmen were engaged in trade or manufacture. Therefore not only was their wealth limited in
amount, but it was also constituted in such a way as to make
its diversion to secondary employments difficult and even
hazardous. A high proportion of their assets were usually
accounted for by trade goods and debts from customers, and
a low proportion by cash or easily negotiable securities. So
Defoe, perhaps remembering his own insolvency of 1692, had
this to say about the dangers attendant upon running into
'projects and heavy undertakings, either out of the common
road which the Tradesman is already engaged in, or grasping
too many undertakings at once':[1]

The consequence of those adventures are generally such as these: first,
that they stock-starve the Tradesman, and impoverish him in his
ordinary business, which is the main support of his family; they lessen
his strength, and as they very rarely add to his credit, so they lessen
the man's stock, they weaken him in the main and he must at last faint
under it.

Secondly, as they lessen his stock, so they draw from it in the most
sensible part; they wound him in the tenderest and most nervous part;
for they always draw away his ready money: and what follows? The
money which was before the sinews of his business, the life of his trade,
maintain'd his shop, and kept up his credit to the full extent of it, being
drawn off, like the blood let out of the veins, his trade languishes, his
credit by degrees flags and goes off, and the Tradesman falls under the
weight.

The safe Tradesman is he, that, avoiding all such remote excursions,
keeps close within the verge of his own affairs, minds his shop or
warehouse, and confining himself to what belongs to him there, goes on
in the road of his business without launching into unknown oceans.

Thus at a time when liquidity was highly prized, discount
facilities were scarce, and the laws of bankruptcy were harsh,
the tradesman was well advised to be cautious.

During the seventeenth and early eighteenth centuries all
these factors tended to inhibit investment in river improvement. Their force was weakened by degrees and with the

also R. Grassby, 'The Personal Wealth of the Business Community in Seventeenth-
Century England', *Econ. Hist. Rev.*, 2nd Ser., xxiii (1970), especially 230–4, for
the small size of provincial business fortunes both absolutely and in relation to
the wealth of Londoners.

[1] [D. Defoe], *The Complete English Tradesman* (3rd edn., 1732), i. 66–7. The
first edition of this work appeared in 1725. Defoe wrote from the point of view
of a Londoner but his strictures would apply even more forcibly in the provinces.

passage of time as the same growth of economic activity which created a need for improved communications provided, after some delay, through the progress of accumulation in the provincial towns, the means with which that need might be met. By the middle of the eighteenth century men's capabilities had been brought more closely into balance with their aspirations than in the past. It is as testimony to this fact that the historical significance of the canal promotions in part consists.

APPENDIX I

Dividend Payments by Canal Companies

IT has been remarked that the 'second generation' of canal promotions was stimulated by the high dividends paid by the more successful promotions of the 'first generation'.[1] Some indication is given here as to what those dividends were. The Birmingham Canal and Loughborough Navigation may serve as examples of the most prosperous undertakings.[2]

Birmingham Canal:	*Rate of Average Annual Dividend Payment (per cent):*
1774–1776	5·0
1777–1779	11·25
1780–1782	13·93
1783–1785	12·0
1786–1788	13·5
1789–1791	17·5

Loughborough Navigation:	
1779–1781	3·3
1782–1784	1·5
1785–1787	13·0
1788–1790	20·0
1791–1793	27·5

The lines of these companies were relatively short. For those with longer ones profits were less spectacular, particularly when completion was delayed. The Trent and Mersey commenced dividend payments in 1781 and was paying 6·5% by 1790;[3] the Coventry began in 1774 and reached 8% by 1791.[4] The Leeds and Liverpool made the following payments on its shares of £114;[5]

1780 £2 10s.	1784 £2 16s.	1788 £5 10s.	1792 £6
1781 Nil	1785 Nil	1789 £6	1793 £7
1782 Nil	1786 £2	1790 £6	1794 £8
1783 Nil	1787 £5	1791 £6	

The situation of some other companies was worse: the ultimately prosperous Oxford Canal declared its first dividend of 2% as late as 1791, the first payment by the Chesterfield, at the rate of 1%, was made in 1789, while throughout its independent existence from 1772

---

[1] Above, p. 87.
[2] Details from Hadfield, *West Midlands*, p. 68; Hadfield, *East Midlands*, p. 84.
[3] Hadfield, *West Midlands*, p. 39.
[4] Hadfield, *East Midlands*, p. 24.
[5] LLC 4/6, Statistical History of the Leeds and Liverpool Canal.

to 1813 the Chester never yielded any revenue to its ordinary proprietors.[1]

The profits distributed by canals, new and old, after the canal mania were various. They are relevant to the subject of this study to the extent that they influenced the rate of further investment, principally through their effect upon the ability of established companies to raise funds. The Grand Junction Canal has been mentioned as a concern whose position in the capital market was strengthened by its good financial prospects.[2] Its early dividend history was as follows:[3]

	Rate of Dividend (per cent)		Rate of Dividend (per cent)
1806	3	1813	7
1807	3	1814	7
1808	4	1815	7·5
1809	5	1816	2
1810	6	1817	6
1811	6	1818	9
1812	7	1819	9

The achievement of most other promotions of the 1790s, in particular of the long-distance or 'agricultural' lines, fell far short of this. Thus the first dividend of the Ashby-de-la-Zouch company, at the rate of 1·8%, was paid in 1827.[4] However, some shorter lines of the 'second generation', for the most part those with access to a considerable mineral traffic, paid well, although without reaching the standards set by their predecessors. Thus the dividend on the Cromford Canal shares of £128 averaged £9 per annum by 1802-3.[5]

In 1825 it was calculated that £13,205,117 of canal capital yielded dividends at the average rate of 5.75%, while £3,734,910 still paid nothing at all.[6] A useful conspectus of the fortunes of the principal undertakings is given by Henry English's account of the capitals, share prices, and dividends, of canal companies in 1826.[7] It is the source of the following statistics of dividend yields which are arranged, as in Chapter II, according to each company's location and the time of its promotion.

[1] Hadfield, East Midlands, pp. 73, 159; Hadfield, West Midlands, pp. 176-9.

[2] Above, pp. 123-5.

[3] Details taken from Hadfield, British Canals, pp. 175-7.

[4] Hadfield, East Midlands, p. 153.

[5] Hadfield, East Midlands, p. 53.

[6] J. H. Clapham, An Economic History of Modern Britain, vol. i, The Early Railway Age 1820-1850, p. 82.

[7] H. English, A Complete View of the Joint Stock Companies formed during the years 1824 and 1825 (1827), pp. 35-7.

England, 1755–1780	Canal	Dividend Rate[1] (per cent)
	Birmingham	71·4*
	Coventry	44*
	Dudley	4·5
	Leeds and Liverpool	16
	Oxford	32*
	Staffordshire and Worcestershire	28·6
	Stourbridge	11·7
	Stroudwater	15·3
	Trent and Mersey	75*
East Midlands, 1780–1815		
	Ashby-de-la-Zouch	Nil
	Barnsley	8·8*
	Grand Junction	13
	Grantham	6
	Leicester	11·4
	Leicestershire and Northamptonshire Union	4·8
	North Walsham and Dilham	Nil
	Wisbech	Nil
West Midlands, 1780–1815		
	Ellesmere and Chester	2·6
	Gloucester and Berkeley	Nil
	Montgomeryshire	2·5[2]
	Shropshire	6·5
	Shrewsbury	8
	Stratford-on-Avon	1·3
	Warwick and Birmingham	11
	Warwick and Napton	11
	Worcester and Birmingham	1·8
	Wyrley and Essington	4·8
Lancashire, 1780–1815		
	Ashton under Lyne	6·5
	Huddersfield	Nil
	Lancaster	3·2
	Manchester, Bolton, and Bury	2·4
	Peak Forest	7·7
	Rochdale	4·7

[1] Payments on ordinary shares, but not on preferential shares or bonds, are included. An * indicates that an unspecified bonus was also paid.

[2] English gives 11% for the Montgomeryshire, but the correct figure is 2·5%: Hadfield, West Midlands, p. 196.

Southern England, 1780–1815

Basingstoke	Nil
Croydon	Nil
Grand Surrey	2
Grand Western	Nil
Kennet and Avon	2·5
Regent's	Nil
Somerset Coal	10
Tavistock	Nil
Thames and Medway	Nil
Thames and Severn	1·05
Wey and Arun	0·9
Wilts and Berks	Nil

South Wales, 1780–1815

Brecknock and Abergavenny	6
Glamorganshire	7·5
Monmouthshire	10
Neath	15
Swansea	14

APPENDIX II

Investment in Inland Navigation

SPACE does not permit me to reproduce the calculations upon which are based the estimates of the sources of navigation finance given on pages 74–5. My estimates of the sums raised by navigation companies are derived from their records, as cited in the text, from Mr. Hadfield's estimates of expenditure printed in the appendices of his regional studies,[1] from the *Canal Returns* of 1888,[2] and from the information given by Priestley about capitals authorized by parliament.[3] From the manner of their compilation they are not, as has already been indicated,[4] accurate measures of capital investment or of company capitalization properly defined. I have excluded from consideration improvements undertaken either without authority from parliament, or on a small scale by private individuals,[5] or primarily in connection with harbours or tidewaters.[6] For a number of minor river navigations, undertaken by commissioners with authority from parliament to borrow on mortgage of the tolls to an unspecified amount, no figure has been found.

Among the navigations of the 'second generation' I have considered the following as 'agricultural': River Adur, River Ancholme, Andover Canal, River Arun, Ashby-de-la-Zouch Canal, River Axe, Bourne Eau River, Brecknock and Abergavenny Canal, Caistor Canal, Chelmer and Blackwater Navigation, Coombe Hill Canal, Dorset and Somerset Canal, River Foss, River Gippen, Grantham Canal, Herefordshire and Gloucestershire Canal, Horncastle Navigation, Ivelchester and Langport Navigation, Leominster and Stourport Canal, Melton Navigation, Montgomeryshire Canal, North Walsham and Dilham Canal, North Wilts Canal, Oakham Canal, River Ouse, River Rother, Salisbury and Southampton Canal, Sleaford Navigation, Stowmarket and Ipswich Navigation, Tamar Manure Navigation, Tavistock Canal, River Thames, Wilts and Berks Canal, Wisbech Canal, Wye and Lugg Rivers Towing Path. All other enterprises of the period 1780–1815 I have considered as 'commercial'.

---

[1] Listed in the Bibliography.
[2] *Parl. Papers 1890*, lxiv, 747–921.
[3] Priestley, *Navigable Rivers, Canals and Railways*.
[4] Above, p. 26.
[5] For example, Sir John Ramsden's Canal, 14 George III *cap.* 13.
[6] For example, the River Ribble, 46 George III *cap.* 121.

APPENDIX III

Subscription to Inland Navigation in Six Towns, 1785-1795

THE following very tentative estimates may be made of the volume of subscriptions to inland navigation schemes at the six principal centres of enthusiasm during the years 1785-95. The italicized figures are approximations based on an examination of the proprietaries named in the relevant Acts of incorporation; for the others the sources are those cited in the text. All figures are in £100s, unless stated otherwise.

Navigation	Birmingham	Town Leicester	Coventry	Market Harborough
Grand Junction	*230*	*440*	*400*	*120*
Ellesmere	*400*	*500*	*100*	*100*
Leics. and Northants. Union	*55*	*480*	*90*	*400*
Rochdale	100	40	290	32
Crinan	20	225	65	159
Leicester		211		13
Ashby	60	60	34	
Melton		18		
Oakham		75		
Chelmer and Blackwater		*18*		*7*
Wisbech		*13*		
Worcester and Birmingham	285			
Dudley	673			
Birmingham (loan)	845			
Stratford	95			
Warwick and Birm.	236			
Warwick and Napton	247			
Coventry (loan)			202	
Total	3,246	2,080	1,181	831
Population at Census of 1801:	73,670	16,953	21,581[1]	1,716
Subscriptions per head of populations (in £s):	4·4	12·3	5·5	48·4

[1] The city, and county, of Coventry.

	Manchester
Manchester, Bolton and Bury	200
Ashton under Lyne	300
Peak Forest	250
Huddersfield	200
Rochdale	1,000
Total	1,950
Population in 1801:	84,020
Subscription per head of population (in £s):	2·3

	Bristol
Kennet and Avon	2,800
Worcester and Birmingham	146
Hereford. and Gloucs	83
South Wales (all canals)	34
Somerset Coal	80
Wilts and Berks	40
Salisbury and Southants	60
Total	3,243
Population in 1801:	63,645
Subscription per head of population (in £s):	5·1

These figures are not to be taken literally, but they suggest that Leicester was surpassed as a centre of canal investment in absolute terms by both Birmingham and Bristol, while for subscriptions per head of population the palm must go to Market Harborough. This last town must be distinguished from the others as essentially a marketing centre, without the large proletarian and artisan population associated with extensive manufactures (though it had a small trade in woollen cloth). Nevertheless, there can be no doubt as to the extraordinary enthusiasm of its trades- and professional men for inland navigation. Of the 160 inhabitants listed in the *Universal British Directory*, 105 have been identified as subscribers to canals, most to the ill-fated Leicestershire and Northamptonshire Union which was intended to give the town access to the North, via the Leicester and Loughborough Navigations, and to the South, via the Grand Junction Canal. Of the 773 persons named in the *Universal British Directory* for Leicester 191 have been identified as subscribers to canals.

Throughout the period covered by this study most canal shares were held by persons with an interest in only one company, as an effect of the localized character of the typical proprietary. A thorough demonstration of this fact by the collation of all available lists of shareholders would be extremely laborious, and not worth the effort involved. Investment by individuals in more than one canal only became common during the canal mania, and even at this time it remained an exception to the rule. The point may be illustrated by a collation of seven proprietaries:[1] those of the Grand Junction, Leicester, Leicestershire and Northamptonshire Union, Rochdale, Crinan, Wisbech, and Chelmer and Blackwater Navigations (including, for the last four of these, only subscribers identified as resident in the Midlands).

> 747 subscribers took shares in one canal
> 131 subscribers took shares in two canals
> 51 subscribers took shares in three canals
> 14 subscribers took shares in four canals
> 3 subscribers took shares in five canals
> 2 subscribers took shares in six canals
> 0 subscribers took shares in seven or more canals

At the centres of enthusiasm multiple subscriptions were proportionately more important. The equivalent figures for the 191 identified Leicester subscribers are:

> 101 subscribers took shares in one canal
> 52 subscribers took shares in two canals
> 28 subscribers took shares in three canals
> 7 subscribers took shares in four canals
> 1 subscriber took shares in five canals
> 2 subscribers took shares in six canals

If a number of other canals, such as the Ellesmere, Ashby, and Oakham, in which local men are known to have taken an interest, were included in these calculations, a few new single subscribers would be added to the list and the proportionate importance of multiple subscriptions would increase. It does not seem likely, however, that the conclusions already reached would be substantially affected.

---

[1] As named in their Acts of incorporation.

APPENDIX IV

Changes in the Character of Proprietaries through the Transfer Shares

IN Chapter II it was asserted that the occupational composition of canal proprietaries did not substantially change following their incorporation. Lists of shareholdings made upon that occasion were therefore useful guides to the sources of the capital which was actually invested in canal companies.[1] Some evidence in support of this opinion was given in the following text;[2] in view of the importance of the matter it is desirable to present more here.

The most satisfactory way of measuring changes in proprietaries is to collate successive lists of shareholders. Of the 101 persons incorporated as proprietors of the Trent and Mersey Canal in 1766, 47 still held its shares in 1782.[3] Of 53 persons resident in or near the city of Oxford recorded in November 1792 as holding 901 shares in the Oxford Canal, 31—holding 609 shares—were among the original proprietors incorporated in 1769.[4] Of the 74 persons mentioned as holding shares in the Swansea Canal company at the time of its general meeting of 4 July 1797, 54 appear in its subscription contract of 1794.[5] Of the 254 proprietors of the Worcester and Birmingham Canal incorporated in 1791, 144 still held shares in the company in 1798.[6] Of the 1,612 new shares in the Huddersfield Canal outstanding in 1804, 1,202 were held by persons named in the subscription contract of 1794.[7]

Another measure of change is the rate of turnover in the stock of companies. It has already been pointed out that often this was low, particularly, in the 1790s, for the 'second generation' of companies.[8] Furthermore, even in those cases where the rate of turnover was relatively high, a large proportion of the transactions were accounted for by a small proportion of the company's shares which were transferred more than once, while much of its stock remained in the same hands over long periods. Thus, as noticed above, many of the Oxford Canal's original proprietors survived from 1769 to the latter part of 1792, even though in the meantime the transfer of nearly 1,100 shares had been recorded in its books while the company's shares totalled about 1,600.[9]

---

[1] Above, p. 19.   [2] Above, pp. 100–5.

[3] TMC 2/2C, List of shareholders and mortgagees.

[4] Oxfordshire R.O., CH. N II/ii/23, List of Oxford Canal proprietors.

[5] H. Pollins, 'The Swansea Canal', p. 139.

[6] Above, p. 47.

[7] Above, p. 61.

[8] Above, pp. 100–5.   [9] Above, pp. 100–2.

Nevertheless, the operation of the secondary market in a canal company's stock did admit the possibility of changes in its occupational character, both through the transfer of shares between classes among the original proprietors and through transactions which involved the admission of new proprietors. The extent to which such changes occurred may be estimated by comparing an occupational analysis of the transferees[1] with a similar analysis of the original proprietary. I have analysed the transferees of shares in four companies during their early years and compared it with the occupational distribution at the time of their incorporation.[2]

Birmingham Canal Distribution of shares in 1768 (total 500):

I	II	III	IV	V	VI	VII	VIII	IX
4%	20%	–	18%	23%	11%	15%	–	10%

Transferees of shares from 1 September 1768 to 7 August 1773 (the total number of shares transferred was 375):[3]

–	6%	2%	26%	14%	17%	19%	1%	15%

Leeds and Liverpool Canal Distribution of shares in 1770 (total 1,919):

–	16%	2%	36%	5%	19%	13%	1%	7%

(Unknown 286)

Transferees of shares from 19 June 1770 to 16 May 1782 (the total number of shares transferred was 1,803):[4]

–	2%	–	54%	5%	17%	7%	5%	11%

(Unknown 362)

Stourbridge Canal Distribution of shares in 1776 (total 300):

14%	10%	1%	13%	34%	10%	10%	1%	7%

Transferees of shares from 1 June 1776 to 31 December 1782 (the total number of shares transferred was 226):[5]

–	6%	1%	17%	31%	23%	6%	2%	14%

Ashby-de-la-Zouch Canal Distribution of shares in 1793 (total 1,500):

8%	26%	7%	10%	5%	20%	10%	6%	8%

Transferees of shares from 1793 to 1805 (the total number of shares transferred was 255):[6]

2%	18%	4%	22%	7%	14%	18%	4%	11%

[1] Principally purchasers, but also transferees by bequest who were often very numerous.

[2] The sources employed for the analyses of the original proprietaries, and the principles of classification, are those employed in Chapter II.

[3] Calculated from BCN 2/36, Book of Transfers 1768–73.

[4] Calculated from LLC 2/1, Transfer Ledger 1770–1819.

[5] Calculated from STN 2/1, Transfer Book 1776–1827.

[6] Calculated from ASCH 2/3, Book of Transfers 1793–1831.

There is, on the whole, a reasonable congruence between the character of the original proprietaries and that of the transferees of shares. Landowners appear less frequently as the latter than as the former, but this probably reflects the fact that their investments, once made, were more stable than those of commercial men. Also, in each of the four companies examined 'capitalists', that is, principally, merchants, appear more often as transferees than as original promoters; it thus appears that they tended to increase their share in companies over the course of time following their establishment. However, only in the case of the Leeds and Liverpool was this disproportion sufficient, given the turnover of the shares in question, to change substantially the character of the original company over the period in which calls were being made on the proprietors, and this has already been noticed in the text as an exception to the general rule of constancy.[1]

[1] Above, p. 35.

APPENDIX V

Bank Finance of Inland Navigation

THIS appendix lists, in tabular form, cases I have noticed in which river navigation or canal companies were granted loans or overdrafts by banks.

ENGLAND, BEFORE 1782

Navigation or Canal	Amount of Loan or Overdraft	Date	Bank[1]	Source
Aire and Calder	£5,235 £5,633	1776 1779	Lodge, Arthington, Beckett (Leeds)	ACN 4/36
Birmingham	A credit balance was maintained with John Kettle, Esquire (who was not a banker), throughout his treasurership from 1768 until 1787, when he relinquished his office to the bankers Taylor and Lloyd of Birmingham			BCN 4/170
Chesterfield	£2,112 Not known £3,000 £3,000	September 1773 3 September 1778 21 July 1778 to 1779 21 July 1778 to 1779	Wilkinson (Chesterfield) and Poplewell (Retford) Crompton (York)* Wright (Nottingham)*	CHC 4/1 CHC 1/1 CHC 1/1 CHC 1/1
Coventry	£155[2]	31 March 1772	Little (Coventry)	CVC 4/23
Lee	£5,000	24 May 1770 to 4 February 1771	Dimsdale, Archer, Byde (London), in return for the treasurership	LEE 1/4
Leeds and Liverpool	£5,000	21 June 1776, for 2 years	Smith, Wright, Gray (London)*	LLC 1/2

[1] The treasurer of the company, unless marked*.
[2] A credit balance was maintained at all other times between 1769 and 1790.

Oxford	Not known	1774	Little (Coventry)	Pressnell, Country Banking, p. 390
Stourbridge	£300	Before 20 August 1782	'Birmingham Banking Company'*	STN 1/3

ENGLAND AND WALES, 1782–1815

Ashby-de-la-Zouch	£2,000 £3,339	20 April 1796 6 February 1798 }	Wilkes, Dickens, Goodall, Fisher (London)	ASCH 1/2
Barnsley	£1,000	27 December 1797	Kennet, Ingram (Wakefield)	BYC 1/3
Birmingham	£4,000	July–August 1790	Taylor, Lloyd (Birmingham)	BCN 4/364
Brecknock and Abergavenny	The company at first had two treasurers, one for Breconshire and one for Monmouthshire. Between 1793 and 1805 large credit balances were maintained with both. After 1805 these balances were much reduced and the Breconshire account was often overdrawn. In 1812 Walter Wilkins of Brecon, banker, was appointed sole treasurer. By 1814 the overdraft on the company's account with him totalled £11,600. This was much reduced in 1815 and paid off in 1816.			BAC 1/1
Coventry	The Treasurer's accounts show credit balances throughout the years 1782–1815			CVC 4/23

Ellesmere	£10,000	5 March 1806	Eyton, Wilkinson (Shrewsbury)	ELC 1/5
Grand Junction	The Treasurer's cash books are extant for 1794–1801 and 1806–11. They show credit balances throughout, except: £5,369 — 22 October 1794 £884 — 29 April 1797 £1,252 — 24 October 1800 £20,465 — 27 May 1801 £6,620 — 24 June 1801 £20,720 — 31 October 1801		Box (Buckingham)	GJC 23/1 GJC 23/2
Grantham	£3,000	27 December 1797	Wright (Nottingham)	GCN 1/1
Horncastle	Not known	1794	Ellison (Lincoln)	Above, p. 112
Huddersfield	£3,400 £5,400 £5,608	7 April 1797 22 March 1798 26 March 1812	Perfect, Seaton, Brook (Huddersfield) Rawson, Rhodes, Briggs (Halifax)	HUC 1/2 HUC 1/3
Kennet and Avon	£6,000	10 April 1797	Worrall, Blatchley (Bristol)	Above, pp. 112–3 KAC 23/1
	After 1801 the Treasurership was held by the bankers Harford, Davis & Co. of Bristol. A credit balance was maintained between 1801 and 1807. Thereafter an overdraft appeared which reached a maximum of £60,631 in November 1815. It was paid off in 1816.			
Lancaster	£15,000	1797	Worswick (Lancaster)	Above, p. 112

Leeds and Liverpool	£8,700	6 June 1800	Peckover, Harris (Bradford)	LLC 1/6
Leicester	£5,627	6 July 1795	Bentley, Buxton (Leicester) Boultbee, Mansfield (Leicester)	LCN 1/2
Monmouthshire	£10,000	1802	Buckle, Williams (Chepstow)	Hadfield, *Canal Age,* p. 47
Nottingham	£3,000	4 June, 5 November 1795	Smith (Nottingham)	NC 1/2
Oxford	£2,000 £2,500	1789 1795	Childs (London) Fletcher, Parsons (Oxford)	Pressnell, *Country Banking,* pp. 390–1
Peak Forest	£4,000	8 July 1796	Jones, Barker (Manchester)	PFC 1/1
Rochdale	£15,167	2 March 1804	Not known	House of Lords Committee Minute Book no. 49, f. 16

				House of Lords Committee Minute Book no. 47, f. 189
Somerset Coal	c. £9,000	14 April 1802	Not known	
Stratford	£2,276	16 November 1812	Battersbee (Stratford)	SCN 1/3
Swansea	£1,197 £3,000	1 January 1800 5 July 1803	Landeg (Swansea) Lynch, Hawkes ('Glamorganshire Banking Co.')	SWC 1/4 SWC 1/1
Warwick and Birmingham	£4,000	16 October 1795	Greenway, Whitehead, Weston (Warwick)	WBC 1/7
Warwick and Napton	£3,000	27 April 1801	Greenway, Whitehead, Weston (Warwick)	WNC 1/1
Wilts and Berks	£8,962	31 December 1810	Mattingley, Kent (Wantage)	Ledger[1]
Worcester and Birmingham	£27,096	1815	Smith, Startin, Smith (Birmingham)	Above, p. 48
Wyrley and Essington	£3,000	17 January 1799	Hordern, Molineux, Bishton (Wolverhampton)	WEC 1/1

[1] Swindon Public Library, Wilts and Berks Canal Collection, no. 32, Ledger 1810–17, f. 11.

APPENDIX VI

Sources for the Indices of Traffic Growth

1. Coasting Trade

Statistics of shipping movements in the coasting trade of certain provincial ports have been compiled from the Exchequer Port Books,[1] supplemented in the case of Hull and King's Lynn by data from the Customs Ledgers for 1789-91.[2] Quinquennial averages have been thus derived for the following ports and periods of years as a basis for the index: Hull, 1670-1739, 1745-94, King's Lynn, 1670-1744, 1750-94, Southampton, 1670-1719, 1745-54, Cowes, 1670-99, Portsmouth, 1670-1719, Minehead, 1670-1734, Bridgwater, 1670-1744, 1755-79, Bristol, 1680-1734, 1750-89, Gloucester, 1670-1729, Caernarvon, 1670-1739, Beaumaris, 1670-1764, Conway, 1670-1729, 1735-64, Chester, 1670-1729, 1740-74, Liverpool, 1670-1719.

From the use which has been made of them by other scholars and random checks of internal consistency which I have made myself, the Port Books appear to be fairly reliable and comprehensive records of traffic. Because of the long-term tendency for the average size of ship to increase, the statistics of shipping movements must of course understate the growth in the volume of goods carried, but as the rate of this increase seems to have been quite uniform over time, they are probably a useful guide to the chronology of economic progress. For the eighteenth century they may be supplemented by statistics of the total tonnage of ships employed in the English coasting trade:[3]

1709	96,929	1730	109,810
1716	101,643	1737	117,743
1723	104,466	1744	123,068

	Quinquennial Average	Per Cent Change on Previous Quinquennium
1751-4	145,033	
1755-9	167,722	+15.6
1760-4	163,110	−2.8
1765-9	204,718	+25.5
1770-4	218,330	+6.7
1775-9	235,854	+8.0
1780-4	247,538	+5.0

[1] P.R.O., E. 190.
[2] P.R.O., CUST 17/11-13.
[3] British Museum, Addit. MS. 11255.

These data contradict my own in suggesting appreciable growth during the 1730s and early 1740s, and late 1770s and early 1780s, but otherwise the degree of conformity between them is considerable.

The indices for navigations and turnpike trusts are based upon revenue statistics derived from their records as listed below. In their calculation, increases of revenue due solely to increases in the rate of toll levied, usually associated in the case of turnpike trusts with the securing of a new Act of parliament, have wherever possible been discounted.

2. Navigations: Southern and Midland Counties

Tone, 1702–1814. Somerset R.O., Tone Conservators MSS., DD/MK, Box 18, General Ledger 1699–1803; Box 16, General Ledger, 1803–31; DD/TC, No. 1.

Avon (Somerset), 1729–1800. AN 23/1–2; AN 23/10–11.

Ouse (Bedfordshire), 1732–1800, 1807–14. Bury St. Edmunds and West Suffolk R.O., Cullum MSS., E 2/17/1, 7; Bedfordshire R.O., Francklin MSS., F.N. 1492.

Lark, 1733–41, 1781–1815. Bury St. Edmunds and West Suffolk R.O., Cullum MSS., E 2/17/1.

Kennet, 1743–58. KN 4/2.

Nene, 1763–94. Welland and Nene River Authority, Oundle, Commissioners' Minute Book No. 2, 1760–1800.

Lee, 1780–1806. LEE 23/2.

Montgomery Canal, 1808–14. MONC 1/12.

Grantham Canal, 1798–1814. GCN 1/3.

3. Navigations: Northern Counties

Aire and Calder, 1704–1814. B.T.H.R. (York), ACN 4/36; R. G. Wilson, 'Transport Dues as Indices of Economic Growth, 1775–1820', Econ. Hist. Rev., 2nd Ser., xix (1966), 117.

Weaver, 1734–99. T. S. Willan, The Navigation of the River Weaver in the Eighteenth Century (Manchester, 1951), pp. 206–7.

Leeds and Liverpool Canal, 1772–1814. LLC 4/6.

Chesterfield Canal, 1777–89. Sheffield Central Library, Jackson Collection, No. 1255.

Trent and Mersey Canal, 1774–83. William Salt Library, Stafford, Hand Morgan Collection, H.M. 37/40.

Trent, 1804–14. TRN 4/2.

4. Turnpike Trusts: Southern and Midland Counties

Edgware, 1729–73. Middlesex R.O., LA/HW/Tp/21.

Bedfont, 1729–56. Middlesex R.O., Tp BED/1.

Maidenhead–Sunning Lane, 1728–34. Berkshire R.O., D/EHy 09/3.

Biggleswade–Alconbury Hill, 1727–69, 1781–1814. Bedfordshire R.O., A.D. 1116; DD X 40/2–4.

Wooburn–Hockliffe, 1730–72. Bedfordshire R.O., X 21/4.

Essex (Chelmsford Division), 1784–1801. Essex R.O., D/TX 2/1.

Ipswich–Southtown, 1789–1810. Ipswich and East Suffolk R.O., EH:50/5/2B/1.

Little Yarmouth, 1796–1814. Ipswich and East Suffolk R.O., EH:50/5/3B/7.

Aldeburgh, 1796–1803, 1813–14. Ipswich and East Suffolk R.O., EH: 50/5/4B.

Taunton, 1753–98. Somerset R.O., D/T/ta, 5, 6.

Wells, 1755–64, 1767–1806. Somerset R.O., D/T/WEL, 8(2), 9(12).

Ilminster, 1760–8, 1781–94. Somerset R.O., D/T/ilm, 1.

Yeovil, 1767–1814. Somerset R.O., D/T/Yeo, 24–5.

Market Harborough–Loughborough, 1725–58. Northamptonshire R.O., Hanbury (Kelmarsh) MSS., 325, 333.

Banbury–Lutterworth (Badby Gate), 1766–77. Northamptonshire R.O., D 2921.

Hardingstone–Old Stratford, 1776–84. Northamptonshire R.O., Misc. Ledger, 755.

Market Harborough–Northampton (Little-Bowden Gate), 1798–1808, 1811–4. Northamptonshire R.O., No. 1484.

Wellingborough–Northampton, 1805–14. Northamptonshire R.O., Box 1023.

Stockenchurch–Oxford, 1755–70, 1789–1806. Oxfordshire R.O., Ch. S. 1, Ch. S. 2/1/2.

Ryton Bridge–Banbury, 1760–1808. Bodleian Library, MS. Top. Oxon. d. 373.

Fyfield–Newbridge (Berkshire), 1789–97. Berkshire R.O., ECR 01.

Stratford–Bromsgrove, 1767–1814. Warwickshire R.O., CR 446/2, 3a.

Spernal Ash–Digbeth, 1777–1814. Warwickshire R.O., CR 347/21.

Droitwich, 1737–63. Worcestershire R.O., 704/3.

Monksbridge–Tenbury, 1781–4. Worcestershire R.O., 4600/300.

Shepherd's Shord–Horsley Upright Gate (Wiltshire), 1736–46. *H.C.J.* xxvi. 317.

Leases of eighteen local trusts recorded in their advertisements in *Jackson's Oxford Journal*, 1772–80, 1783–5, 1790–3.

5. Turnpike Trusts: West Riding of Yorkshire

West Riding County Council Offices, Wakefield: Collection of Turnpike MSS.:

Redhouse–Wakefield, 1742–1814. Box 54, Minutes 1741–1830; Accounts 1741–1812.

Boroughbridge–Ripon, 1752–1812. Box 27, Accounts 1752–1814.

Tadcaster–York, 1753–89, 1794–8. Box 54, Minutes 1745–99.

Ripon–Pateley Bridge, 1756–85, 1790–6. Box 27, Accounts 1756–1852.

Keighley–Kirkby-in-Kendal, 1756–63, 1787–1812. Box 22, Minutes 1753–63, 1787–1815.

Harrogate–Hutton Moor, 1759–1800. Box 27, Minutes 1752–1814.

Knaresborough–Pateley Bridge, 1759–63, 1769–82, 1790–1813. Box 27, Accounts 1759–1881.

Halifax–Wakefield, 1759–1813. Box 32, Cash Book 1758–77; Minutes 1762–1822.

Harrogate–Boroughbridge, 1760–1813. Box 27, Minutes 1752–1870.

Toller Lane End–Colne, 1762–1812. Box 50, Minutes 1755–1823.

Wakefield–Weeland, 1763–88, 1793–1814. Box 54, Minutes 1741–1826.

Doncaster–Tadcaster, 1767–85, 1794–1814. Box 54a, Minutes 1741–1835.

Leeds–Wakefield, 1770–1814. Box 45, Minutes 1758–79, 1779–94, 1794–1821.

Knaresborough–Green Hammerton, 1775–7, 1795–1814. Box 27, Minutes 1752–1878.

Knaresborough–Wetherby, 1776–8, 1784–1814. Box 27, Minutes 1775–1870.

Huddersfield–Penistone, 1778–1814. Box 72, Accounts 1771–1811.

Collingham–York, 1788–1811. Box 27, Minutes 1771–1875.

Keighley–Halifax, 1790–1814. Box 8, Minutes 1789–1815.

Worksop–Attercliffe, 1794–1814. Box 24, Minutes 1782–1824.

Standedge–Oldham, 1794–1810. Box 63, Minutes 1792–1812.

Oldham–Ripponden, 1799–1808. Box 46, Minutes 1795–1808.

Marsden–Long Preston, 1805–7, 1811–13. Box 9, Minutes 1803–60.

Sheffield–Wakefield, 1766–75. Sheffield Central Library, T.C. 364.

Tadcaster–Otley, 1778–83, 1788–1814. Leeds Central Library, Harewood Estate MSS. (Turnpike Trusts), Account Book 1778–1831, and papers.

Halifax–Wakefield, 1781–1808. Halifax Central Library, Lister MSS., R.&.W. 1, 7, 12, 13, 20.

R. G. Wilson, 'Transport Dues as Indices of Economic Growth', p. 115: toll leases on six turnpike roads around Leeds 1772–1820, compiled from the files of the *Leeds Mercury* and *Leeds Intelligencer.*

BIBLIOGRAPHY

A. MANUSCRIPT SOURCES

BRITISH TRANSPORT HISTORICAL RECORDS (LONDON)

Ashby-de-la-Zouch Canal (ASCH)
1/1 Minutes of the Subscribers 1792-4
1/2, 3 Committee Minutes 1794-9, 1799-1807
2/1 Share Register
2/2 Register of Mortgages
2/3 Book of Transfers

Ashton under Lyne Canal (AC)
1/1 Committee Minutes 1798-1815

Avon River Navigation (AN)
1/5 Minutes of the Commissioners 1725-1822
2/1 Transfer Register 1726-1823
23/1, 2 Ledgers 1725-51, 1751-77
23/10, 11 Cash Books 1775-86, 1786-1800

Bath and Bristol Canal and Bristol Waterworks (BBC)
1/1 Proceedings of the Committee of Management and the Company of
   Proprietors 1811-19

Birmingham Canal Navigations (BCN)
1/1, 2, 5 Committee Minutes 1767-71, 1771-2, 1784-8
1/41 General Assembly Minutes 1771-87
2/26 Transfer Ledger 1768-1835
2/36 Book of Transfers 1768-73
4/17 Loan Ledger 1784-1819
4/170 Ledger 1767-70
4/364, 365 Abstracts of Accounts 1775-95, 1795-1810

Brecknock and Abergavenny Canal (BAC)
1/1 General Assembly Minutes 1793-1823
1/3 Committee Minutes 1793-1800
1/4 Committee Minutes 1802-10
4/3 Rough Journal 1808-20
4/6 Cash Book 1812-18

Chester Canal (CC)
1/3 Committee Minutes 1775-9

Chesterfield Canal (CHC)
1/1 General Assembly and Committee Minutes 1771-80
4/1 Ledger 1769-80

Coventry Canal (CVC)
1/1 General Assembly and Committee Minutes 1768-71
1/2 General Assembly and Committee Minutes 1771-7

1/3 General Assembly and Committee Minutes 1777-90
4/23 Treasurer's Accounts 1767-1860
Cromford Canal (CRC)
1/1 General Assembly and Committee Minutes 1789-99
Dudley Canal (DDC)
1/2 Committee Minutes 1776-85, General Assembly Minutes 1776-1846
Dun River Navigation (DUN)
2/1 Share Ledger 1730-41
Ellesmere Canal (ELC)
1/4 Minutes of the Promoters 1791-3
1/5 General Assembly Minutes 1793-1812
1/1, 2, 3 Committee Minutes 1793-6, 1796-1804, 1804-13
Ellesmere and Chester Canal (ECC)
1/7 Minutes of the Subcommittee of Accounts and Finance 1805-46
Erewash Canal (EWC)
1/1 General Assembly and Committee Minutes 1777-98
Gloucester and Berkeley Canal (GBC)
1/1 General Assembly Minutes 1794-1823
1/3, 4 Committee Minutes 1793-8, 1798-1818
2/1 Calls Book 1792-1829
Grand Junction Canal (GJC)
1/39 General Assembly and General Committee Minutes 1793-8
1/40, 41, 42, 43 General Committee Minutes 1798-1800, 1800-5, 1805-12, 1812-28
23/1, 2 Treasurer's Cash Books 1794-1801, 1807-10
Grand Union Canal (GJC)
2/2 Share Register 1809-37
Grantham Canal (GCN)
1/1, 3 Committee and General Assembly Minutes 1793-1809, 1835-54
Herefordshire and Gloucestershire Canal (HGN)
1/1 General Assembly Minutes 1791-1882
2/5 Calls Book 1791-8
Huddersfield Canal (HUC)
1/1 General Assembly Minutes 1794-1815
1/2, 3 Committee Minutes 1794-1801, 1801-19
2/1 'A Book Containing an Account of the New or Additional Shares in the Huddersfield Canal' 1801-4
Kennet and Avon Canal (KAC)
1/1 Minutes of the Promoters 1788-94
1/7 Minutes of the Committee for the Eastern Extension 1809-16
1/9, 10 Minutes of the General Committee of Management 1794-1805, 1805-18
2/1 Register of Unclaimed Dividends 1814-51
23/1 Ledger 1793-1822

Kennet River (KN)
1/1 Minutes of the Undertakers 1720- 7
4/2 Account Book 1743- 58

Lancaster Canal (LC)
1/8 General Assembly Minutes 1792- 1822
8/2 3 Letter Books 1794- 7, 1797- 1808

Lee River (LEE)
2/6 Register of Assignments of 4% Securities 1768- 1846
23/2 General Account Book 1779- 1806

Leeds and Liverpool Canal (LLC)
1/1 Minutes of the Subscribers 1766- 70
1/2, 3, 4, 5, 6, 7, 8 General Assembly and Committee Minutes
    1770-82, 1782-90, 1790-3, 1793-8, 1798-1802, 1802-9, 1809-17
1/49 Minutes of the London Proprietors 1794
1/50 Minutes of the Meetings of the Delegates of Proprietors of Inland
    Navigations 1797
2/1 Transfer Ledger 1770- 1819
2/11 'Leeds and Liverpool Canal Mortgage Book' 1820- 30
4/6 Statistical History of the Leeds and Liverpool Canal

Leicester Navigation (LCN)
1/1, 2, 3 General Assembly and Committee Minutes 1790- 1, 1791- 5,
    1795- 1801

Leicestershire and Northamptonshire Union Canal (LNC)
1/1 Committee Minutes 1792- 3 1/9 General Assembly Minutes
    1803- 44

Loughborough Navigation (LBN)
1/1 General Assembly and Committee Minutes 1776- 97

Montgomeryshire Canal (MONC)
1/1 General Assembly Minutes 1794- 1839
1/11, 12 Committee Minutes 1794- 7, 1798- 1817
2/1 Register of Proprietors 1817- 45

Nottingham Canal (NC)
1/2 General Assembly and Committee Minutes 1792- 7

Oxford Canal (OXC)
1/2 General Assembly and Committee Minutes 1769- 75
1/3, 4 Committee Minutes 1775- 87, 1787- 97
2/2, 3, 4 Counterfoils of Mortgage Securities 1775- 79
2/5, 6 Counterfoils of Mortgage Securities 1786- 90

Peak Forest Canal (PFC)
1/1, 2 Committee Minutes 1794- 1800, 1800- 7

Shrewsbury Canal (SHRC)
1/1 General Assembly and Committee Minutes 1793- 1847

Shropshire Canal (SHPC)
1/1 General Assembly and Committee Minutes 1788- 1858

Staffordshire and Worcestershire Canal (STW)
1/1 Committee Minutes 1766-85

Stourbridge Canal (STN)
1/1 General Assembly Minutes 1776-1826
1/3 Committee Minutes 1776-83
2/1 Transfer Book 1776-1827

Stratford-upon-Avon Canal (SCN)
1/1 General Assembly Minutes 1793-1856
1/3 Committee Minutes 1798-1829

Swansea Canal (SWC)
1/1 General Assembly Minutes 1794-1822
4/1 Ledger 1794-1813

Trent River Navigation (TRN)
4/2 Accounts 1814-54

Trent and Mersey Canal (TMC)
2/2A, 2B, 2C Lists of Shareholders and Mortgagees 1781-4

Warwick and Birmingham Canal (WBC)
1/1 Minutes of the General Assembly 1793-1812
1/7 Committee Minutes 1793-8

Warwick and Napton Canal (WNC)
1/1 General Assembly Minutes 1794-1810
1/2, 3 Committee Minutes 1793-4, 1794-7

Witham Navigation (WTN)
1/1 Minutes of the Proprietors 1762-1817

Worcester and Birmingham Canal (WOBC)
1/1 General Assembly Minutes 1791-1834
1/4, 5, 6 Committee Minutes 1791-1800, 1800-12, 1812-16

Wyrley and Essington Canal (WEC)
1/1 General Assembly Minutes 1793-1840

BRITISH TRANSPORT HISTORICAL RECORDS (YORK)

Aire and Calder Navigation (ACN)
1/5 General Assembly Minutes 1774-87
2/14 List of Creditors 1775
4/112/5 File of Correspondence 1770s

Barnsley Canal (BYC)
1/3 Minutes of the Committee and General Assembly 1792-1806

Calder and Hebble Navigation (CHN)
1/1 Committee Minutes 1756-8
4/12 Cash Book 1775-80

Pocklington Canal (POC)
2/1 Register of Shareholders 1815-49

PUBLIC RECORD OFFICE

B.1 Court of Bankruptcy, Order Books
B.3 Court of Bankruptcy, Files of Proceedings

C.5 Chancery Proceedings, Bridges, before 1714
C.12 Chancery Proceedings, 1758-1800
C.108/204 (Chancery Masters' Exhibits) Printed List of Shareholders in the Birmingham and Liverpool Junction Canal, 7 July 1827
CUST 17 Customs Ledgers
E.112 Exchequer K.R., Bills, Answers
E.136 Exchequer K.R., Decree Books
E.171/1 Wey Navigation Claims
E.190 Exchequer K.R., Port Books
PROB 2 Prerogative Court of Canterbury, Registers of Wills
PROB 3, 4 Prerogative Court of Canterbury, Inventories

SCOTTISH RECORD OFFICE, H.M. REGISTER HOUSE, EDINBURGH

BR/CRC/1/1 Crinan Canal, Minutes of the General Meetings and Board of Directors 1793-1819
BR/CRC/2/1 Crinan Canal, Lists of Proprietors 30 December 1797

HOUSE OF LORDS RECORD OFFICE

Deposited Plans (Subscription Contracts).

Montgomeryshire Canal 1794	Warwick and Braunston Canal 1794
Peak Forest Canal 1794	Huddersfield Canal 1794
Rochdale Canal 1794	Kennet and Avon Canal 1794
Swansea Canal 1794	Wilts and Berks Canal 1795
Dorset and Somerset Canal 1796	Grand Union Canal 1810
Bristol and Taunton Canal 1811	North Wilts Canal 1813

House of Lords Committee Minute Books, Nos. 47, 49

BANK OF ENGLAND

Four Per Cent Consolidated Annuities for 28 Years: Index volumes 1780-93

BRITISH MUSEUM

Additional Manuscript 11255, 'An Account of the Tonnage of all Ships and Vessels belonging to each respective Port in England . . .'

BEDFORDSHIRE RECORD OFFICE

A.D.1116, 'An Account of the Biggleswade Turnpike Road', 1725-69
DD X 40/2-4, Biggleswade Turnpike Trust Account Books, 1780-1819
Francklin MSS., F.N.1492, Accounts of the Ouse Navigation, 1732-1800

BERKSHIRE RECORD OFFICE

D/E Hy 09/3, Maidenhead Bridge-Sunning Lane Turnpike Trust, Statement of Income 1728-34
ECR 01, Fyfield-Newbridge Turnpike Trust Minute Book, 1787-1819

BIRMINGHAM REFERENCE LIBRARY

Jewell Baillie MSS.:
  83b/10, Proceedings before the Commissioners of the Worcester and
    Birmingham Canal
  308, Warwick and Birmingham Canal agent's notebook
568603, Canal papers of the Revd. John Rose Holden

BODLEIAN LIBRARY, OXFORD

Dep. a.16, Oxford Canal Accounts 1772-1800
Dep. c.102, 103, Oxford Canal Transfer Books, 1769-93, 1793-1800
MS. Eng. Misc. b.41, Account Book of Jacob Hagen 1736-74
MS. Eng. Misc. c.144, 'An Essay Concerning the Decay of Rents, &
    their Remedys, written by Sir William Coventry abt. the year 1670'
MS. Top. Oxon. d.373, Ryton Bridge-Banbury Turnpike Trust
    Account Book, 1758-1808

BRISTOL UNIVERSITY LIBRARY

Pinney MSS.:
  Letter Book No. 11, John Pinney 1792-6
  Ledger No. 11, John Pinney 1789-1800

BUCKINGHAMSHIRE RECORD OFFICE

Way MSS., D/W, 94; 96/12, Grand Junction Canal circulars to pro-
    prietors
Lee MSS., D/LE, 1/732, 734, Deeds

BURY ST. EDMUNDS AND WEST SUFFOLK RECORD OFFICE

Cullum MSS.:
  E2/17/1, Accounts of the Ouse Navigation 1732-42, 1807-23, and
    of the Lark Navigation 1733-41, 1811-17
  E2/17/7 Lark Navigation Account Book, 1780-1810

DERBY CENTRAL LIBRARY

Derby Canal Collection:
  Committee Minutes, 1793-1820
  Transfer Book
  No. 15, Deeds of the River Derwent Navigation 1720-1
  No. 48, Account of shares taken by landowners

ESSEX RECORD OFFICE

D/TX 2/1, Essex Turnpike Trust, Chelmsford Division, Treasurer's
    Accounts, 1783-1802

GLAMORGANSHIRE RECORD OFFICE

D/D NCa 84, Neath Canal Minute Book, 1791-1856

GLOUCESTERSHIRE RECORD OFFICE

D. 1180 3/1, Stroudwater Navigation, Register of Shares and Share
    Transfers, 1774-1809

T.S. 166, Thames and Severn Canal, Minutes of the General Assembly, 1783-1822

HALIFAX CENTRAL LIBRARY

Lister MSS., R. & W. 1, 7, 12, 13, 20, Halifax-Wakefield Turnpike Trust Accounts, 1781-1808
Parker Collection, No. 2264, Declaration of Trust concerning shares in the Calder and Hebble Navigation, 1768

IPSWICH AND EAST SUFFOLK RECORD OFFICE

EH: 50/5/2B/1, Ipswich-Southtown Turnpike Trust Minute Book, 1785-1821
EH: 50/5/3B/7, Little Yarmouth Turnpike Trust Account Book, 1796-1839
EH: 50/5/4B, Aldeburgh Turnpike Trust Minute Book, 1792-1846

LANCASHIRE RECORD OFFICE

DD Bo/289-292, Papers of a Shareholder in the Rochdale Canal

LEEDS CENTRAL LIBRARY

Harewood Estate MSS. (Turnpike Trusts), Tadcaster-Otley Turnpike Trust, Papers and Account Book, 1778-1831

LEICESTERSHIRE RECORD OFFICE

Acc. No. 336/1, Melton Navigation, Register of Shareholders
Q.S. 50/1, Enrolments of Bargains and Sales to the Companies of Proprietors of Navigations, vol. i, 1792-1808
Q.S. 72/3, Grantham Canal, Book of Reference, 1793

LINCOLNSHIRE ARCHIVES OFFICE

T.L.E.:
    I/1/1, Horncastle Navigation Committee Minutes, 1792-1803
    I/1/7, Share Register
    I/1/9, Dividend Book, 1813-61
Lincolnshire River Board Records, I 1/1, Witham Drainage Committee Minutes, 1762-76

MIDDLESEX RECORD OFFICE

Deposited Plans, Grand Junction Canal, Book of Reference, 1793
LA/HW/Tp/21, Edgware Turnpike Trust Account Book, 1733-1811
Tp BED/1, Bedfont Turnpike Trust Minute Book, 1728-57

NATIONAL LIBRARY OF WALES, DEPARTMENT OF MSS.

Deposit 91B, Glamorganshire Canal Minute Book, 1790

NORTHAMPTONSHIRE RECORD OFFICE

Ellesmere (Brackley) MSS.:
    1460, General Account of the Duke of Bridgewater's Lancashire and Cheshire Estates, 1759-90

1461, 'General State of his Grace the Duke of Bridgewater's Navigation, Colliery, Lime and Farm Concerns in Lancashire and Cheshire from Midsummer 1759.'

Cartwright (Aynho) MSS., 3408–3487, Deeds

Hanbury (Kelmarsh) MSS., 325, 333, Accounts of the Tolls of the Market Harborough–Loughborough Turnpike Trust, 1725–58

D. 2921, Banbury–Lutterworth Turnpike Trust Account Book, 1765–78

Box 1023, Wellingborough–Northampton Turnpike Trust Account Book, 1797–1818

Box 1484, Market Harborough–Northampton Turnpike Trust, Leases of Tolls, 1798–1808, 1811–14

Misc. Ledger 755, Hardingstone–Old Stratford Turnpike Trust Account Book, 1775–1800

NOTTINGHAMSHIRE RECORD OFFICE

DDVC 67/12–16, Five Shares in the Basingstoke Canal belonging to Peter Vere of Kensington

OXFORDSHIRE RECORD OFFICE

CH/III/9, Oxford Canal Subscription Deed, 1768

CH. N II/ii/23, List of Oxford Canal Proprietors resident at or near Oxford, November 1792

Ch. S. 1, 2/1/2, Stokenchurch Turnpike Trust Minute Books, 1740–93, 1793–1807

Stockton and Fortescue Collection, Box 33, Bundles B, I

DIL/II/c/5d–9

Dash IX/iii/16/1, X/ii/xx/1, XIII/i/27, XVIII/ii/13

PRIOR'S KITCHEN, DURHAM

Backhouse MSS., 247–8, 289–90, Deeds concerning shares in the Leeds and Liverpool Canal, 1780

SHEFFIELD CENTRAL LIBRARY

Jackson Collection, No. 1255, Chesterfield Canal Abstract of Tonnage, 1774–89

T.C. 362, Considerations relating to the proposed Sheffield–Derbyshire turnpike, c, 1758

T.C. 364, Sheffield–Wakefield Turnpike Trust Accounts, 1766–75

SOMERSET RECORD OFFICE

DD/MK, Boxes 16, 18, Tone Navigation General Ledgers, 1699–1803, 1803–31

DD/TC, No. 1, Tone Navigation Treasurer's Memorandum Book

DD/TC, Box 24, Copy of the assignment of interest in the Tone, 1698

D/T/ta 5–7, Taunton Turnpike Trust Minute Books, 1752–77, 1778–90, 1791–1805

D/T/ilm 1, Ilminster Turnpike Trust Minute Book, 1759–1803

D/T/wel 8(2), 9(12), Wells Turnpike Trust Account Books, 1753–66, 1766–1806

D/T/Yeo 24, 25, Yeovil Turnpike Trust Ledgers, 1777–1808, 1808–20

SWINDON PUBLIC LIBRARY

Wilts and Berks Canal Collection:
  No. 1, Copy Book of Conveyances, 1798–1815
  No. 2, Account of Receipts and Disbursements, 1795–1805
  No. 12, Register of Optional Notes, 1802–3
  No. 13, Subscription Ledger, 1793–1803
  No. 32, Ledger, 1810–17

STAFFORDSHIRE RECORD OFFICE

Baldwyn MSS., Deeds and papers relating to the navigation of the Stour, Parcel 43, Bundles 3, 10; Parcel 59, Bundle 3; Parcel 61, Bundle 5

Q/SO 7, Order Book of the Staffordshire Quarter Sessions, 1659/60–1667

D 1734/2/5/1s, Addresses of the inhabitants of the town of Burton on Trent concerning the navigation of the Trent, c. 1692 and 1694

WARWICKSHIRE RECORD OFFICE

C.R. 136A/7, Diary of Sir Roger Newdigate, 1763–76

C.R. 347/21, Spernal Ash-Digbeth Turnpike Trust Minute Book, 1767–1859

C.R. 446/2, 3a, Stratford–Bromsgrove Turnpike Trust Minute Books, 1767–1806, 1806–50

C.R. 580, Box 50, 'Canal agency' papers of William Pratt

WELLAND AND NENE RIVER AUTHORITY, OUNDLE

Nene Navigation MSS.:
  Commissioners' Minute Book No. 2, 1760–1800
  'Entries of the Original Assignments from the Commissioners of the Western Division of the Navigation of the River Nene or Nen to the several Proprietors of Navigation Joint Stock', 1 vol., 1762

WEST RIDING COUNTY COUNCIL OFFICES, WAKEFIELD

Collection of Turnpike MSS.:
  Box 8, Keighley–Halifax Turnpike Trust Minute Book, 1789–1815
  Box 9, Marsden–Long Preston Turnpike Trust Minute Book, 1803–60
  Box 22, Keighley–Kirkby-in-Kendal Turnpike Trust Minute Book, 1753–63, 1787–1815
  Box 24, Worksop–Attercliffe Turnpike Trust Minute Book, 1782–1824
  Box 27, Boroughbridge–Ripon Turnpike Trust Account Book, 1752–1814
  Collingham–York Turnpike Trust Minute Book, 1771–1875

Harrogate–Boroughbridge Turnpike Trust Minute Book, 1752–1870

Harrogate–Hutton Moor Turnpike Trust Minute Book, 1752–1814

Knaresborough–Green Hammerton Turnpike Trust Minute Book, 1752–1878

Knaresborough–Pateley Bridge Turnpike Trust Account Book, 1759–1881

Knaresborough–Wetherby Turnpike Trust Minute Book, 1775–1870

Ripon–Pateley Bridge Turnpike Trust Account Book, 1752–1814

Box 32, Halifax–Wakefield Turnpike Trust Cash Book, 1758–77, Minute Book, 1762–1822

Box 45, Leeds–Wakefield, Turnpike Trust Minute Books, 1758–79, 1779–94, 1794–1821

Box 46, Oldham–Ripponden Turnpike Trust Minute Book, 1795–1808

Box 50, Bradford–Keighley Turnpike Trust Minute Book, 1755–1823

Box 54, Redhouse–Wakefield Turnpike Trust Minute Book, 1741–1830, Account Book, 1741–1812

Tadcaster–York Turnpike Trust Minute Book, 1745–99

Wakefield–Weeland Turnpike Trust Minute Book, 1741–1826

Box 54a, Doncaster–Tadcaster Turnpike Trust Minute Book, 1741–1835

Box 63, Standedge–Oldham Turnpike Trust Minute Book, 1792–1812

Box 72, Huddersfield–Penistone Turnpike Trust Account Book, 1771–1811

WILLIAM SALT LIBRARY, STAFFORD

HM 37/40, Notebooks of Edward Sneyd of Lichfield, 1770s, including accounts of the Trent and Mersey Canal, 1774–83

WORCESTERSHIRE RECORD OFFICE

614/56, Droitwich Borough Records, Agreements of the Droitwich Canal Company with proprietors for the purchase of land, c. 1770

704/3, Droitwich Turnpike Trust Account Book, 1736–64

4600/300, Monksbridge–Tenbury Turnpike Trust Accounts, 1781–4

B. PRINTED SOURCES

Calendar of State Papers, Domestic.
House of Commons Journals.
House of Lords Journals.
English Reports.

British Parliamentary Papers:

1825 (403), v, pp. 551-566. *Western Ship Canal. Minutes of Evidence Taken before the Committee on the Bill.*

1830 (251), x, pp. 719-865. *Report from the Committee on the Birmingham and London Junction Canal Petitions.*

1837-8 (108), xxv. *Thirty-Second Report of the Commissioners for Inquiring Concerning Charities, Part I.*

1850 (508), xix, pp. 169-294. *Report from the Select Committee on Investments for the Savings of the Middle and Working Classes.*

1890 (6083), lxiv, pp. 747-923. *Returns made to the Board of Trade . . . in respect of the Canals and Navigations of the United Kingdom for the year 1888.*

DIRECTORIES

(Henry KENT), *The Directory for the year 1738* [for London].

Kent's Directory for the year 1780 [for London].

G. T. and I. SHAW (eds.), *Liverpool's First Directory* (1907) [a reprint of John Gore's *The Liverpool Directory for the Year 1766*].

Sketchley & Adam's Tradesman's True Guide: or an Universal Directory for . . . Birmingham, Wolverhampton, Walsall, Dudley & the Villages in the Neighbourhood . . . (Birmingham, 1770).

Bailey's British Directory . . . for . . . 1784 (4 vols., 1784).

William TUNNICLIFF, *A Topographical Survey of the Counties of Stafford, Chester & Lancaster* (1787).

The Universal British Directory of Trade, Commerce and Manufacture . . . (5 vols., 1790-8).

Matthew's New Bristol Directory for . . . 1793-4 (Bristol, 1793).

(John ROBINSON), *A Directory of Sheffield including . . . Adjacent Villages (Sheffield, 1797).*

Holden's Triennial Directory (Fifth Edition) for 1809, 1810, 1811 (1809).

Pigot and Co's London and Provincial New Directory for 1823-4 (1823).

NEWSPAPERS AND PERIODICAL PUBLICATIONS

Annual Register	*Leeds Mercury*
Aris's Birmingham Gazette	*Leicester Journal*
Felix Farley's Bristol Journal	*London Gazette*
Gentleman's Magazine	*Manchester Mercury*
Gore's General Advertiser	*Northampton Mercury*
Halifax Journal	*Sheffield Iris*
Jackson's Oxford Journal	*Williamson's Liverpool Advertiser*

BOOKS AND ARTICLES
Published before 1850

An Address to the Public on the New Intended Canal from Stourbridge to Worcester with the Case of the Staffordshire and Worcestershire Canal Company (n.p., 1786).

J. AIKIN, *A Description of the Country from thirty to forty miles round Manchester* (1795).

W. ALLEN, *Ways and Means to raise the Value of Land* (1736).

E. ASHMOLE, *The Antiquities of Berkshire* (1719).

T. BADESLADE, *The History of the ancient and present state of the navigation of the port of King's Lynn* (1725).

T. BAIRD, *General View of the Agriculture of the County of Middlesex* (1793).

J. W. BUCK, *Cases in Bankruptcy*, i, (1820).

P. COLQUHOUN, *A Treatise on the Wealth, Power and Resources of the British Empire* (1814).

T. CONGREVE, *A Scheme or Proposal for making a navigable Communication between the Rivers of Trent and Severn in the County of Stafford* (1753).

[D. DEFOE], *The Complete English Tradesman* (3rd edn., 1732).

J. DONALDSON, *General View of the Agriculture of the County of Northampton* (Edinburgh, 1794).

C. DUPIN, *The Commercial Power of England* (2 vols., 1825).
The Earl of Plimouth's Case (n.p., n.d.).

S. EDWARDS, *Extracts from Harrod's History of Stamford relating to the Navigation of the River Welland* ... (1810).

W. ENFIELD, *An Essay towards the History of Liverpool* (1774).

H. ENGLISH, *A Complete View of the Joint Stock Companies formed during the years 1824 and 1825* (1827).

E. H., *Reasons for the Abatement of Interest to Four in the Hundred* (1692).

J(ames) H(ELY), *A Modest Representation of the Benefits and Advantages of Making the River Avon Navigable* (1672).

T. HEYWOOD (ed.), *The Norris Papers* (Chetham Society, Manchester, ix, 1846).

The History of Inland Navigations, Particularly those of the Duke of Bridgewater in Lancashire and Cheshire (1st edn., 1766; 3rd edn., 1779).

J. HOUGHTON, *A Collection for the Improvement of Husbandry and Trade* ed. R. Bradley (3 vols., 1727).

J. LATIMER, *Annals of Bristol in the Eighteenth Century* (Frome, 1893).

A List of the Proprietors of the Worcester and Birmingham Canal Navigation on the First Day of June, 1798 (n.p., n.d.).

A List of the Proprietors of the Worcester and Birmingham Canal Navigation on the 26th November 1808 (n.p., n.d.).

W. MAVOR, *General View of the Agriculture of Berkshire* (1813).

J. MIDDLETON, *View of the Agriculture of Middlesex* (1807).

J. S. MILL, *Principles of Political Economy* (1848).

Observations on a scheme for extending the Navigation of the Rivers of Kennett and Avon ... *by a Canal from Newbury to Bath* (Marlborough, 1788).

J. PHILLIPS, *A General History of Inland Navigation* (4th edn., 1803).

W. PITT, *General View of the Agriculture of the County of Leicester* (1813).
—— *A Topographical History of Staffordshire* (Newcastle-under-Lyme, 1817).
J. PRIESTLEY, *An Historical Account of the Navigable Rivers, Canals and Railways throughout Great Britain* (1831).
W. RICHARDS, *The History of Lynn* (King's Lynn, 2 vols., 1812).
O. RUFFHEAD (ed.), *The Statutes at Large* (18 vols., 1763-1800).
P. THOMPSON, *Collections for a Topographical and Historical Account of Boston* (1820).
J. THROSBY, *The History and Antiquities of the Ancient Town of Leicester* (Leicester, dated 1791, but published later).
J. E. TOMLINS and J. RAITHBY (eds.), *The Statutes of the United Kingdom of Great Britain and Ireland* (5 vols., 1804-14).
J. WEDGE, *General View of the Agriculture of Warwick* (1794).
A. YARRANTON, *England's Improvement by Land and Sea* (1677).
A. YOUNG, *An Enquiry into the Progressive Value of Money in England* (1812).
—— *General View of the Agriculture of Sussex* (1794).

BOOKS AND ARTICLES
Published after 1850

W. I. ALBERT, *The Turnpike Road System in England* (Cambridge, 1972).
T. S. ASHTON, *Economic Fluctuations in England 1700-1800* (Oxford, 1959).
—— *The Industrial Revolution* (rev. edn., Oxford, 1968).
T. C. BARKER, 'The Beginnings of the Canal Age in the British Isles', in L. S. Pressnell (ed.), *Studies in the Industrial Revolution* (1960).
—— 'Lancashire Coal, Cheshire Salt and the Rise of Liverpool', *Transactions of the Historic Society of Lancashire and Cheshire*, ciii (1951), 83-101.
—— 'The Sankey Navigation', ibid. c (1948), 121-55.
H. BRAUN, 'The Salisbury Canal. A Georgian Misadventure', *Wiltshire Archaeological and Natural History Magazine*, lviii (1962) 171-80.
S. A. BROADBRIDGE, 'The Early Capital Market. The Lancashire and Yorkshire Railway', *Econ. Hist. Rev.*, 2nd Series, viii (1955), 200-12.
G.E.C., *The Complete Peerage* (13 vols., 1910-40).
C. W. CHALKLIN, 'Navigation Schemes on the Upper Medway 1600-1655', *Journal of Transport History*, v (1961), 105-15.
W. H. Chaloner, 'The Cheshire Activities of Matthew Boulton and James Watt of Soho, near Birmingham 1776-1817', *Transactions of the Lancashire and Cheshire Antiquarian Society*, lxi (1949), 121-36.
J. D. CHAMBERS, *The Vale of Trent 1670-1800*, Econ. Hist. Rev. Supplement No. 3 (n.p., n.d.).

S. G. CHECKLAND, 'Finance for the West Indies, 1780-1815', *Econ. Hist. Rev.*, 2nd Ser., x (1957-8), 461-9.

I. R. CHRISTIE (ed.), *The Correspondence of Jeremy Bentham*, vol. 3, 1781-8 (1971).

J. H. CLAPHAM, *The Economic History of Modern Britain*, vol. i, *The Early Railway Age 1820-1850* (Cambridge, 1939).

R. CRAIG, 'Some Aspects of the Trade and Shipping of the River Dee in the Eighteenth Century', *Transactions of the Historic Society of Lancashire and Cheshire*, cxiv (1962), 99-128.

D. A. E. CROSS, 'The Salisbury Avon Navigation', *Industrial Archaeology*, vii (1970), 121-30.

F. CROUZET, 'La Formation du capital en Grande-Bretagne pendant la revolution industrielle', in *Deuxième Conférence Internationale d'Histoire Economique, Aix-en-Provence, 1962* (Paris, 1965), ii. 589-642.

W. CUDWORTH, 'The First Bradford Bank', *The Bradford Antiquary*, New Series, ii (1903), 232-7.

J. F. CURWEN, 'The Lancaster Canal', *Transactions of the Cumberland and Westmoreland Antiquarian and Archaeological Society*, New Series, xvii (1917), 26-47.

P. DEANE, *The First Industrial Revolution* (Cambridge, 1965).

———— and W. A. COLE, *British Economic Growth 1688-1959* (Cambridge, 1962).

P. G. M. DICKSON, *The Financial Revolution* (1967).

A. B. DUBOIS, *The English Business Company after the Bubble Act 1720-1800* (New York, 1938).

G. H. EVANS, *British Corporation Finance 1775-1850* (Baltimore, 1936).

A. EVERITT, 'Social Mobility in Early Modern England', *Past and Present*, no. 33 (April 1966), 56-73.

K. E. FARRER (ed.), *Letters of Josiah Wedgwood 1762 to 1770* (n.p., n.d.).

M. W. FLINN, *Men of Iron. The Crowleys in the Early Iron Industry* (Edinburgh, 1962).

———— *The Origins of the Industrial Revolution* (1966).

A. D. GAYER, W. W. ROSTOW, and A. J. SCHWARTZ, *The Growth and Fluctuation of the British Economy 1790-1850* (2 vols., Oxford, 1953).

J. E. GINARLIS, 'Capital Formation in Road and Canal Transport', in J. P. P. Higgins and S. Pollard (edd.), *Aspects of Capital Formation in Great Britain 1750-1850* (1971).

R. GRASSBY, 'English Merchant Capital in the Late Seventeenth Century. The Composition of Business Fortunes', *Past and Present*, no. 46 (February 1970), 87-107.

———— 'The Personal Wealth of the Business Community in Seventeenth-Century England', *Econ. Hist. Rev.*, 2nd Series, xxiii(1970), 220-34.

—––– 'The Rate of Profit in Seventeenth-Century England', *English Historical Review*, lxxxiv (1969), 721-51.

H. J. HABAKKUK, 'Economic Functions of English Landowners in the Seventeenth and Eighteenth Centuries', *Explorations in Entrepreneurial History*, vi (1953), 92-102.

—––– 'The Long-term Rate of Interest and the Price of Land in the Seventeenth Century', *Econ. Hist. Rev.*, 2nd Series, v (1952-3), 26-45.

C. HADFIELD, *British Canals* (2nd edn., 1959).

—––– *The Canal Age* (Newton Abbot, 1968).

—––– *The Canals of Southern England* (1955).

—––– *The Canals of South Wales and the Border* (London and Cardiff, 1960).

—––– *The Canals of the West Midlands* (Newton Abbot, 1966).

—––– and G. BIDDLE, *The Canals of North West England* (2 vols., Newton Abbot, 1970).

—––– and J. NORRIS, *Waterways to Stratford* (Dawlish, 1962).

H. HAMILTON, *An Economic History of Scotland in the Eighteenth Century* (Oxford, 1963).

A Handlist of Inclosure Acts and Awards relating to the County of Oxford, Oxfordshire County Council Record Publications, No. 2 (1963).

J. R. HARRIS, 'Liverpool Canal Controversies 1769-1772', *Journal of Transport History*, ii (1956), 158-74.

J. W. F. HILL, *Tudor and Stuart Lincoln* (Cambridge, 1956).

E. J. HOBSBAWM, *Industry and Empire* (1968).

W. G. HOFFMANN, *British Industry 1700-1950*, translated by W. O. Henderson and W. H. Chaloner (Oxford, 1955).

G. G. HOPKINSON, 'The Development of Inland Navigation in South Yorkshire and North Derbyshire 1697-1850', *Transactions of the Hunter Archaeological Society*, vii (1956), 229-51.

—––– 'The Inland Navigation of the Derbyshire and Nottinghamshire Coalfield 1777-1856', *Journal of the Derbyshire Archaeological and Natural History Society*, lxxix (1959), 22-41.

H. G. W. HOUSEHOLD, *The Thames and Severn Canal* (Newton Abbot, 1969).

B. C. HUNT, *The Development of the Business Corporation in England 1800-1867* (Cambridge, Mass., 1936).

Index to Wills Proved in the Prerogative Court of Canterbury, 1686-1693 (Index Library, lxxvii, 1955-6).

W. ISON, *The Georgian Buildings of Bristol* (1952).

W. T. JACKMAN, *The Development of Transportation in Modern England* (2nd edn., 1962).

A. H. JOHN, 'Insurance Investment and the London Money Market in the Eighteenth Century', *Economica*, New Series, xx (1953), 137-58.

M. F. KEELER, *The Long Parliament, 1640–1641* (Philadelphia, 1954).

J. R. KELLETT, *The Impact of Railways on Victorian Cities* (1969).

E. KERRIDGE, *The Agricultural Revolution* (1967).

H. F. KILLICK, 'Notes on the Early History of the Leeds and Liverpool Canal', *The Bradford Antiquary*, New Series, Part II (1897), 169–238.

J. R. KILLICK and W. A. THOMAS, 'The Provincial Stock Exchanges, 1830–1870', *Econ. Hist. Rev.*, 2nd Series, xxiii (1970), 96–111.

H. G. LEWIN, *Early British Railways . . . 1801–1844* (1925).

J. LINDSAY, *The Canals of Scotland* (Newton Abbot, 1968).

J. D. MARSHALL, *Furness and the Industrial Revolution* (Barrow-in-Furness, 1958).

P. MATHIAS, *The Brewing Industry in England, 1700–1830* Cambridge, 1959).

————— *The First Industrial Nation* (1969).

————— 'The Social Structure in the Eighteenth Century: a Calculation by Joseph Massie', *Econ. Hist. Rev.*, 2nd Series, x (1957–8), 30–45.

E. METEYARD, *The Life of Josiah Wedgwood* (2 vols., 1865).

W. E. MINCHINTON, 'Bristol—Metropolis of the West in the Eighteenth Century' *Transactions of the Royal Historical Society*, 5th Ser., iv (1954), 69–89.

G. E. MINGAY, *English Landed Society in the Eighteenth Century* (1963).

B. R. MITCHELL and P. DEANE, *Abstract of British Historical Statistics* (Cambridge, 1962).

L. MOFFIT, *England on the Eve of the Industrial Revolution* (2nd edn., 1963).

E. V. MORGAN and W. A. THOMAS, *The Stock Exchange: its history and function* (1962).

L. B. NAMIER, *England in the Age of the American Revolution* (1930).

J. U. NEF, *The Rise of the British Coal Industry* (2 vols., 1932).

R. NEWTON, 'Society and Politics in Exeter 1837–1914', in H. J. Dyos (ed.), *The Study of Urban History* (1968).

NORTON, TRIST, and GILBERT, 'A Century of Land Values: England and Wales', *Journal of the Royal Statistical Society*, liv (1891), reprinted in E. M. Carus-Wilson (ed.), *Essays in Economic History*, iii (1962).

P. K. O'BRIEN, 'British Incomes and Property in the Early Nineteenth Century', *Econ. Hist. Rev.*, 2nd Series, xii (1959–60), 255–67.

C. C. OWEN, 'The Early History of the Upper Trent Navigation', *Transport History*, i (1968), 233–59.

E.M.S.P., *The Two James's and the Two Stephensons* (1861. New edition, Dawlish, 1961).

R. PARES, *Merchants and Planters*, Econ. Hist. Rev. Supplement No. 4 (Cambridge, 1960).

————— *A West-India Fortune* (1950).

C. N. PARKINSON, *The Rise of the Port of Liverpool* (Liverpool, 1952).

A. T. PATTERSON, *Radical Leicester* (Leicester, 1954).

H. PERKIN, *The Origins of Modern English Society 1780-1880* (1969).

J. A. PICTON, *Memorials of Liverpool, Historical and Topographical* (2 vols., 1873).

S. POLLARD, 'Fixed Capital in the Industrial Revolution in Britain', *Journal of Economic History*, xxiv (1964), 299-314.

———— 'The Growth and Distribution of Capital in Great Britain', in *Third International Conference of Economic History, Munich, 1965* (Paris, 1968).

H. POLLINS, 'A Note on Railway Constructional Costs 1825-1850', *Economica*, New Series, xix (1952), 395-406.

———— 'The Swansea Canal', *Journal of Transport History*, i (1954), 135-54.

M. M. POSTAN, 'Recent Trends in the Accumulation of Capital', *Econ. Hist. Rev.*, 1st Series, vi (1935), 1-12.

L. S. PRESSNELL, *Country Banking in the Industrial Revolution* (Oxford, 1956).

———— 'The Rate of Interest in the Eighteenth Century', in L. S. Pressnell (ed.), *Studies in the Industrial Revolution* (Manchester, 1960).

A. RAISTRICK, *Dynasty of Ironfounders; the Darbys and Coalbrookdale* (1953).

———— and B. JENNINGS, *A History of Lead Mining in the Pennines* (1965).

H. A. SHANNON, 'Bricks—A Trade Index, 1785-1849', *Economica*, New Series, iii (1934), 300-18.

W. SLATCHER, 'The Barnsley Canal: Its first Twenty Years', *Transport History*, i (1968), 48-66.

S. SMILES, *Lives of the Engineers* (5 vols., 1874-9).

J. E. H. SPAUL (ed.), *The Andover Canal* (Andover Local Archives Committee, Andover Documents No. 1, 1968).

H. SPENCER, *London's Canal. The History of the Regent's Canal* (1961).

H. A. C. STURGESS (ed.), *Register of Admissions to the Honourable Society of the Middle Temple 1501-1944* (3 vols., 1949).

D. H. TEW, *The Oakham Canal* (Wymondham, 1968).

F. S. THACKER, *Kennet Country* (1932).

A. L. THOMAS, 'Geographical Aspects of the Development of Transport and Communications Affecting the Pottery Industry of North Staffordshire during the Eighteenth Century', *Collections for a History of Staffordshire* (1934), 1-157.

H. THORPE, 'Lichfield: A study of its growth and function', *Collections for a History of Staffordshire* (1954), pp. 139-211.

V. I. TOMLINSON, 'The Manchester, Bolton and Bury Canal', *Transactions of the Lancashire and Cheshire Antiquarian Society* lxxv-lxxvi (1965-6), 231-99.

—— 'Salford activities connected with the Bridgewater Navigation', ibid. lxvi (1956-7), 57-86.

G. S. L. TUCKER, *Progress and Profits in British Economic Thought 1650-1850* (Cambridge, 1960).

G. UNWIN, *Samuel Oldknow and the Arkwrights. The Industrial Revolution at Stockport and Marple* (Manchester, 1924).

R. W. UNWIN, 'The Aire and Calder Navigation. Part I: The Beginning of the Navigation', *The Bradford Antiquary*, New Series, xliii (1964), 53-87.

A. P. USHER (ed.), *Two Manuscripts by Charles Davenant* (Baltimore, 1942).

Victoria County History: Berkshire, iv (1924).

Victoria County History: Leicestershire, iii (1955).

Victoria County History: Worcestershire, ii (1906).

P. A. L. VINE, *London's Lost Route to Basingstoke* (Newton Abbot, 1968).

—— *London's Lost Route to the Sea* (2nd ed., Newton Abbot, 1966).

A. P. WADSWORTH and J. De L. MANN, *The Cotton Trade and Industrial Lancashire 1600-1780* Manchester, 1931).

E. WELCH, *The Bankrupt Canal* (Southampton Corporation Civic Record Office, Southampton Papers, No. 5, 1966).

T. S. WILLAN, *The Early History of the Don Navigation* (Manchester, 1965).

—— *The Navigation of the Great Ouse between St. Ives and Bedford in the Seventeeth Century* (Bedfordshire Historical Record Society, Aspley Guise, xxiv, 1946).

—— *The Navigation of the River Weaver in the Eighteenth Century* (Chetham Society, Manchester, 3rd Series, iii, 1957).

—— 'The Navigation of the Thames and Kennet 1600-1750', *Berkshire Archaeological Journal*, xl (1936), 146-56.

—— 'River Navigation and Trade from the Witham to the Yare 1600-1750', *Norfolk Archaeology*, xxvi (1938), 296-309.

—— *River Navigation in England 1600-1750* (Oxford, 1936).

—— 'Salisbury and the Navigation of the Avon', *Wiltshire Archaeological and Natural History Magazine*, xlvii (1935-7), 592-4.

A. F. WILLIAMS, 'Bristol Port Plans and Improvement Schemes in the Eighteenth Century', *Transactions of the Bristol and Gloucestershire Archaeological Society*, lxxxi (1962), 138-88.

O. C. WILLIAMS, *The Historical Development of Private Bill Procedure and Standing Orders in the House of Commons* (1948).

F. WILLIAMSON, 'George Sorocold of Derby', *Journal of the Derbyshire Archaeological and Natural History Society*, lvii (1936), 43-63.

E. A. WILSON, 'The Proprietors of the Ellesmere and Chester Canal Company in 1822', *Journal of Transport History*, iii (1957), 52-4.

R. G. WILSON, 'Transport Dues as indices of Economic Growth, 1775-1820', *Econ. Hist. Rev.*, 2nd Series, xix (1966), 110-23.

UNPUBLISHED THESES

P. J. CAINE, 'A History of the Chelmer Navigation down to 1830' (Dissertation, St. John's College, York, 1961: Copy in Essex R.O.).

H. G. W. HOUSEHOLD, 'Thames and Severn: Birth and Death of a Canal' (Bristol University M.A. Dissertation, 1958).

R. M. SIMPSON, 'Walter Spencer Stanhope: Landlord, Business Entrepreneur and M.P.' (Nottingham University M.A. Dissertation, 1959).

T. S. WILLAN, 'English Coasting Trade and River Navigation, 1600–1750', (Oxford University D. Phil. Thesis, 1934).

INDEX

Abbot, Woolstone, of Salisbury, gentleman, 6
Abingdon, 69
Adams, William, of the Middle Temple, Esquire, 2 n. 4.
Adur, River, 179
Aire and Calder Navigation, 7, 43, 108-9, 186
Alanson, Edward, of Liverpool, surgeon, 95
Aldridge, Richard, of Stroud, tallow chandler, 64
Ancholme, River, 179
Anderdon, J. P., of Bristol, attorney, 140
Andover, 66
Andover Canal, 66, 179
Annuity, 48-9, 122-3
Anson, Lord, 151
Arkwright, Richard, the elder, cotton manufacturer, 149
Arkwright, Richard, the younger, cotton manufacturer, 59-60
Arun, River, 179
Ashby-de-la-Zouch, 87, 118 n. 2.
Ashby-de-la-Zouch Canal, 19, 42, 87, 153, 160, 176-7, 179-80, 182, 184, 187
Ashley, Henry, of Eynesbury, Hunts., tanner and gentleman, 2
Ashton, John, of Liverpool, merchant, 26-7
Ashton under Lyne, 57-8, 60
Ashton under Lyne Canal, 57-8, 82, 85, 95, 121 n. 1, 177, 181
Atherstone, 30
Attorneys, see Lawyers
Aufrere, George, of London, merchant, 65 n. 2
Avon, River (Hampshire), 5-7
Avon, River (Somerset), 10
Avon, River (Warwickshire), 2-3, 15-16
Axe, River, 179
Aylesbury, 45

Bailiss, Thomas, of Stroud, clothier, 64
Baker, Nicholas, of Worcester, mercer, 3

Baldwyn, Benjamin, of Stoke Castle, Salop, gentleman, 4
Baldwyn, Samuel, of the Inner Temple, Esquire, 4-5
Baldwyn, Timothy, Doctor of Laws, 4
Banbury, 32, 45, 97
Banks and Navigation Finance, 48, 73, 80-2, 98, 109-13, 186-90
Bankruptcy, 9, 61, 82, 113, 118, 173
Barnard, Charles, of Leeds, attorney, 108
Barnsley, 34, 43, 88, 97
Barnsley Canal, 42-3, 88, 119, 120 n. 5, 157 nn. 2-3, 177, 187
Bartlett, Richard, of Old Stratford, dyer, 3
Basingstoke Canal, 80-1, 116-17, 178
Bath, 10, 68, 94, 142
Bath and Bristol Canal, 83
Bath City Bank, 109 n. 9
Battersbie, of Stratford, banker, 190
Bawtry, 9
Bayley, William, of London, gentleman, 9
Beaufort, Duke of, 73
Beaumaris, 163 n. 1, 191
Beaumont, Thomas, of Nottingham, clerk, 98
Bedford, 2, 158
Bedford, Duke of, 158
Bedfordshire, 141
Bennet, Sir Humphrey, 3 n. 2.
Bennet, Thomas, of Salisbury, gentleman, 6
Bentley and Co., of Leicester, bankers, 40, 189
Berkshire, 66-7, 141, 148
Bewdley, 29
Bicester, 32
Bingley, 145
Birmingham, 29, 30, 37-40, 42, 45-52, 54, 63, 69, 72-3, 79 n. 3, 84, 86, 88, 90, 97, 100-1, 127, 130, 133, 142, 180-1
Birmingham Banking Company, 187
Birmingham Canal, 30-1, 87 n. 1, 115-16, 122, 127, 175, 177, 180, 184, 186-7

Birmingham and Liverpool Junction Canal, 85
Blackburne, John, of Liverpool, merchant, 26
Blisworth, 124
Boissier, John Lewis, Captain of Dragoons, 65 n. 3
Bollo Pill Railway, 71
Bolton, 55
Boott, James, of Loughborough, auctioneer, 107
Boston, 13, 41
Boultbee and Co., of Leicester, bankers, 40, 189
Boulton, Matthew, of Birmingham, manufacturer, 160
Bourne, Cornelius, of Liverpool, merchant, 95
Bourne Eau River, 179
Box, Philip, of Buckingham, banker, 44, 188
Bradford, 34, 97, 128
Bradford Canal, 36
Brain, James, of London, merchant, 12
Brecknock and Abergavenny Canal, 73, 113, 145, 178-9, 187
Brecon, 72-3
Bridgewater, Duke of, and the Bridgewater Navigations, ix, 27-8, 73-4, 79, 127, 144, 150-3
Bridgwater, 162, 191
Bridgwater and Taunton Canal, 109
Brindley, James, engineer, 97, 150-1, 152 n. 1
Bristol, 10, 46-8, 53, 66-70, 76, 83, 86, 92-4, 96, 108, 110, 138-40, 142, 152, 155 n. 1, 181, 191
Bristol and Cirencester Canal, 139
Bristol and Gloucester Canal, 96
Bristol and Taunton Canal, 83, 93
Bristol and Worcester Canal, 93
Bristol, Earl of, 3
Broadwood, Bazile, Esquire, 10
Brockwell, Wingfield, 6
Brooke, Sir Richard, 144
Brown, James, of Liverpool, surgeon, 95
Buck, Charles, of Leeds, attorney, 108
Buckingham, 45
Buckinghamshire, 141
Buckle and Williams, of Chepstow, bankers, 189
Burke, Edmund, M.P., 171

Burman, Mr., 12
Burroughs, Samuel, of Crownest, Yorkshire, Esquire, 14 n. 1
Burton-on-Trent, 8, 88, 97
Bury, 55
Bury and Sladen Canal, 90

Caernarvon, 191
Caistor Canal, 135, 179
Calder and Hebble Navigation, 13-14, 98
Caldon (Staffordshire), 29
Cambridgeshire, 141
Canal mania, ix, 44, 51-2, 66, 78, 86-96, 101-2, 104, 106-8, 135-8, 140, 154-6, 160, 180-2
Capell, William, of Stroud, clothier, 64
Capital market, imperfections in, 171-2
Carlisle Canal, 134 n. 3
Carron Iron Company, 132
Carter, Edward, of Leicester, attorney, 40
Cartwright, Francis, of Aynho, Esquire, 159
Cartwright, Thomas, of Aynho, Esquire, 159
Chambers, Rolleston, and Sargent, of London, merchants, 65
Chambers, Christopher, of London, merchant, 65 n. 2
Chard, 83
Chard Canal, 109
Charlbury, 32
Chelmer and Blackwater Navigation, 89, 91 n. 3, 92, 179-80, 182
Chelmsford, 89
Cheshire, 29, 53, 60, 85, 141-2
Chester, 191
Chester Canal, 52, 109, 115, n. 3, 121-2, 133, 175-6
Chesterfield, 9, 36, 97
Chesterfield Canal, 36, 79, 109, 115 n. 2, 133, 175, 186
Cheyne, George, of Bath, Doctor of Physic, 12
Chichester, Bishop of, 6
Chiffinch, William, 6
Child, Robert, of London, banker, 159
Childs and Co., of London, bankers, 28, 79, 189
Chippenham, 67, 69
Chipping Norton, 32
Christchurch, 5

Cirencester, 36
Cirencester and Westerleigh Canal, 93
Clarendon, Earl of, 6, 144, 147
Clarke, Godfrey, M.P. for Derbyshire, 37
Clements, John, of Symons Inn, London, gentleman, 6
Clergymen, 12, 18, 22-3, 29, 33, 55, 57, 66, 70, 74-6, 81 n. 1, 98
Clerke, Sir Clement, of Rudge, Salop, 4
Coal, and coal trade, 4 n. 2, 17, 28, 31, 39, 43, 64, 95, 127, 134, n. 3, 137 n. 2, 143, 154, 157
Coasting trade, 162-3, 165, 191-2
Coalbrookdale, 35, 51
Colchester, 7
Colne, River (Essex), 7
Colne (Lancashire), 34, 97
Congleton, 97
Conway, 191
Cooke, Isaac, of Bristol, attorney, 109
Cooke, John, of Fisherton Anger, Salisbury, silkweaver, 6
Coombe Hill Canal, 179
Cornwall, 141
Cotton manufacturers, 24, 57-60, 63, 77-8
Coventry, 31-2, 40 n. 3, 42, 45-6, 52, 63, 86-8, 91, 140, 180
Coventry Canal, 31-2, 79 n. 2, 115 nn. 2-3, 120, 130, 133, 144, 159, 169 n. 1, 175, 177, 180, 186-7
Cowes, 163 n. 1, 191
Cowslade, Richard, of East Woodhay, Hampshire, Esquire, 10
Cowslade, Thomas, of the Inner Temple, Esquire, 10
Crawshay, Richard, ironmaster, 72-3
Crinan Canal, 90-1, 114 n. 5, 180, 182
Cromford Canal, 39, 109, 115 n. 6, 136, 149, 176
Crompton, of York, banker, 186
Crosbie, James, of Liverpool, merchant, 26
Crown and Anchor Tavern, London, 80
Croydon Canal, 123, 178
Cumberland, 141
Currie, James, of Liverpool, M.D., 95

Dale, William, of Covent Garden, 11-12
Daranda, Paul, of London, merchant, 9.

Dashwood, Sir Henry, of Kirtlington, 159
Dashwood, Sir James, of Kirtlington, 159
Daventry, 45, 69, 84
Dawson, Edward, steward of the Earl of Huntingdon, 38
Dean, Forest of, 71
Dearne and Dove Canal, 88, 157 n. 2
Debenture, 48
Dee, River, 17 n. 3
Denew, Nathaniel, of Canterbury, Esquire, 11 n. 6
Dennet, Thomas, of Salisbury, gentleman, 6
Derby, 9, 42, 45-6, 52, 56, 88, 97
Derby Canal, 42, 88, 103, 115 n. 6
Derbyshire, 38-41, 141, 172
Derbyshire, Mr., attorney, 109
Derwent, River (Derbyshire), 9
Devizes, 67
Devon, 141
Devonshire, Duke of, 37
Dillon-Lee, the Hon. Charles, later Viscount Dillon, 159 n. 6, 160
Dilworth, John, of Lancaster, merchant, 55
Dimsdale, Archer, and Byde, of London, bankers, 186
Dividends of canal companies, 52-3, 101-4, 115-6, 122, 132-8, 175-8
Dobbs, Mr., 145-6
Don Navigation, 12-13, 88
Doncaster, 13, 34, 97
Dorset, 141
Dorset and Somerset Canal, 94, 139, 155, 179
Douglas Navigation, 11 n. 6
Dovegang Committee, 79 n. 5
Droitwich, 3
Droitwich Canal, 146
Drought, Henry, of Oxford, brewer, 110
Dudley Canal, 37-8, 136 n. 3, 153, 160, 177, 180
Dudley, Lord, 145
Dunsford, James, of Oxford, clerk to the Oxford Canal Co., 106
Durham, Co., 141

Eagle, John, of Bradford, attorney, 109
Eastern and Wirral Canal, 90

Egerton, Samuel, of Tatton Park, Cheshire, 29, 128
Ellesmere, later Ellesmere and Chester, Canal, 51, 82, 90, 91 n. 3, 92, 99 nn. 4, 6, 121 n. 1, 155 n. 2, 157, 177, 180, 182, 188
Ellison, of Lincoln, banker, 188
English and Bristol Channels Ship Canal, 83
Erewash Canal, 38, 87 n. 1, 88
Essex, 89, 141
Essex, Earl of, 144, 147
Evans, Francis, of Nottingham, attorney, 109
Evans, Thomas, 12
Exchequer Bill Loan Commissioners, 54
Exe, River, 9 n. 1
Exeter, 9 n. 1, 25
Eyton and Wilkinson, of Shrewsbury, Bankers, 188

Farmers, see Yeomen
Fazeley, 30, 116
Fern, Lady, 73
Ferne, James, of London, surgeon, 12
Finch, the Hon. Charles, 144
Foljambe, F. F., 14 n. 1
Forbes, William Lord, 12
Forth, John, of London, citizen and alderman, 4
Forth and Clyde Canal, 82, 132-3
Fosdyke Navigation, 3 n. 3
Foss, River, 179
Fry, Henry, of London, attorney, 82
Fuller, William and Thomas, of London, bankers, 110
Funds, the public, 129-30, 140-2

Gainsborough, 36, 97
Garbett, Samuel, of Birmingham, manufacturer, 132-3, 134 n. 3
Garraway's Coffee House, London, 68, 82
Gell, Francis, of London, merchant, 17 n. 3
Gibbons, John, of Birmingham, japanner, 130 n. 1
Gilbert, John, agent of the Duke of Bridgewater, 27
Gippen, River, 179
Girton, Thomas, of Westminster, vintner, 2

Glamorganshire Canal, 72, 178
Glenton, J. W., of Liverpool, landwaiter, 96
Gloucester, 53-4, 163 n. 1, 191
Gloucester and Berkeley Canal, 54, 149 n. 4, 156, 169 n. 1, 177
Gloucestershire, 38, 53-4, 141-2
Gore, Charles, of Liverpool, merchant, 26
Gower, Lord, 151
Grand Junction Canal, 43-6, 71, 81-4, 88, 91 n. 3, 99 n. 5, 104-5, 108, 120 n. 3, 121 n. 1, 123-5, 130, 147, 149 n. 5, 153, 157, 176-7, 180-2, 188
Grand Surrey Canal, 122, 178
Grand Union Canal, 46 n. 3, 83, 99, 105, 144
Grand Western Canal, 178
Grand Western Ship Canal, 85
Grantham, 41
Grantham Canal, 41, 109, 119, 157 n. 2, 177, 179, 188
Great Barford, 2
Green, James, of Salisbury, gentleman, 6
Green, Joshua, of Banbury, shagmanufacturer, 130
Greenway, Whitehead, and Weston, of Warwick, bankers, 190
Gurneys, the, Quaker family, 35

Hagen, Jacob, of London, timbermerchant, 36, 79 n. 5.
Halifax, 13-14
Hampshire, 141
Harbour improvement, 164
Hardcastle, William, of Bradford, banker, 110 n. 5
Harfords, the, of Bristol, merchants and ironmasters, 94 n. 7
Harford, Davis, and Co., of Bristol, bankers, 188
Harrison, Edward, of Leicester, attorney, 118 n. 4
Harvey, Sir Eliab, 6
Hawtyn, Joseph, of Banbury, auctioneer, 106-7
Hayne, George, of Wirksworth, gentleman, 8
Hebden, Mr., clerk of Aire and Calder Navigation, 108-9
Hedges, Henry, of Salisbury, surgeon, 6

Hereford, 53
Herefordshire, 53, 141
Herefordshire and Gloucestershire Canal, 53-4, 79 n. 2, 92-3, 122, 179, 181
Hertfordshire, 141
Hewer, William, of Clapham, 7
Heyrick, William, of Leicester, attorney, 107
Highworth, 71
Hill, Humphrey, of London, merchant, 12
Hinckley, 87
Hoare, Jonathon, of London, merchant, 110
Hobbs, John, of Bristol, timber merchant, 10
Holden, Revd. John Rose, of London, 81 n. 1
Homer, Thomas, auditor of Grand Junction Canal, 124-5
Hordern, Molineux, and Bishton, of Wolverhampton, bankers, 190
Hore, John, of Newbury, engineer, 10-11
Horncastle, 41
Horncastle Navigation, 41, 112, 117, 122, 150 n. 2, 179, 188
Huddersfield, 60
Huddersfield Canal, 60-2, 85, 119-20, 177, 181, 183, 188
Hughes and Anderdon, of Bristol, attorneys, 140 n. 1
Hull, 14, 34, 97, 152, 162, 163 n. 1, 191
Hunt, Richard, of Stratford, mercer, 3
Huntingdon, Earl of, 38
Huntingdonshire, 141
Hustler, John, of Bradford, woolstapler, 35, 105, 110
Huxley, George, of London, attorney, 9

Inkersole, Joseph, of Market Harborough, draper, 91
Insolvency, 52, 61, 118-19, 173
Interest, rate of, and canal building, 161-9
Iron manufacture, 4 n. 2, 17, 51, 72-3, 94 n. 7, 132, 137 n. 2
Itchen, River, 3 n. 2, 9
Ivelchester and Langport Navigation, 179

Jackson, John, of Oxford, printer, 129
Jackson, John, of St. Neots, dyer, 2
James, William, of London and Stratford, speculator, 84
Jemmatt, Samuel, mayor of Reading, 2
Joint-stock mania of 1807-11, 82-4
Jones and Barker, of Manchester, bankers, 189
Jones, Landor, of Lincoln's Inn, 11 n. 6
Jowett, Nathaniel, of Clockhouse, 110 n. 5

Keighley, 34, 97
Kendal, 55-6, 112
Kennet Navigation, 10-12, 115 n. 4, 151
Kennet and Avon Canal, 66-9, 80-1, 83-4, 94, 102, 112-13, 115 n. 4, 118, 120 n. 6, 121 n. 1, 131, 149 n. 3, 157, 178, 181, 188
Kennet and Ingram, of Wakefield, bankers, 187
Kent, 141
Kenyon, Lord, 119
Kettle, John, of Birmingham, Esquire, 186
Kidderminster, 4, 29, 48, 172
Kidlington-Deddington Turnpike, 130
King's Lynn, 24-5, 162, 163 n. 1, 191
Kingswinford, 37

Lancashire, 33-5, 60-1, 84 n. 2, 102, 108, 141-2, 158
Lancaster, 55-6, 112, 188
Lancaster, Bax, and Ellil, of London, lead merchants, 36
Lancaster Canal, 55-7, 85, 95, 106, 112, 117, 120 n. 6, 169 n. 1, 177, 188
Landeg, of Swansea, banker, 190
Landowners and river navigations, 5, 7-9, 13-15, 152, 171
Landowners and canals, 40-4, 52, 54, 73-6, 88, 128, 137-8, 143-60, 185
Lansdowne, Marquis of, 70
Lawyers and river navigation finance, 2-4, 6, 9-10, 11 n. 6, 12
Lawyers and canal finance, 40, 82, 98-9, 106-9
Lax, Anthony, attorney, 109
Leach, Thomas, of Riddlesden, banker, 110 n. 5

Lead trade, 36, 79 n. 5
Ledbury, 53
Lee, Sir William, of Hartwell, 159 n. 6
Lee, River, 134, 186
Leeds, 7, 34, 86, 97, 108-9
Leeds and Liverpool Canal, 33-6, 79, 82, 90, 94, 97-8, 100-2, 105-6, 109-10, 115-16, 120 n. 3, 123, 128, 132, 136, 140, 145, 151-3, 169 n. 1, 175, 177, 184-6, 189
Leicester, 40-2, 45-6, 52, 63, 86-92, 107, 180-2
Leicester Navigation, 40, 111-12, 115 n. 6, 122, 135-6, 177, 180-2, 189
Leicester and Swannington Railway, 92
Leicestershire, 38-41, 52-3, 88, 141-2, 146-8
Leicestershire and Northamptonshire Union Canal, 40, 84, 88, 91 n. 3, 99 n. 3, 118 n. 4, 130, 153, 177, 180-2
Leigh, 151
Leominster and Stourport Canal, 179
Leregoe, William, agent of the Stour Navigation, 5, 6 n. 1
Lewis, Stoughton, Buckle, and Co., of Chepstow, bankers, 109-10
Lichfield, 29, 52, 97, 128-9
Lincoln Bank, 112
Lincolnshire, 141
Little, of Coventry, banker, 186
Liverpool, 10, 26-8, 33-4, 46, 55-6, 85-7, 92, 94-7, 108, 138-40, 142, 151-2, 163 n. 1, 191
Lodge, Arthington, and Becket, of Leeds, bankers, 186
London, 14-15, 83, 136, 167, 171-2, 173 n. 1
London Lead Company, 36, 79 n. 5
Londoners and river navigation finance, 2-4, 9-12, 17, 171-2
Londoners and canal finance, 29, 32, 35-6, 38, 40-2, 45-8, 53, 56-7, 61, 64-6, 68, 70-3, 76, 78-87, 91, 97, 105, 123-5, 128, 140, 160
London and Birmingham Canal, 86
Longbottom, John, of Halifax, engineer, 151
Loughborough, 38, 40 n. 3, 45, 52
Loughborough Navigation, 38-9, 87 n. 1, 115 n. 1, 175, 181

Lowe, Jeremiah, of Coventry, merchant and manufacturer, 44, 130
Luxford, Stephen, mayor of Bedford, 2
Lyon, Dr., of Liverpool, 95
Lynch and Hawkes ('Glamorganshire Banking Co.'), 190

Malet, John, 15
Manchester, 9-10, 14, 28, 55-8, 60-3, 85-6, 97, 108, 127, 142, 181
Manchester, Bolton and Bury Canal, 55, 177, 181
Manchester Theatre, 108
Mansfield, J., of the Inner Temple, 120 n. 5
Manufacturers, 18, 22, 24, 37, 48, 51, 55, 57-60, 62, 66, 72, 74-8, 127-8, 132
Market Bosworth, 87
Market Harborough, 40 n. 3, 45, 52, 86, 88-9, 91-2, 180-1
Marlborough, 67
Marlborough, Duke of, 33, 159
Marple, 59
Marsden, William, of Barnsley, gentleman, 98
Martin, Bendal, Esquire, 12
Martin, Henry, of the Middle Temple, Esquire, 10-12
Martyn, William, of London, attorney, 12
Mattingley and Kent, of Wantage, bankers, 190
Measham Sick Club, 42
Melton Navigation, 40, 87, 103-4, 115 n. 6, 179-80
Melton Mowbray, 45
Merchants, 3, 7-14, 18, 22, 24, 26-7, 33-5, 43-4, 55, 62, 65-7, 70, 80-1, 98, 128, 139-40, 151, 171, 185
Mersey, 8
Mersey and Irwell Navigation, 9
Middlesex, 141, 147-8
Middleton, Lord, 154
Midford, John, of London, merchant, 12
Mildred, Daniel, of London, banker, 110
Milner, James, Esquire, 12
Milsom, Thomas, gentleman, 10
Minehead, 162, 163 n.1, 191

Mogeridge, Matthias, of Birmingham, attorney, 106
Monmouthshire Canal, 178, 189
Montgomery, 53
Montgomeryshire Canal, 53, 89, 137-8, 157 n. 2, 177, 179
Moorhouse, John, of Keighley, attorney, 98
Morgan, William, of Chepstow, banker, 109-10
Morgan, William, of Mamhilad, 145
Mortgage of tolls, loans on, 6, 12, 28-33, 35-6, 38, 40-2, 47-9, 54-7, 60-1, 63, 66, 73, 85, 108-9, 114-17, 120, 123, 134 n. 2
Neath, 73
Neath Canal, 72, 178
Nene, River, 13
Newark, 88, 97
Newbury, 10, 68, 83
Newcastle, Duke of, 37, 154
Newcastle upon Tyne, 167 n. 2
Newcastle-under-Lyne, 97
Newdigate, Sir Roger, 146, 159
Newry Canal, 151
Newtown, 53
Nicholas, Sir John, 6
Norfolk, 35, 79, 141-2
Northampton, 13, 40 n. 3, 46, 52, 88
Northamptonshire, 141, 147
Northumberland, 141
North Walsham and Dilham Canal, 177, 179
North Wilts Canal, 71-2, 179
Norwich, 35, 140
Nottingham, 9, 39, 41, 52, 88, 97, 154
Nottingham Canal, 39, 115 n. 6, 149, 153-4, 157 nn. 2-3, 189
Nottinghamshire, 38-40, 141-2
Nourse, Sir Charles, of Oxford, surgeon, 130

Oakham Canal, 41, 82, 87, 119, 146, 157 n. 2, 179-80, 182
Oldham, 60, 82
Oldknow, Samuel, of Stockport, cotton manufacturer, 59-60, 77-8
Oldswinford, 37
Optional notes, 45-6, 52, 67, 70-1, 121, 123-5
Ottley, 34, 97
Ouse, Great, 2, 14, 15 n. 3

Ouse, Little, 3 n. 3, 15 n. 3
Ouse, River (Sussex), 179
Oxford, 32-3, 46, 86-7, 129, 183
Oxford Canal, 32-3, 87, 95, 97, 98 n. 3, 100-2, 106, 110, 115 n. 2, 129-30, 133, 146, 150 n. 1, 153, 159, 169 n. 1, 175, 177, 183, 189
Oxfordshire, 141, 153

Paget, Sir William, later Lord, 8
Pane, Clement, of Birmingham, japanner, 130
Parliament and navigation acts, 17-19, 86, 148, 160, 171
Parsons, Joseph, of Oxford, barber, 129
Patten, Thomas, of Bank Hall, Warrington, merchant, 8
Peak Forest Canal, 20, 58-60, 82, 85, 95, 120, 177, 181, 189
Peckovers, the, Quaker family, 35
Peckover and Harris, of Bradford, bankers, 189
Pennsylvania Land Company, 79 n. 5
Pensnett Chase, 145
Perfect, Seaton, and Brook, of Huddersfield, bankers, 188
Peterborough, 13,
Phillips, Richard, of Leicester, canal share broker, 95-6, 107-8
Pinney, John, of Bristol, merchant, 139-40
Pitt, Thomas, of the Inner Temple, Esquire, 6
Pitt, William, Prime Minister, 136
Plymouth, Countess of, 16 n. 6
Plymouth, Earl of, 5, 16 n. 6
Pocklington Canal, 85, 114 n. 1
Pocock, Thomas, gentleman, 10
Pollard, William, of Halifax, banker, 110 n. 5
Pontefract, 34, 97
Poole, 155 n. 1
Poplewell, of Retford, banker, 186
Portsmouth, 163 n. 1, 191
Portsmouth and Arundel Canal, 82 n. 4
Poyntz, Sir John, of Iron Acton, Gloucestershire, knight, 4
Praed, William, of Tyringham and London, banker, 44
Pratt, William, of Banbury, innkeeper, 106

Pre-emption, right of, 46, 48, 61, 71, 120 n. 5, 121, 125
Preston, 57, 112
Profit, rate of on river navigations, 16, 170
Promissory notes, 57, 63

Quakers and canal finance, 34-6, 51, 79, 140

Radnor, Earl of, 70
Railways, 71, 92, 97, 124, 169 n. 1
Ramsden's Canal, Sir John, 179 n. 5
Rathbones, the, of Liverpool, merchants, 51
Rawlinson, Abraham, of Lancaster, merchant, 55
Rawson, Rhodes, and Briggs, of Halifax, bankers, 188
Read, Francis, of Willington, Bedfordshire, gentleman, 2
Regent's Canal, 76 n. 1, 125, 178
Rennie, John, engineer, 91, 115 n. 4
Retford, 36
Reynolds, the, of Coalbrookdale, ironmasters, 51
Ribble, River, 179 n. 6
Ripponden, 14
River navigations, 1-17, 26, 151-2, 161-73, 192
Rochdale, 14, 63
Rochdale Canal, 20, 63-4, 90, 91 n. 3, 95, 107, 122, 130, 177, 180-2, 189
Rolleston, Robert, of London, merchant, 65 n. 2
Rollestone, Christopher, of London, canal share broker, 81, 106
Rose, Christopher, of Cambridge, Esquire, 2
Rother, River, 179
Ruding, Walter, of Merton College, 129
Rugby, 45, 69
Runcorn, 8
Rutland, 39, 141

Saddleworth, 61
Salford, 151
Salisbury, 5-6
Salisbury, Bishop of, 6
Salisbury, Lady, 14 n. 1
Salisbury and Southampton Canal, 81, 93-4, 109 n. 9, 153, 179, 181
Salwarpe, River, 3-4, 17 n. 3

Sandys, Henry, 3 n. 2
Sandys, William, of Warwickshire, M.P., 2, 15
Sankey Navigation, 26-7, 94, 151
Sargent, John, of London, merchant, 65 n. 2
Savile, Sir George, 14 n. 1
Say, William, of the Middle Temple, Esquire, 2
Scarsdale, Lord, 37
Scotland, 90-1, 142
Scott, Mr., of London, share broker, 82
Seagar, Stephen, of Birmingham, grocer, 107
Settle, 34, 97
Shares, canal:
—forfeiture of, 49-50, 58, 61, 67-70, 118
—form of, 100 n. 2
—market in, 81-3, 85-7, 95-108, 183-5
—prices of, 44, 46-7, 49, 54, 56, 58, 67-8, 70, 86, 92, 101, 102 n. 3, 104, 106, 119-21, 124-5, 133, 154-6, 160
See also: Preference shares, Optional notes, Promissory notes.
Shaftesbury, Earl of, 6
Sheffield, 13, 34, 88, 97, 172
Shrewsbury, 52
Shrewsbury Canal, 51, 118 n. 2, 177
Shropshire, 51, 53-4, 85, 141
Shropshire Canal, 51, 82, 114 n. 1, 177
Skipp, George, of Ledbury, Esquire, 4
Skipton, 34, 97
Sleaford Navigation, 179
Smith, Abel, of Nottingham, banker, 98, 189
Smith, Edward, of Birmingham, 106
Smith, Startin, and Smith, of Birmingham, bankers, 190
Smith, Wright, and Grey, of London, bankers, 35, 186
Smyth, Thomas, of the Middle Temple, Esquire, 3
Sneyd, Edward, of Lichfield, Esquire, 130
Soame, Richard, of London, merchant, 9
Solicitors, see Lawyers
Somerset, 141-2
Somerset Coal Canal, 94, 178, 181, 190

Southampton, 9, 94, 163 n. 1, 191
South Sea Bubble, 10
Spencer, Arnold, of Bedfordshire and London, 2, 14
Spencer, Lord, 150 n. 1
Stafford, 97
Staffordshire, 29-31, 38, 47-9, 51, 85, 128, 141-2
Staffordshire and Worcestershire Canal, 5, 20, 29-30, 64, 115 n. 1, 130, 133, 148, 152, 177
Stainforth and Keadby Canal, 119
Stamford, 3, 82 n. 4
Stamford, Earl of, 145
Stanhope, Walter Spencer, 88-9
Starr, Mary, of Salisbury, widow, 6
Startin and Smith, of Birmingham, bankers, 48
Stirrop, Nathaniel, of London, 2
Stock Exchange, 46, 82, 85-6, 99
Stockport, 9, 58
Stony Stratford, 44, 52, 69
Stour, River (Essex), 7
Stour, River (Worcestershire), 3-5, 17
Stourbridge, 3-4, 29, 37
Stourbridge Canal, 37, 114 n. 6, 115 n. 1, 145, 177, 184, 186
Stowmarket and Ipswich Navigation, 179
Stratford-upon-Avon, 2-3, 49, 84
Stratford-upon-Avon Canal, 49, 84-5, 106, 122-3, 169 n. 1, 177, 180, 190
Stroud, 38, 64
Stroudwater Navigation, 38, 64, 92, 115 n. 1, 177
Sudbury, 7
Suffolk, 141
Sunderland, 167 n. 2
Sun Fire Insurance Company, 28, 79
Surrey, 141
Surrey Iron Railroad, 82
Sussex, 141
Swansea, 73
Swansea Canal, 72-3, 178, 183, 190
Swindon, 71

Tamar Manure Navigation, 179
Tamworth, 30, 97
Taunton, 7
Tavistock Canal, 178-9
Tavistock, Marquis of, 158
Taylor and Lloyd, of Birmingham, bankers, 186-7

Tewkesbury, 2
Thames, River, 15 n. 3, 71, 179
Thames and Medway Canal, 178
Thames and Severn Canal, 64-6, 71, 80-1, 117, 122, 140, 146, 169 n. 1, 178
Thomas, Mr., of Bristol, canal share broker, 108
Thompson, John, of Manchester, canal share broker, 108
Thonhaugh, Francis, 14 n. 1
Thornhill, Thomas, of Fixby, Esquire, 14 n. 1
Tone, River, 7, 15 n. 3, 16
Towcester, 69
Trafford, Richard, of Liverpool, merchant, 26
Trafford, William, of Liverpool, merchant, 27
Trent, River, 8, 15, 88
Trent and Mersey Canal, 28-9, 31, 78-9, 88, 95, 97-8, 114 n. 5, 115 n. 2, 128, 130, 132-4, 148, 150, 152-3, 169 n. 1, 175, 177, 183
Turton, Richard, of London, gentleman, 3
Turner, Henry, of Blenheim Park, gentleman, 129
Turnpike Trusts, 130, 164-5, 192-4
Twells, Charles, of Nottingham, attorney, 109

Ulverston Canal, 95, 114 n. 5
Uxbridge, 147

Vere, Peter, of Kensington, 81 n. 1
Vernon, Lord, 72

Wakefield, 7, 13, 34, 43, 97
Wales, 142
Walker, John, of Oxford, attorney, 106
Walsall, 97
Wantage, 69
War and canal building, ix, 31, 33, 101-2, 113, 115, 125, 140, 156, 168
Warrington, 8-10
Warwick, 50-1
Warwick and Birmingham Canal, 50-1, 81 n. 1, 96, 106, 146-7, 177, 180, 190
Warwick and Napton Canal, 50-1, 106, 114 n. 1, 177, 180, 190

Warwickshire, 32, 49-51, 85, 141-2, 147, 153

Watt, James, of Glasgow and Birmingham, engineer, 90

Waveney, River, 3 n. 3, 15 n. 3

Weald of Kent Canal, 82 n. 4, 118 n. 4

Weaver, River, 9

Webb, Edward, of Leicester, tallow chandler, 135

Wedgwood, Josiah, of Etruria, potter, 78-9, 128, 132-4

Welland, River, 3, 15 n. 3, 16

Welshpool, 53, 89

Westmoreland, 141

Wetherell, Nathan, Vice-Chancellor of Oxford University, 33

Wey, River, 15 n. 3, 16, 17 n. 3

Wey and Arun Canal, 76 n. 1, 178

Whitbread, Samuel, M.P., 158

Whitehead, Messrs., of London, bankers, 83

Wigmore, Daniel, of Stamford, wine-merchant, 3, 3 n. 3, 16

Wilcocks, Barnaby, 6

Wilden Ferry, 8

Wilkes, Dickens, Goodall, and Fisher, of London, bankers, 187

Wilkins, Walter, of Brecon, banker, 73, 187

Wilkinson, of Chesterfield, banker, 186

Wilkinson, J., of Leicester, canal share broker, 107

Wilkinson, John, of Coalbrookdale, ironmaster, 51

Willis, Captain Francis, 12

Wilts and Berks Canal, 69-72, 81-2, 84, 94, 103-4, 120 n. 6, 147, 153, 178-9, 181, 190

Wiltshire, 66-70, 141

Winchester, 9

Windsor, Thomas Lord, 2-3, 5

Wisbech Canal, 89 n. 4, 177, 179-80, 182

Witham, River, 13

Witney, 32

Wolverhampton, 29-30, 42, 49, 97

Wood, Simon, of London, citizen and haberdasher, 17 n. 3

Woodin, John, of Stratford, 3

Woodstock, 32

Woodward, Robert, Doctor of Laws, 6

Woolfe, Mr., of London, share broker, 82

Worcester, 47-8

Worcester and Birmingham Canal, 47-8, 85, 93, 96, 106, 120 n. 6, 122-3, 145-6, 169 n. 1, 177, 180-1, 183, 190

Worcestershire, 38, 47-8, 54, 141-2

Worksop, 36

Wormleighton, 150 n. 1

Worrall, Blatchley, and Co., of Bristol, bankers, 112-13, 188

Worrall, Samuel, of Bristol, attorney and banker, 93, 112-13

Worswick, Thomas, of Lancaster, banker, 112, 188

Worthing, 82

Worthington, Dr., of Liverpool, 95

Wray, Sir Cecil, M.P. for Retford, 37

Wright, of Nottingham, banker, 186, 188

Wyan, Jacob, 12

Wye and Lugg, Rivers, 3 n. 2, 179

Wykeham, W. H., of Swalcliffe, Esquire, 159 n. 6

Wyrley and Essington Canal, 49, 115 n. 6, 130, 177, 190

Yarranton, Andrew, 3-4, 6 n. 1, 16

Yeomen, 18, 21-2, 34, 36, 58 n. 3, 74-6

York, 34, 97

York, Duke of, 2

Yorkshire, 33-6, 46, 60-1, 108, 141, 153, 158, 165